English for Academic Purposes

STUDENTS' BOOK

KATHY COX ▪ DAVID HILL

PEARSON
Education Australia

Pearson Education Australia
Unit 4, Level 3
14 Aquatic Drive
Frenchs Forest NSW 2086

www.pearsoned.com.au

Senior Acquisitions Editor: Andrew Brock
Senior Project Editor: Rebecca Pomponio
Copy Editor and Proofreader: Jane Tyrrell of Editing Solutions
Cover and internal design by Peta Nugent
Cover photographs supplied by the authors and publisher with permission
Typeset by Midland Typesetters, Australia

Printed in Malaysia (CTP-VVP)

7 8 9 10 13 12 11 10 09

National Library of Australia
Cataloguing-in-Publication Data

Cox, Kathy, 1945– .
EAP now! : English for academic purposes : preliminary.

Includes index.
ISBN 9780733978050 (student bk.).

1. English language – Study and teaching – Australia – Foreign speakers. 2. English language – Problems, exercises, etc. I. Hill, David, 1969– . II. Title.

428.2407094

An imprint of Pearson Education Australia
(a division of Pearson Australia Group Pty Ltd)

PREFACE

EAP Now! Preliminary has been created for those of you who have academic aims and need to learn more English. It is an *introduction* to a higher level of English for Academic Purposes (EAP), and may also help students who would like to go into vocational courses at colleges. It offers the kinds of topics, themes and language that you will find and use at university and college, given at an appropriate English language level.

Each unit has a different topic. The topics were chosen to include many situations that people experience. They will help you with your conversational English as well as introducing you to more academic English.

The course covers the areas of grammar in General English course books under the title: Language Spotlight. The grammar is presented to you in context as is vocabulary learning. The course connects critical thinking with Reading, Listening, Writing and Speaking activities as well as with learning technologies like the world wide web. Ideas and suggestions for you to have more practice of English, and to extend your knowledge, are included at the end of each unit.

Listening exercises from the audio CDs are linked to each unit's theme. The topics are meant to get you thinking about what you hear, and to help you understand how to listen and understand what you hear. Grammar from the listening also helps you understand why you are listening to something and how to make the best sense of it.

At the end of the book, there are Appendices which include some self-correction sheets and an academic word guide with parts of speech. There are also peer-editing worksheets for you and your classmates to check your own and one another's writing, as well as information that you will use while doing some of the activities in the book. There is also a list of references.

Compared with other Intermediate General English course books, *EAP Now! Preliminary* has more written work for you to do, and a lot of speaking practice as well. Some speaking tasks are open-ended, which means sometimes many different answers are correct. You must use your own knowledge and experience. There is also guided practice. Academic topics and introductions to college and university tasks help those of you who wish to follow higher education and further education courses taught in English.

AIMS AND FOCUS OF *EAP NOW! PRELIMINARY*

EAP Now! Preliminary is designed to help you learn English language skills, vocabulary and grammar. It is an *introduction* to academic English. It is for those who wish to succeed in EAP (English for Academic Purposes) and then continue that success in a further or higher education course taught in English, at university or college.

The aims of this Students' Book are to help you to learn vocabulary and grammar, to improve reading, to write texts for different purposes, to listen and understand what you hear, to question and give opinions, and to become familiar with some academic contexts.

Each unit contains seven areas of learning which are linked to the unit theme. These are:

- Speaking
- Reading
- Writing
- Listening
- Language Spotlight (grammar and vocabulary)
- Critical Thinking
- English for the Internet Age

Reading, Writing, Speaking, Listening and Language Spotlight have separate sections within each unit, and additionally there are extra speaking activities in most sections. Tasks to help you with Critical Thinking and English for the Internet Age are included in other sections. You are asked to think critically in many of the speaking, reading, writing and listening tasks, and the *Reading, Films and Fun* section at the end of each unit has topics that you can research on the internet.

Most units have the following sections:

Speaking

The first task in each unit introduces you to the topic of the unit through speaking activities. They help you 'build the field' in your mind. Most Reading, Writing, Listening and Language Spotlight sections also include tasks in which you speak with other students. In addition, there are extra Speaking sections in each unit which have a special focus on a useful function of speaking, for example, making requests, or talking about experiences. They may also give more practice of the English you learned earlier in the unit.

Reading

This section helps you with skills that are useful for reading any kind of text, and introduces you to the kinds of texts you will have to read at college or university. The texts are shorter than you will find at college or university, but longer than those on General English courses at Intermediate level. Sometimes you will find parts that are difficult to understand – but the tasks will help you with the important meanings. Remember, you won't understand everything in college or university readings the first time you see them, so this book gives you the skills to understand as much as possible, and to become more confident at dealing with longer and more complicated texts.

Writing

Most units introduce a new genre (that is, type of writing) or review a genre from one of the previous units. The tasks in this section show you the stages in each genre, and help you to write examples of the genre.

Listening

You will hear many different accents – because your lecturer at college or university might be from any part of the world. As with the texts in the Reading sections, some of it will be difficult – but the tasks will help you to cope with the lectures, tutorials and social situations at college or university.

Language Spotlight

The first Language Spotlight section in each unit focuses on grammar and/or vocabulary from the reading, and gives you some practice. The reading gives a context and meaning for the new language, making it easier to learn. The second Language Spotlight in each unit focuses on language from the listening. Again, seeing the language in context makes it easier to learn.

Further practice

This section appears at the end of each unit and lists films, books or articles to read and points to talk or write about, all connected with the topic of the unit. Your teacher may give you ideas about using this section, or you could use it for self study.

We wish you luck with your studies, and hope you enjoy using this book.

Kathy K Cox and David Hill

ABOUT THE AUTHORS

KATHY K COX

was born in California and settled in Australia in 1970. Educated in Florida when shocking racial segregation was the norm, she became a committed exponent of equality. Attending the Universities of Hawaii and Wollongong, Australia, deepened and widened that commitment. After teaching in Pago Pago, American Samoa, she travelled throughout Asia and the Pacific. She was Director of Studies at APC, Sydney, for a decade and has enjoyed a life long career in TESOL and in the writing of English learning materials.

DAVID HILL

grew up in the north west of England. After studying at the University of Durham, his fascination for other cultures took him around the world and eventually inspired him to become a teacher of English. David has previously taught in the UK, Turkey and Japan. He now lives in Australia, where he has worked in various teaching and management positions, including Director of Studies.

ACKNOWLEDGEMENTS

Kathy would like to thank the students and colleagues from around the world who throughout many years have provided the impetus for creating English language books. Thank you to Diane Larsen-Freeman and Mary Kalantzis for their inspiration as researchers and writers who justify and illuminate a true student based approach.

Kathy also extends personal thanks to her good friends Peter and Rosemary for their patient work-shopping of ideas and interest in her projects; to David & Susan from APC; to teachers and administrators who have trialled materials and provided useful feedback; to Murray, for his ongoing support and encouragement; and to her mother, K.C., loving thanks for being a life long linguistic and personal mentor.

•••

David would like to thank the numerous students, friends and colleagues he has worked with and learned so much from over the years, and in particular those who have assisted with the review process for this book – you know who you are! He would also like to thank the editorial and production team for their valuable contributions to the project. David also extends his special thanks to Chie, whose help, encouragement and support has been immensely valuable.

CONTENTS

CONTENTS MAP

Critical Thinking and English for the Internet Age are incorporated into the Reading, Writing, Listening and Speaking activities throughout. Extra speaking practice is included in the Reading, Writing, Listening and Language Spotlight activities.

Bonus CD Tracks from *EAP Now!*
CD 2 – T4 The new student
CD 2 – T5 Going down fighting (a play)

1 CUSTOMS

'when in Rome, do as Rome does'

BY THE END OF THIS UNIT, YOU SHOULD:

- know more vocabulary for talking about customs, culture, romance and marriage .... Speaking 1: Task A **2**; Listening: Task A **8**
- be more fluent and confident when talking about customs, culture, romance and marriage .... Speaking 1: Task B **2**; Listening: Task G **10**
- be able to predict when reading and listening, and be aware of the usefulness of this skill ... Reading: Task A **2**; Listening: Task B **8**
- be able to skim (read quickly to get the main ideas) .... Reading: Task B **3**
- be more aware of different written genres and their purpose .... Reading: Task C **3**
- be prepared to think about five standard questions every time you read .... Reading: Task D **5**
- be able to correct and avoid mistakes in sentence structure and clause structure .... Language Spotlight 1: Tasks A and B **5–6**
- be aware of staging in written texts and how this relates to genre .... Writing: Task A **8**
- have practised writing to follow a particular genre .... Writing: Task B **8**
- have improved your ability to predict and listen for main ideas and specific information .... Listening: Tasks B, C, D and F **8–10**
- be aware of the reasons why you don't always have to understand every word when listening .... Listening: Task E **10**
- be able to use phrasal verbs correctly, and be aware of their informality .... Language Spotlight 2: Tasks A and B **11**
- be able to discuss ideas on specific topics and understand how you like to learn a language .... Speaking 2: Tasks A, B and C **12**
- have a better understanding of your learning style, and know some different ways to improve your English ... Speaking 2: Task C **12**

CUSTOM n. pl., CUSTOMS [UNCOUNTABLE AND COUNTABLE]: something that is done by people in a particular society because people have been doing it the same way for a long time.

BUILDING THE FIELD

Task A | Vocabulary about customs

1. Look at the pictures. Working in pairs, say as much as you can about each.

2. In pairs, match the following words to their meanings. Share your knowledge – but use an English–English dictionary if you need to.

WORDS

ceremony

celebration

festival

parade

religion (n) / religious (adj)

society (n) / social (adj)

tradition (n) / traditional (adj)

MEANINGS

- an event where musical bands, decorated trucks, dancers, etc pass down the street
- an important event in which traditional actions are performed in a formal way
- a way of doing things that has been the same for a very long time
- an event or party when many people show they are very happy about something (eg winning a sporting event, a birthday)
- a belief in one or more gods
- all the people in a country, sharing the same customs, laws, etc
- an occasion when there are performances of dancing, music, films, plays, parades, etc, usually happening in the same place every year.

Task B | Talking about customs

1. Tell your partner about a time you saw or participated in:

   a ceremony

   a festival

   a parade

   a religious event

2. What do people in your culture do around each of these traditions? Tell your group about your experiences. Is it the same for you and for your grandparents' generation?
   - Sending cards for birthdays, New Year or other special days
   - Having parties for birthdays
   - Greeting people the first time you meet them (eg bowing)
   - Going outside the house to meet friends (eg to restaurants, pubs).

INTRODUCTION TO A GLOBAL APPROACH TO READING (PREDICTING, SKIMMING, PURPOSE AND CRITICAL READING) – A TRAVEL BROCHURE

Task A | Introduction to prediction

To understand something well, it can be VERY helpful to make some guesses.

1. Look quickly at the first page of the text on the next page and answer the following questions. It is part of a brochure.

   [a] Look at the pictures. What is the topic?

   [b] Look at the title. Who is the brochure for . . .

   (i) students?
   (ii) tourists?
   (iii) religious people?

   [c] Use the headings. Which from the following list does the brochure NOT tell you about?

   (i) where the festivals are
   (ii) the cheapest supermarket
   (iii) why the places are interesting
   (iv) information about local schools
   (v) information about the festivals
   (vi) the kind of transport to be used.

COME AND DISCOVER SOME ANCIENT MAGICAL TRADITIONS (DAY TRIP)

. . .

N US ON THE TOUR OF A LIFETIME AND DISCOVER THE TRADITIONAL CULTURE OF PAN, AS WE TAKE YOU TO SOME THOUSAND-YEAR OLD FESTIVALS IN SOME OF THE OLDEST AREAS OF THE COUNTRY.

. . .

ake part in a Buddhist fire-walking ceremony on the famous island of Miyajima before travelling inland through spectacular scenery to Midori, where ou will view a festival of age-old Kagura performances, with their glorious multi-coloured costumes and charming, centuries-old acting style.

For more information about this add-on tour, please call 042 796 2548 or visit www.japantours.co.za

OUR TOUR – THE HISTORY AND HE MAGIC OF THE FESTIVALS

s stunning tour begins with a journey by luxury coach from your el to the magical island of Miyajima, famous for its 1400 year-old ines, its mystical temples and its spectacular views. Here you will o see the romantic view of the 'floating torii', a religious symbol nding like an enormous orange gate in the sea. You have probably en this in photographs – it is one of the three most famous views Japan. You will have the opportunity to go up the mountain in e centre of the island by cable car. From the top you will see agnificent views over the thousand islands of the inland sea.

After a delicious lunch of a local speciality in a traditional-style staurant, your knowledgeable and experienced guide will explain e history of Daisho-in Temple. This ancient mountain-side temple a main centre of Shingon Buddhism, and continues the customs d traditions brought to Japan from China and Tibet over 1200 ears ago. Here you will see the ancient fire-walking ceremony, erformed twice every year by the monks. If you are feeling brave, ou can walk across the fire as well!

At the end of this amazing experience, your luxury coach will whiz ou to the village of Midori, famous for performances of traditional Kagura plays. These have been performed at Shinto shrines since he beginning of time, and have evolved into many different styles in different parts of Japan (Shinto is the traditional religion of Japan, with many interesting stories about gods and goddesses). The local style is one of the most exciting, with characters in spectacular costumes fighting fire-breathing dragons, while awe-struck children watch on. And the music is something you'll remember for the rest of your life!

At the end of the day your coach will return you to your hotel.

ITINERARY

09.00 Pick up from your hotel. Travel to Miyajima by luxury coach.
10.00 Arrive at Miyajima island. View the famous 'floating torii'.
11.00 Take the cable car to the top of Mt Misen, for views over the spectacular inland sea.
12.30 Lunch: A local speciality in one of the best local restaurants
14.00 Start of the firewalking festival at the centuries-old Daisho-in Temple
16.00 Return to your luxury coach for the journey to the Kagura village
18.00 Traditional dinner in the village
19.00 Kagura performance begins
21.30 Return by coach to your hotel, to arrive about 22.30.

WHAT THE PRICE INCLUDES

The price (see back page of brochure) includes entry fees, the ferry fare to the island, the cable car fee, lunch and dinner (not including drinks).

WHAT TO BRING

- Camera – make sure it has plenty of memory space – you will probably take many photographs!
- Bottled water
- Enough cash to cover the cost of extra drinks, snacks and souvenirs
- An umbrella in case of rain.

Page 2

❷ Say whether you think the following statements are most likely to be true or false. (You will have to use clues from the title, headings, pictures, and what you already know about package tours, to help. This kind of guessing is called *predicting* or *making predictions*, and can help you quickly understand the text.)

[a] The tour will visit a very modern shrine.
[b] In one of the festivals on this tour, you will see people walking on fire.
[c] The festivals on the tour are very boring to watch.
[d] The tour will use only public transport.
[e] The tour operates every weekend of the year.
[f] The tour visits more than one festival.

*

SKIMMING IS READING QUICKLY (WITHOUT READING EVERY WORD) TO FIND THE MAIN IDEAS.

Task B | Introduction to skimming

When reading, it isn't always helpful to read every word. Sometimes you only need to find the main ideas – reading only for main ideas is called ***skimming***. At other times, skimming helps to find the right part of the text quickly, ie the part that might have the information you're looking for. On the next page is the brochure you looked at previously.

❶ Look at it quickly. What can help you find the main ideas?

❷ Which section on page two of the brochure would you read to find out the following information?

[a] The time the trip finishes.
[b] Information about the festivals.
[c] Whether you have to pay for meals.
[d] How you will be travelling (train? walking?)
[e] What is special about the places on the tour?

Task C | Texts and their purpose

There are many different kinds of text. Each kind of text has different features—for instance, titles, pictures, headings and different kinds of grammar in the writing. Also each type of text has a purpose, ie a reason the author wrote it. For example, the purpose of an advertisement is to make people want to buy something. Each type of text has different features from other text types. For example, advertisements usually have lots of photographs but little writing.

In this book, a type of text is called a genre, and the features of the text type are called generic features.

❶ Match the following types of text to their purpose. Note that each might have more than one purpose.

TEXT TYPE

- advertisement
- information leaflet about a library
- information leaflet about a tourist attraction
- map
- bus timetable
- newspaper article
- this course book
- orientation booklet for your language school
- shopping list
- dictionary
- encyclopaedia article

PURPOSE

- to help you remember what to buy
- to give information about recent events
- to help you know where to go
- to help people use English in their future study
- to make something sound interesting
- to help students understand what they have to do and why
- to give information
- to give information about times and routes
- to sell something
- to help people find the pronunciation of words, see examples of how they are used and find out their meaning
- to give information about how to use the services

COME AND DISCOVER SOME ANCIENT MAGICAL TRADITIONS (DAY TRIP)

...

JOIN US ON THE TOUR OF A LIFETIME AND DISCOVER THE TRADITIONAL CULTURE OF JAPAN, AS WE TAKE YOU TO SOME THOUSAND-YEAR OLD FESTIVALS IN SOME OF THE OLDEST AREAS OF THE COUNTRY.

...

We will take part in a Buddhist fire-walking ceremony on the famous island of Miyajima before travelling inland through spectacular scenery to Midori, where you will view a festival of age-old Kagura performances, with their glorious multi-coloured costumes and charming, centuries-old acting style.

For more information about this add-on tour, please call 042 796 2548 or visit www.japantours.co.za

YOUR TOUR – THE HISTORY AND THE MAGIC OF THE FESTIVALS

This stunning tour begins with a journey by luxury coach from your hotel to the magical island of Miyajima, famous for its 1400 year-old shrines, its mystical temples and its spectacular views. Here you will also see the romantic view of the 'floating torii', a religious symbol standing like an enormous orange gate in the sea. You have probably seen this in photographs – it is one of the three most famous views in Japan. You will have the opportunity to go up the mountain in the centre of the island by cable car. From the top you will see magnificent views over the thousand islands of the inland sea.

After a delicious lunch of a local speciality in a traditional-style restaurant, your knowledgeable and experienced guide will explain the history of Daisho-in Temple. This ancient mountain-side temple is a main centre of Shingon Buddhism, and continues the customs and traditions brought to Japan from China and Tibet over 1200 years ago. Here you will see the ancient fire-walking ceremony, performed twice every year by the monks. If you are feeling brave, you can walk across the fire as well!

At the end of this amazing experience, your luxury coach will whiz you to the village of Midori, famous for performances of traditional Kagura plays. These have been performed at Shinto shrines since the beginning of time, and have evolved into many different styles in different parts of Japan (Shinto is the traditional religion of Japan, with many interesting stories about gods and goddesses). The local style is one of the most exciting, with characters in spectacular costumes fighting fire-breathing dragons, while awe-struck children watch on. And the music is something you'll remember for the rest of your life!

At the end of the day your coach will return you to your hotel.

ITINERARY

09.00 Pick up from your hotel. Travel to Miyajima by luxury coach.
10.00 Arrive at Miyajima island. View the famous 'floating torii'.
11.00 Take the cable car to the top of Mt Misen, for views over the spectacular inland sea.
12.30 Lunch: A local speciality in one of the best local restaurants
14.00 Start of the firewalking festival at the centuries-old Daisho-in Temple
16.00 Return to your luxury coach for the journey to the Kagura village
18.00 Traditional dinner in the village
19.00 Kagura performance begins
21.30 Return by coach to your hotel, to arrive about 22.30.

WHAT THE PRICE INCLUDES

The price (see back page of brochure) includes entry fees, the ferry fare to the island, the cable car fee, lunch and dinner (not including drinks).

WHAT TO BRING

- Camera – make sure it has plenty of memory space – you will probably take many photographs!
- Bottled water
- Enough cash to cover the cost of extra drinks, snacks and souvenirs
- An umbrella in case of rain.

Page

2 Before your next class, try to notice as many texts as you can (eg in newspapers, on signs). Make a list, and write the purpose of each.

Task D | Introduction to critical reading – The five questions for any reading

1 Look at the text below and circle the correct answer.

EXPERIENCE THE WONDERFUL CULTURE OF JAPAN!

Have a once-in-a-lifetime experience!

Travel with the best travel company — we guarantee no other company can do this better!

Departing: 6th March, 8th May, 10th July, 11th September 2007

Only £8995!!

[a] **What is it?** (What type of text is it)?
- i. a sign
- ii. an advertisement
- iii. an information leaflet.

[b] **What is the source?** (Where is it from?)
- i. a writer
- ii. an encyclopaedia
- iii. a travel company.

[c] **Who is the writer?**
- i. a government employee
- ii. someone working for a travel company
- iii. a famous writer.

[d] **What purpose does the writer have for writing it?**
- i. to give information
- ii. to make you want to buy the tour
- iii. to make you interested in Japanese culture.

[e] **Who is the intended audience?** (Who was it written for? Who should read it?)
- i. ordinary people who like travelling
- ii. children
- iii. ordinary people who don't have much money.

*

THINKING ABOUT WHERE THE INFORMATION COMES FROM, WHO THE WRITER IS, WHY THE TEXT WAS WRITTEN, AND WHO IT WAS WRITTEN FOR, CAN HELP US TO FIND OUT HOW THE WRITER WANTS TO INFLUENCE US.

THINKING LIKE THIS IS ONE WAY OF *CRITICAL THINKING*. IN YOUR FUTURE COLLEGE OR UNIVERSITY COURSE, YOU WILL HAVE TO SHOW CRITICAL THINKING SKILLS.

2 Now, look back at the part of the travel brochure on page 4. Answer the questions below:

[a] What is it?

Part of a travel brochure

[b] What is the source?

____

[c] Who is the writer?

____

[d] What purpose does the writer have for writing it?

____

[e] Who is the intended audience?

____

CLAUSE AND SENTENCE STRUCTURE

Task A | Clause structure

1 A clause must have a subject and a verb (or verb group). It can sometimes have an object. In the examples below, mark ||| at the end of each clause and underline the verb group.

There are many famous views in Japan. In one of them, there is an orange gate in the sea. It is at a place called Miyajima, near the city of Hiroshima. This kind of gate is called a torii, and there is one of these at the entrance to most Shinto shrines. Shinto is one of the main religions in Japan, and the places of worship in Shinto are called shrines. When people go through the torii, they are entering the shrine. The one at Miyajima is unusual because you have to go through it by boat. In fact, most people walk into the temple through other torii.

2. There may also be extra parts of the sentence giving extra information about the clause. This may give information about where, when, why or how something happens, etc. There are many grammatical words for these groups of words, but a very useful one is *Circumstance*. Circumstances usually begin with a preposition (unlike the subject and object) and sometimes they are just an adverb.

In the following paragraph, mark the subjects and objects in one way, and the circumstances in another way (eg single and double underlining, or different colours).

There are many famous views in Japan. In one of them, there is an orange gate in the sea. It is at a place called Miyajima, near the city of Hiroshima. This kind of gate is called a torii, and there is one of these at the entrance to most Shinto shrines. Shinto is one of the main religions in Japan, and the places of worship in Shinto are called shrines. When people go through the torii, they are entering the shrine. The one at Miyajima is unusual because you have to go through it by boat. In fact, most people walk into the temple through other torii.

3. Find and correct the mistakes in the following sentences.

[a] When I go to another country, I want to travel to many places, because like learning about other cultures.

[b] However, my friend he likes beaches, and he just stays in one place.

[c] One of the most interesting cultures in the world, it is Japanese culture.

[d] In Japan have many shrines.

[e] If you go to Japan should visit Miyajima.

[f] Some people they don't like travelling.

Task B | Sentence structure

1. Look at the following sentences. How many clauses are there in each? Can you see differences in the clause structure in each sentence?

[a] We will take you on a tour to the island of Miyajima.

[b] We will take you on a tour to the island of Miyajima, and you'll see some wonderful views.

[c] We think you'll enjoy your tour of Miyajima because there are some wonderful views.

DISCUSSION

[a] A simple sentence – it has just one clause

[b] A compound sentence. There are two clauses, and each makes sense by itself.

[c] A complex sentence. There are two clauses, but if you remove the first clause, the second makes no sense. We call the second clause a dependent clause because it depends on the first clause (the main clause) to make meaning. We can also call it a subordinate clause.

IN YOUR ACADEMIC WRITING, TRY TO USE LOTS OF SUBORDINATE CLAUSES. IF YOU DO THIS, YOUR WRITING WILL LOOK BETTER, AND YOU WILL GET HIGHER MARKS IN EXAMS!

2 Look at the following sentences. Mark whether they are simple, compound or complex.

[a] Fire walking ceremonies are held in many cultures around the world, in countries such as India, Africa, South Eastern Europe, North America and Japan. [b] These ceremonies are usually connected with religion, and have many purposes including healing sick people and making people spiritually clean. [c] It looks dangerous but usually no one gets hurt. [d] However, if you walk too slowly or stand still, your feet might get burnt!

[e] Taking part in a fire-walking ceremony is not dangerous for several reasons. [f] Firstly, because you walk quickly, your feet don't spend much time on the hot wood. [g] Also, the wood has usually cooled a little before the fire walk starts.

[a] ______________________

[b] ______________________

[c] ______________________

[d] ______________________

[e] ______________________

[f] ______________________

[g] ______________________

3 Put the words below in the table that follows (subordinators begin subordinating clauses; coordinators connect clauses in compound sentences). Reading other texts in this unit may help – these words or similar words have been used there.

but	and
even if	if
because	before
after	when
until	or
whenever	while

COORDINATORS	SUBORDINATORS
(used in compound sentences)	*(used in complex sentences – they begin subordinating clauses)*

4 Correct the punctuation and capital/small letters in the following two paragraphs.

When you visit London. You will find people of many different cultures. It is one of the most culturally diverse cities in the world. And the people living there speak over 300 languages between them.

Because of this variety of cultures. You will easily be able to find food from many different countries. Different cultural groups often live in specific areas. For example. If you feel like having Chinese food. Just go to Chinatown, near Leicester Square. Where there are many Chinese restaurants. There are also many festivals in London, the biggest one of the year is the Notting Hill Carnival. Which includes Caribbean music and dancing. If you like variety. London is a very good place to live.

GENRE

Task A | Putting ideas in order

1. Look again at the brochure about tours in Japan, in the Reading section of this unit.
   - [a] Which section of the brochure gives the most general information?
   - [b] Which sections give the most detailed information?
   - [c] What patterns do you notice?

2. Look at (i) the paragraph on the first page of the brochure, (ii) the *Your tour* section on the second page, and (iii) the *Itinerary* section also on the second page. Do they:
   - [a] start with general information and become more detailed?
   - [b] start with detailed information and become more general?
   - [c] follow a time order (eg from first to last)?
   - [d] jump about, without any order?

Task B | Writing to follow a genre

You are going to write information brochure pages about a tour in your country, city or home town. Your brochure should follow the pattern shown in the example in the reading section.

1. Choose a place to write about.
2. Make a rough itinerary.
3. Tell your partner about your tour. Your partner will ask questions.
4. Write the brochure, checking that the paragraphs and ideas follow the patterns you found earlier in this unit.
5. Swap your brochure with someone else. Check that – (a) the paragraphs move in time order (chronological order), and (b) each section has the same purpose as the example.

MAIN IDEAS AND SPECIFIC INFORMATION – LECTURE ON WEDDING CUSTOMS; CONVERSATION BETWEEN TWO STUDENTS

Task A | Vocabulary around romance and marriage

1. Help each other to put the following in time (chronological) order (some may happen at the same time).
   - have a wedding/a wedding ceremony
   - get engaged
   - have the stag night/have the hen's party
   - go on a honeymoon
   - get married
   - start going out with each other/start dating
   - choose the best man and the bridesmaids
   - have a wedding reception.

2. What's the difference between:
   - [a] a wedding and a marriage?
   - [b] a bride and a groom?
   - [c] a groom and a husband?
   - [b] a partner, a husband and a wife?

3. In small groups, guess the meaning of the following and (if necessary) check the meaning in a dictionary.
   - [a] a registry office wedding
   - [b] to elope
   - [c] to get a divorce/to get divorced/to divorce.

   In what situations might these happen? For each, say whether they are good or bad – and give reasons.

Task B | Discussion and prediction

1. Talk with a partner or small group about wedding ceremonies in your own culture. Think especially about:
   - what happens during the ceremony and at the party afterwards
   - any symbols and their meanings (eg wedding rings)
   - any people who have a special role (eg to look after the wedding ring)
   - the people who come to the wedding ceremony and the reception.

   What new vocabulary did you find out from your partner(s), your teacher or your dictionary during this activity?

2. In the next task, you are going to listen to part of a university lecture. Here are the lecture notes from the student handbook, which summarises each lecture.

Lecture 3: We will look at some of the traditions of weddings, with examples from countries such as India, Japan and China, as well as the traditionally English-speaking countries. We will see that many of the symbols in weddings can help us understand other aspects of a country's culture.

[a] Think of as many symbols in weddings as you can. What is each symbolic of?
[b] What do you know about weddings in the countries listed in the box above?

Task C | Listening for main ideas

CD 1

Listen to the first part of the recording. Tick the ideas below when you hear them. One idea is not mentioned – which is it?

Main topic of the lecture:
[a] Wedding customs in different cultures

To be mentioned later:
[b] Religious and spiritual beliefs
[c] Differences in wedding customs within a country
[d] Recent changes in wedding customs

To be mentioned in the next part of the lecture:
[e] Wedding clothes
[f] Rituals – bride leaves family or joins another
[g] How to stop bad luck
[h] Symbol of promises
[I] Religious part of the ceremony
[j] Wedding reception.

*

AT THE BEGINNING OF A TALK OR LECTURE, THE LECTURER OFTEN GIVES THE MAIN IDEAS TO BE TALKED ABOUT LATER.

Task D | Listening for specific information

Read the questions below. Then, listen to the next part of the recording, section by section, and answer the following questions.

1. Who is the centre of attention, the bride or the groom?

____

2. What did the white colour of wedding dresses symbolise in the past?

____

3. What colour do Chinese brides traditionally wear? What does this colour symbolise?

____

4. Do Chinese brides change clothes during the wedding day?

____

5. Name one country in which the bride 'changes family'?

____

6. Who is with a Western bride when she enters the church?

____

7. Who is with her when she leaves?

____

8. What is worn to symbolise the marriage in India?
[a] a ring
[b] a necklace
[c] a special colour of clothing
[d] a special hair style.

9. What is a spelling of this Indian symbol of marriage?

____

10. Traditionally, did the man give the woman a wedding ring (in Western weddings)?

____

11. In what country are the bride and groom's hands sometimes tied together?

____

12. Throwing confetti is a wish for fertility (fertility: ability to have babies):
[a] true
[b] false
[c] no information given.

13. Before confetti, people used to throw ______________ over the couple.

14. Other symbols of fertility are ______________ and ___

____

15. Which are longer, wedding parties in India or in Western countries?

____

____

16. Western weddings don't have which of the following:
    [a] special seating arrangements
    [b] people making speeches
    [c] people giving money, not presents
    [d] the bride and groom cutting the cake together.
17. According to the lecturer, the longest weddings in Islamic cultures are ________________ days long.

Task E | Do you need to understand every word?

1. Look at the underlined words in the sentences below – these sentences are from the recording. Did you need to understand these words while listening for the answers to the questions in Tasks C and D?
   - … we'll start with the most obvious visual elements – the costumes, and especially the choice of clothes …
   - In many Western cultures, and more and more often in Eastern cultures, elaborate white dresses are worn …
2. How do you know the main point of the sentences?
3. Do you always need to understand every word, to understand the main points?

Task F | Listening to compare

CD 1

Listen to two students talking together after the lecture you heard before. They are talking about weddings in Japan. Fill in the gaps below, which show some differences and similarities between a typical Japanese wedding and a typical Western wedding.

Kaori's sister (Japanese style wedding)	What Michael is used to (Western style wedding)
ceremony in a [1]__________	ceremony in a religious building, eg a church
traditional weddings usually follow Shinto style __________	traditional weddings are usually Christian
modern weddings are often [2]__________ style	
the priest performed a ritual with a [3]__________ __________ while chanting	
the [4]__________ made a promise to the [5]__________	the bride and groom make promises to each other
the bride and groom exchange [6]__________	the bride and groom exchange rings
the wedding party is in a [7]__________	
people give [8]__________ as a wedding present	people give household goods as wedding presents
the bride wore [9]__________ dresses	the bride wears the same dress all the time

Task G | Discussion

1. What is the difference between weddings in your culture and:
   [a] Kaori's wedding in Japan?
   [b] Western weddings, such as those Michael was used to?
2. Think about weddings in your culture. Tell your partner about the following:
   [a] What costumes are worn in weddings in your country (eg by the bride and groom, best man, bridesmaids, family members)?
   [b] What rituals (if any) and symbolic actions happen during the weddings?
   [c] Is anything special done for good luck?
   [d] What happens during the wedding reception?
3. What differences between wedding ceremonies in different parts of your country do you know about?
4. What changes have happened to wedding ceremonies and customs in your country?

PHRASAL VERBS

Task A | About phrasal verbs

1 Look at the short conversation below:

[a] Circle each verb.
[b] Which verbs have more than one word (these are called phrasal verbs)?
[c] What is the meaning of each phrasal verb?
[d] For each phrasal verb, does each word in the verb help you find the meaning?

A: Hey, Libby, have you heard? Tom's going out with Rebecca!

B: Really! I know they get on well with each other, that's good news!

A: Yeah, they got together at a party last week

B: I was going to drop in on Rebecca later … can't wait to hear the whole story!

2 Match the following phrasal verbs with a regular verb with the same meaning. Which feels more formal? (Help each other and use a dictionary only if necessary.)

PHRASAL VERBS	REGULAR VERBS
bring up (eg children)	admire
carry on (doing something)	awaken
carry out	continue
drop in (on someone)	disrespect
die out	do
give up (something/doing something)	investigate
look up to (someone)	raise
look down on (someone)	stop doing
look into (something)	stop happening (eg a tradition)
put up (with something)	test
try out (something)	tolerate
wake up	visit

3 Look at the following. Crossed out sentences are incorrect. What do you notice about the second word of the phrasal verb?

____

____

give up
Tom should give up smoking.
Tom should give smoking up.
Tom's still smoking? He should give it up.
Tom's still smoking? ~~He should give up it~~.

put up
Rebecca might not put up with Tom's unusual sense of humour.
~~Rebecca might not put with Tom's unusual sense of humour up.~~
Tom's got an unusual sense of humour. ~~Rebecca might not put with it up~~.
Tom's got an unusual sense of humour. Rebecca might not put up with it.

Task B | Practice

1 Replace a regular verb in the following sentences with a phrasal verb. Separate them if possible. An English-English dictionary will help you find out which are separable. Special symbols may be used – for example the *Longman Dictionary of Contemporary English* uses ⇔ to show a verb is separable.

[a] Her father was well known for working for charities. She admired him.
[b] His mother awakens him early every morning.
[c] The town's traditional festival has fewer and fewer people taking part each year. However, the mayor doesn't want the town to stop it.
[d] People ask the surgeon to perform many operations every year. He still does them, even though he's seventy.
[e] Japan has many interesting festivals. The university professor is investigating how they began.
[f] Their children are very respectful. Their parents are raising them in traditional ways.
[g] Before he buys a new computer, he wants to test it at home.
[h] Your snoring's terrible! I won't tolerate it any more!
[i] Visit our house any time! You're very welcome!

2 *Play this game in small groups.* Each group should have a ball – the last person holding the ball loses the game. Choose a topic to talk about, and start talking. When you use a phrasal verb, throw the ball to another student in your group. This person should complete your sentence and continue talking on the same topic. Keep doing this until the teacher stops the game – the person holding the ball at this time loses. Repeat several times.

3 *Play this game in pairs.* Tell a story. Your teacher will give you some ideas to talk about, or ask you to think of some yourself. Talk about it for up to two minutes, trying to use as many phrasal verbs as possible. Your partner will count them. Then swap roles.

SPECIFIC AND GENERAL QUESTIONS; LEARNING STYLES QUIZ

Task A | Specific questions

1. Tell your partner about some time when you visited another country (perhaps where you are studying, if it isn't your own country) and were surprised by a cultural difference. Also, what cultural similarities surprised you?

2. Tell your partner about a festival that you went to in your country. Then your partner will ask you questions about the festival.

3. Imagine your speaking partner is a friend from another country, and will visit your family soon. Tell your friend about the customs they will need to know. Your friend will ask you what to do in certain situations.

Task B | General questions

INSTRUCTIONS

1. Spend a few minutes making notes about each of the questions below (these notes are only to help with ideas for speaking).
2. Tell your group your ideas.
3. Discuss the ideas you heard from others in your group.

QUESTIONS

[a] Do you think it is important to continue the traditions of the past?

[b] Do you think that traditions should change with the influence of other cultures? (Perhaps think about the effect of US culture on the rest of the world)

[c] How much do you think movies and music from other cultures have changed your culture from when your grandparents were young?

[d] Has the culture in your country changed a lot over the last 50 years?

[e] Do you expect your country's culture will change a lot in the future?

Task C | How do you like to learn languages?

Take the following quiz. Your answers will help you understand how you learn English best. Circle the letter that is your answer and that is closest to your feeling.

1. In my English class
- A. I would rather write most things down that I hear
- B. I would rather practise with a partner out loud
- C. I would rather sit quietly until I know the answer
- D. I would rather get the chance to speak than be quiet

2. When working in pairs in class
- A. I like to write what is going on
- B. I like to be the leader
- C. I like to be quiet and let the other person speak
- D. I like to speak

3. When speaking in class
- A. I always want to be corrected
- B. I like the teacher to allow me to finish without corrections in the middle
- C. I feel embarrassed and know I am making mistakes
- D. I want mistakes corrected immediately

4. When in class
- A. I wish I were outside walking or swimming or enjoying myself
- B. I enjoy working and learning English
- C. I don't enjoy it, but I know I must study hard
- D. I like my classmates and know my English will improve if I try by completing work

5. When it comes to grammar
- A. I like to memorise the rules by heart
- B. I seem to use grammar correctly most of the time without memorising
- C. I like to keep practising until the rule is not in my mind
- D. I don't need rules, because I can hear changes in speech and see them in the writing

6. When it comes to vocabulary
   A. I like to memorise all vocabulary
   B. I like to try to use new words as soon as I have heard them
   C. I like to write down new words before I use them
   D. I like to practise new words outside class

7. Outside of class
   A. I hate making mistakes when talking
   B. I like to try to talk to people as much as I can
   C. I always worry and feel embarrassed to speak because I will make mistakes
   D. I don't care too much about mistakes, I just enjoy talking with someone

8. When I'm listening
   A. I can't hear well because I'm nearly always nervous
   B. I don't hear every word, but can usually follow the gist of what's being said
   C. I want to hear every word so I know I understand the conversation
   D. I try to follow even when I don't know all the words

On the next page, check your score to find the 'type' of learner you are. Read the box indicated by your score, and think about the advice it gives you.

If your score is between 8 and 10 inclusive, look at box Y
If your score is between 11 and 13, look at box X
If your score is between 14 and 16, look at box Z

BOX X

Like many people, you have a combination of learning styles and ways in which you like to learn. You are relaxed and confident in some situations, but like to be accurate and speak correctly in others.

Your task will be to work on study patterns that make the most of both these qualities.

BOX Y

Your learning style is communicative. You like to make friends easily and want to talk to everyone.

Your style is relaxed and you are fairly comfortable in new situations. You will try to talk, even if you make mistakes.

You may need to work harder towards accuracy in your writing when it comes to academic English.

BOX Z

Your learning style is accuracy driven. You like to be sure you are right before speaking and writing. You may be a little shy when it comes to communicating, particularly in unfamiliar situations.

You are probably an analytical person and are neat and tidy with your notes and personal dictionary.

If you take more risks, your English may improve more quickly. Try to communicate in English even when you aren't completely sure whether your grammar and vocabulary are correct.

DISCUSSION

1. Form groups of different learning styles and discuss what you think are the strengths and weaknesses of each learning type.
2. Make a list for yourself of suggestions that you think you might try after discussion with that person. Can you think of ways to add to your learning style? How could you experiment with a new idea after speaking to someone different from yourself?

HOW TO CALCULATE YOUR SCORE

As = 2
Bs = 1
Cs = 2
Ds = 1

Add all your answers together.

Score ________

FURTHER PRACTICE: READING, FILMS AND FUN

READING

Travel guides can give some good information about cultures. For example, try:

http://www.lonelyplanet.com/worldguide/ or **http://travel.roughguides.com/destinationshome.html**.

For more specific information about countries, you can look at:

http://www.infoplease.com/countries.html and **http://www.cia.gov/cia/publications/factbook/**

http://www.shaadi.com/wedding/rituals/wedding.php explains several different wedding traditions common in India.

http://weddings.lovetoknow.com/wiki/Main_Page has quite a lot of information on Western weddings,

http://www.central-mosque.com/fiqh/Wedding.htm lists and explains some of the rules of Islamic weddings.

FILMS

There are many films showing people dealing with living in different cultures. For example:

Bend it like Beckham, directed by Gurinder Chanda. A comedy about a girl who is a member of a family from India living in London. She wants to play soccer, but her family have other ideas.

Seven Years in Tibet, directed by Jean-Jacques Annaud. An Austrian is lost in Tibet.

Dances with Wolves, directed by Kevin Costner. An American soldier learns about Native American culture.

Weddings were the topic of part of this unit, and the following films show weddings in different cultures:

India: *Monsoon Wedding*, directed by Mira Nair.

Australia: *Muriel's wedding*, directed by PJ Hogan.

USA: *Father of the Bride*, directed by Charles Shyer.

QUESTIONS

1. What happens on a child's birthday in your country?
2. Describe a typical baby naming ceremony in your culture. Are there sometimes variations (differences) from the traditional ceremonies? If so, describe the differences.
3. When some people get married, they choose to make the ceremony different from what is traditional in their culture. For example, they hold the ceremony on a beach at sunset, or the wedding dress is a different colour. What would happen at your ideal wedding, and why?
4. Many countries have national days on which people might dress in traditional costumes, eat special food, or take part in ceremonies and processions. Describe a day like this from your own culture.
5. Should marriage be for life? Or is it OK for people to be married more than once during their lifetime?

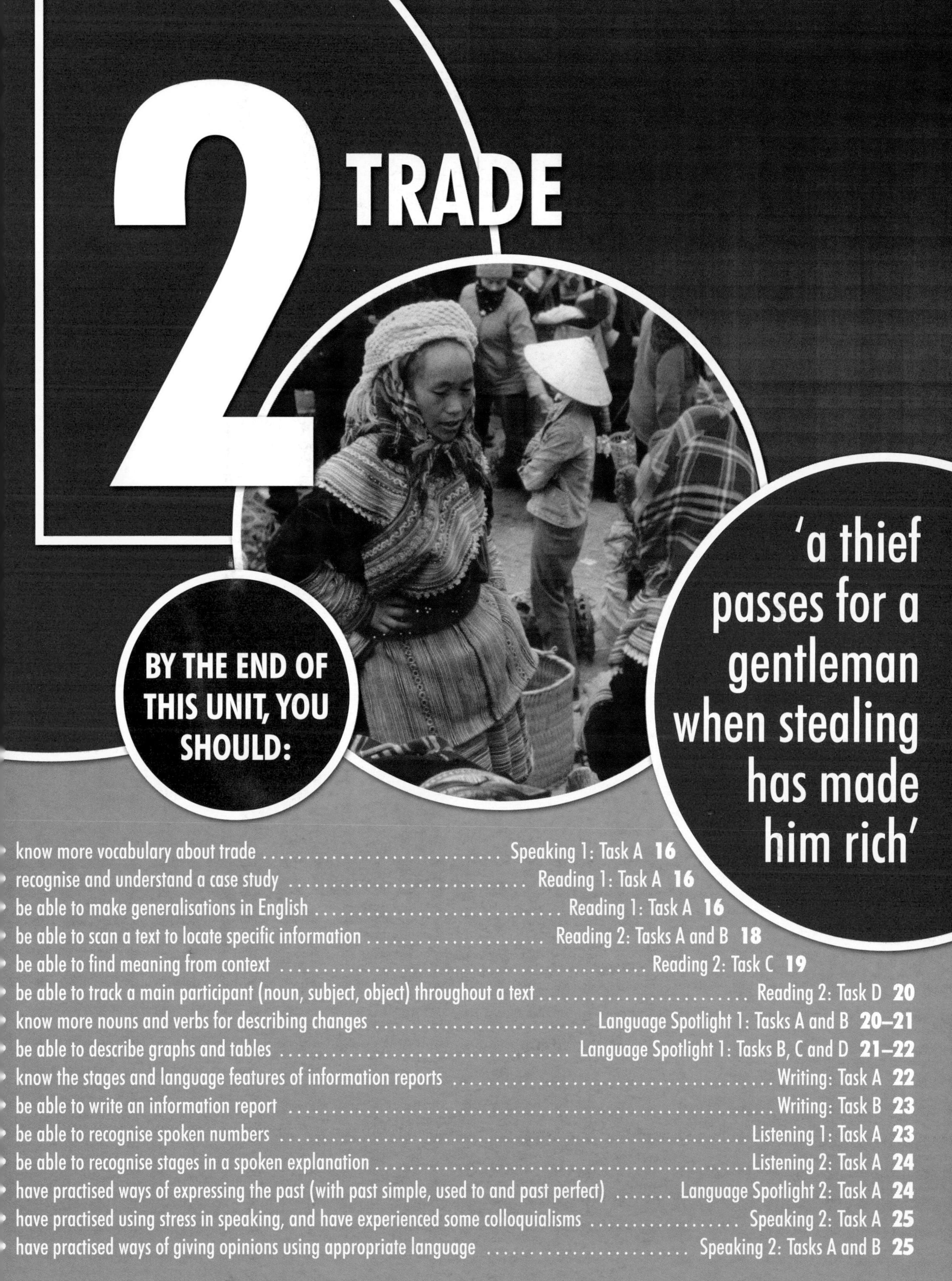

2 TRADE

'a thief passes for a gentleman when stealing has made him rich'

BY THE END OF THIS UNIT, YOU SHOULD:

RADE [UNCOUNTABLE]: 1 **Buying/Selling** the activity of buying, selling, or exchanging goods within a country or between ountries; = commerce; *There has been a marked increase in trade between East and West.* 2 **The hotel/tourist etc trade** the usiness done by companies, hotels etc; 3 **Amount of business** [U] *BrE* business activity, especially the amount of goods or products hat are sold; = business: *A lot of pubs nowadays do most of their trade at lunchtimes.* 4 **An exchange of things** [sing.] *AmE* when ou exchange something you have for something that someone else has: *Let's **make a trade**.*

BUILDING THE FIELD

Task A | Asking questions about trade

1. In pairs, ask the following questions. Then swap roles and repeat.

[a] Student A: Do you know what trade means?
Student B: (yes or no)

[b] Student A: Have you traded something in your life?
Student B: (yes or no)

[c] Student A: What items did you trade and how old were you when you did this?
Student B: I traded ______________________ (answer truthfully)

[d] Student A: Can you give me a definition – Can you tell me what the word 'trade' means?
Student B: I think 'trade' means ______________ ______________ (tell in your own words)

[e] Student A: What country do you come from?
Student B: I'm from ______________________ (answer truthfully)

[f] Student A: What is your country famous for trading?
Student B: It's famous for trading ______________.

[g] Student A: What does your country export?
Student B: I think we send (sell) ______________ to ______________

[h] Student A: What does your country import?
Student B: I think we bring in (buy) ______________ from ______________

Now, work together to define 'export' and 'import'. Use your dictionary if you don't know what the words mean. Write their definitions.

Export

____

Import

____

Swap places. Student B now asks the same questions of Student A.

2. What question words were used by Student A? Write them below: Some examples of question words are: What, when, who, how, where, can you, do you and have you?

[a] ______________ [e] ______________

[b] ______________ [f] ______________

[c] ______________ [g] ______________

[d] ______________ [h] ______________

MAKING GENERALISATIONS – CASE STUDY

Task A | Making generalisations from a case study

Case studies are used on many kinds of courses to show how some general rules (or a theory) can be used in a real situation.

This case study is from a text book for business studies courses (Hartley, 2002). It shows the effect of bad customer service on trade.

1. Before reading the case study, answer the following questions:

[a] Have you ever had bad service in a shop?
[b] What was the problem?
[c] What did you do?
[d] How did the problem make you feel about buying from the shop again?

2. Read the text on the following page. While reading, think about whether the staff are doing a good job or a bad job.

THE PRICE PAID FOR IGNORING THE CUSTOMER

1 With a wallet in one hand and a broken plate in the other, Kevin entered the shop.

As he walked around the store, he noticed that it was empty; he was the only customer on both floors. The only other people in the building were three sales people standing around one of the sales counters.

5 At first, Kevin was quite happy to browse because he hated pushy sales people who approach every new customer as soon as they start looking at something and ask 'Can I help you?'. However, as time passed, Kevin started to become a little irritated, especially when he noticed that the three staff were all standing around the sales counter discussing the choice of music being played over the in-store PA system.

10 Kevin was confused. There was no-one else in the shop; people could see him easily and, for good measure, his wallet and broken plate made his purpose for being in the shop very clear. His intention to buy a new plate could not have been more clear.

All the tried and tested attempts to attract the staff's attention like coughing, picking up the goods on sale and rattling the cutlery failed. So did walking directly past the front

15 counter where the staff were still talking about themselves.

After 15 minutes of being ignored, what else could Kevin do? He left the shop.

Source: Stephen Hartley, *The Trainers Toolbox*. Sydney: Pearson Education Australia, p. 31. Reproduced with permission.

3 In pairs, ask and answer the following questions (about your personal reaction):

[a] If you were Kevin, would you do the same? If something different, what?

[b] What do you think of the attitude of the staff?

[c] If you were a staff member, would you do the same? If something different, what?

4 **(i)** For each statement below, use a tick (✓) if it is an appropriate conclusion from the case study, and put a cross (✗) if it isn't. Explain your reasons using sentences and quotes from the study.

[a] If a salesperson asks a customer as soon as they enter the shop 'May I help you?', they might make the customer feel uncomfortable.

[b] In Kevin's culture, shop sales people don't try to help customers.

[c] Customers who don't ask for help don't get served.

[d] In Kevin's culture, customers don't ask for help.

[e] In Kevin's culture, if people want to replace something that's broken, they bring the broken thing to the shop.

[f] A shop might sell more things if the sales people speak to customers.

(ii) Which of these statements do you think is the main point of the case study? Why?

5 The statements in Question 4 are called generalisations, because they say that something is generally true.

[a] Which tenses/verb forms are used in these generalisations? (These are commonly used in other generalisations.)

____

____

[b] Do generalisations use specific words for people (like *me*, *he* or the person's name), or do they use general words (eg *customers*, *people*)?

____

[c] Do generalisations use singulars or plurals?

____

6 Personalised practice. Tell your partner some generalisations about the following:

[a] Prices in your current country

[b] Prices in your own country (if different from [a])

[c] Customer service in your current country

[d] Customer service in your own country

[e] Anything else about shopping in your own country and your current country

[f] The weather in your current country and your own country

[g] What you do in your free time in your own country and the country where you live now.

READING 2 SCANNING, FINDING MEANING FROM CONTEXT, TRACKING PARTICIPANTS – INFORMATION REPORT

Task A | Introduction to the Silk Road

1. In small groups, discuss the following questions:
   - [a] What products is China famous for?
   - [b] What products was China famous for in the past?
   - [c] How did China export its products in the past?
   - [d] Look at the map below. Have you heard about the trade route shown? What is it called in your own language? Can you translate that into English?

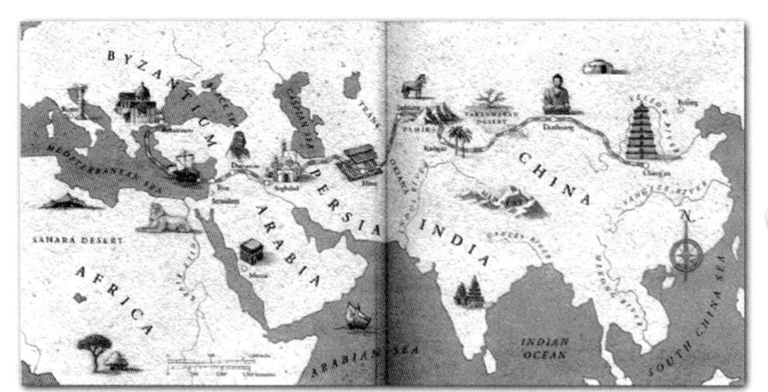

Source: The Oracle Education Foundation (ND), '*The Silk Road: Linking Europe and Asia by Trade*'. Available: http://library.thinkquest.org/13406/sr/, accessed 8 January 2007.

Task B | Introduction to scanning

If you are looking for specific information (eg numbers, dates, answers to specific questions), you don't have to start at the beginning of a text and read every word – it will take too long. You can find the answers much more quickly by *scanning*, that is, reading quickly for specific words or ideas. Don't use a dictionary when scanning.

1. Read questions [a] to [h] below. Scan for the key words (in **bold** in the questions) in the Silk Road text on the next page. Write only the line number where you find the key words – this is where you are likely to find the answers to the questions.

__	[a] How were **goods** carried?
__	[b] Why did Chan Ch'ien make **alliances** with the local tribes?
__	[c] Was silk **lucrative**?
__	[d] Which **commodities** were silk traded for?
__	[e] What effect did high **duties** have on the cost of silk in the Roman Empire?
__	[f] When did trade along the Silk Road first **decline**? Why?
__	[g] When did trade **increase**?
__	[h] Why did Silk Road trade finally **decrease**?

2. After finding the line numbers in Question 1, write the answers to the questions here.

[a] ______________________________

____

[b] ______________________________

____

[c] ______________________________

____

[d] ______________________________

____

[e] ______________________________

____

[f] ______________________________

____

____

[g] ______________________________

____

____

[h] ______________________________

____

3. Did you read the whole text to find these answers?

4. For each of the following situations, mark whether you would scan, skim or read everything in detail (look back at Unit 1 to review skimming).

[a] finding someone's number in a phone book ________
[b] finding out about a bank account by reading a small leaflet ________
[c] finding the interest rate of a bank account by reading a small leaflet ________
[d] finding a price in a leaflet ________
[e] understanding a complicated explanation ________
[f] looking for a date in a text ________
[g] finding all the reasons that the Silk Road trade declined ________
[h] finding the main points covered in a book chapter ________
[i] finding a paragraph in a book chapter about the first Silk Road traders ________.

Task C | Introduction to finding meaning from context

In the previous task, maybe you didn't know some of the words before. However, you probably have a better idea about their meaning now. This is because you used:

- the meaning of the sentence containing the unknown word
- the meaning of the paragraph and the text as a whole, and
- your knowledge of the topic

to help you find the meaning.

This is called FINDING MEANING FROM CONTEXT.

The Silk Road: Linking Europe and Asia through Trade

The Silk Road is one of the best known ancient trading routes. It was a major link between East and West, and for this reason, it has been very important in history.

Origins

Originally, the Chinese traded silk within its own empire. Caravans, which were large groups of animals carrying goods for trade, would carry silk from the empire's interior to the western edges of the region. Often thieves would attack these caravans hoping to capture the traders' valuable goods. As a result, the Han Dynasty extended its military defences further into Central Asia from 135 to 90 BC to protect these caravans.

Chan Ch'ien, the first known Chinese traveller to make contact with the Central Asian tribes, later thought of expanding the silk trade to include these smaller tribes and therefore made alliances with them. Because of this idea, the Silk Road was born. The route grew with the rise of the Roman Empire, because the Chinese gave silk to the Roman and Asian governments as gifts.

Spanning Two Continents

The 11,000 kilometre route spanned China, Central Asia, Northern India, and the Parthian and Roman Empires. It connected the Yellow River Valley to the Mediterranean Sea and passed through the present-day countries of Iran, Iraq and Syria.

People who lived in the North West of India, near the Ganges River, played important roles as middlemen in the China-Mediterranean silk trade because as early as the third century AD, they understood that silk was a lucrative product of the Chinese Empire. The trading relationship between the Chinese and the Indians grew stronger with increased Chinese expansion into Central Asia. The Chinese would trade their silk with the Indians for commodities such as jade, gold, and silver, and the Indians would trade the silk with the Roman Empire. Silk proved to be an expensive import for the Roman Empire since heavy duties were collected across India and Central Asia by the Parthian Empire.

Social Consequences of the Silk Road

Because of the number of people travelling along the Silk Road not only goods but also ideas were conveyed. One of the most important effects of the trade route was that Buddhism spread from India to China.

The Silk Road's Decline

As table 1 shows, by 760 AD, trade along the Silk Road had declined. This was because robbers had started to attack the caravans again. Trade revived considerably in the eleventh and twelfth centuries when China became largely dependent on its silk trade. In addition, trade to Central and Western Asia as well as Europe increased from 1276 to 1368 when the Mongols controlled China. However, after that, overland trade became increasingly dangerous, and sea routes became more popular, so trade along the Silk Road decreased.

Period	Years	Trade activity
Warring States Period	before 206BC	none
Roman Empire/Han Dynasty	206BC – AD220	some
Early T'ang Dynasty	6th –7th century AD	the highest of all
Middle of T'ang Dynasty	AD760	less
Song Dynasty	11th–12th century AD	higher again
Yuan Dynasty	AD1276–1368	even higher
Ming Dynasty	15th century AD	much lower

TABLE 1: Trade activity along the Silk Road

Source: adapted from The Oracle Education Foundation (ND), *'The Silk Road: Linking Europe and Asia by Trade'*. Available: http://library.thinkquest.org/13406/sr/, accessed 8 January 2007.

To check that you did this, match the following words to their meanings, without using a dictionary. Some of the words are about trading, and others are about numbers getting higher or lower.

WORDS	MEANINGS
goods	• to get lower, to go down
alliances	• things that are traded
lucrative	• to get higher, to go up
commodities	• things that are bought and sold – usually something natural, eg metal or food.
duties	• to get lower, to go down
decline	• countries or people that have decided to work together to help each other
increase	• something that makes lots of money
decrease	• taxes on things imported into a country

Task D | Tracking participants

Study the two examples below, then do Question 1.

Example 1: Tracking participants 1

Track the word 'road'. Follow the word throughout the text. In English, we use substitution as well as repetition (repeating a word).

> The road is long. It was made by men. The road is famous around the world. The road is really a silk route. It is a trading route. It is the Silk Road.

Example 2: Tracking participants 2

Track the word 'history'. Follow the word throughout the text.

> History repeats itself. If we study it, we are supposed to learn from it. The past is supposed to be a guide for humans. Without it, we lose our way. Without knowledge of prior events, we can repeat our mistakes. We need to study history to have better societies.

Track the participant – 'the *Silk Road* ' – throughout the reading (see page 19), (a historical report – *The Silk Road: Linking Europe and Asia through Trade*). Circle each reference to it. The first paragraph is done for you below.

> The Silk Road is one of the best known ancient trading routes. It was a major link between East and West, and for this reason, it has been very important in history.

Task E | The five questions for any reading

Using the following text, answer the questions below.

[a] What are you reading? What is it? (an article, poem, a review, an extract from somewhere, a definition, a short story, an essay?)

____

[b] What is the source? In other words, where does the text come from? (Newspaper, journal, text book, novel, dictionary, thesaurus, magazine?)

____

[c] Who is the writer?

____

[d] What purpose does the writer have for writing the text?

____

[e] Who is the intended audience?

____

VOCABULARY DESCRIBING GRAPHS AND TABLES

Task A | Further vocabulary for describing graphs and tables

1. In the previous section, you looked at some words that show that numbers get higher and lower. Here are some more. Put them into two groups, each with a similar meaning.

decline	fall	drop
increase	climb	rise
decrease	grow	reduce

HIGHER	LOWER

2 Write the past tense form of each of the words below, and the past participle.

BARE INFINITIVE	PAST SIMPLE FORM	PAST PARTICIPLE
climb		
decline		
decrease		
drop		
fall		
grow		
increase		
reduce		
rise		

Task B | Noun forms of the verbs

1 Rewrite the following sentences using the verb form of the word highlighted in bold. Two examples are given.

[a] There was an **increase** in the number of robberies on the Silk Road

➔ *The number of robberies on the Silk Road increased*

[b] After this, there was a **decline** in trade on the Silk Road.

➔ *After this, trade on the Silk Road declined*

[c] There was a **decline** in Silk Road trade to almost nothing when travel by ship became safer than the overland route.

➔ ____________________

[d] There was significant **growth** in Australia's exports of iron during 2005.

➔ ____________________

[e] There was a **rise** in the number of overseas students in New Zealand between 1985 and 2005.

➔ ____________________

[f] There has been a **growth** in my vocabulary since I started using this book.

➔ ____________________

[g] I'm hoping there will be an **increase** in my English level over the next year.

➔ ____________________

2 What pattern do you notice in the noun and verb forms of most of these words?

3 Put appropriate words in the correct form into the gaps in the paragraph below. Hint: These words can be found in the word list in Task A.

I started learning English in junior high school, but I wasn't very good and my level ____________________ [🡅] very slowly. I think this was because I couldn't see a good reason to learn English at that time. However, I became more interested in English later and my level ____________________ [🡅] more quickly. Then, when I studied for the university entrance exams, my English ability ____________________ [🡅] even faster. But, when I was at university, I didn't need to use English at all, so my level ____________________ [🡇].

After university, I worked with people from East Asia, and I had to use English with them. Therefore my English ____________________ [🡅] again. After a couple of years, I decided to study in the UK, so I had to study for an English exam. Therefore there was another ____________________ [🡅] in my English level, but not as fast as I wanted. When I went to the UK, though, there was a much faster ____________________ [🡅] in my English level, because I could practise outside class, and because when I learnt something in lessons, it wasn't long before I heard or saw examples in real life. Now, I'm studying hard – I think my reading ability is ____________________ [🡅] because I have to read many journal articles every day, but my speaking level is ____________________ [🡇]!

Task C | Practice – Describing graphs and tables

1. Do this in pairs. Student A: look on page 161. Student B: look on page 163 of Appendix 4. You will both see a graph, but they are a little different: they have the same axes but show different things (axes are the lines at the bottom and left side of a graph). Do not show the graphs to each other.
2. Student A: describe your graph to student B. Student B should draw the graph following student A's instructions only, without looking.
3. Swap. Now, student A will draw student B's graph without looking.

Task D | Have a go!

1. Draw graphs to show each of the following over time:
   [a] Your English level
   [b] Your feelings since you started this course
   [c] Your feelings about your further studies
   [d] How hungry you are through the day
   [e] How awake/tired you are through the day.
2. Without showing the graphs to your partner, describe them to him or her. Your partner should ask you questions about what you say.

INFORMATION REPORT

Task A | Generic features of an information report

The *Silk Road* text in the previous section is an information report. The main purpose of an information report is to give facts (not opinions). It says what happened, or what exists.

1. Read the following table carefully. It shows the stages in information reports.

STAGE	SUB-STAGE	PURPOSE
Introduction	General statement	To introduce the topic of the information report, and to define it.
	Justification (optional)	To show why the topic is important
Points (in logical order)	*for each point:*	
	Theme	To introduce the point
	Elaboration	To give further information about the point

Note: *the theme is sometimes a sentence. When it is a sentence it is often called a* ***topic sentence****.*

2. Draw boxes around (or colour) the stages in the *Silk Road* text. The introduction has been done for you as an example:

General statement

Introduction

The Silk Road is one of the best known ancient trading routes.

It was a major link between East and West, and for this reason, it has been very important in history.

Originally, the Chinese traded silk within ......

Justification

3. Which of the following best describes the kind of logical order in this text?
   [a] time order (chronological)
   [b] order of importance (most important first, least important last)
   [c] different stages in a circle of events (cyclical)
4. From the following list of topics, choose the type of logical order that fits best:
   [a] life cycle of a frog
   [b] history of China
   [c] stages in your English learning
   [d] the members of your favourite sports team.

5. Which tense is used the most? Why, do you think this?

6. Look at the nouns in the text. Are they mostly general (eg *Chinese people*, *trade*) or specific (eg *someone's name*)?

Task B | Write an information report

1. Choose a topic from the following list, or a list your teacher gives you:
   [a] Stages in your English learning
   [b] A very short history of your country
   [c] The members of your favourite sports team or music band
   [d] Where you can go shopping in your city.

2. Write an information report on the topic you chose. Use the following checklist and make sure you include all the points while writing it.
   - it has a clear introduction and a few points
   - the introduction has a general statement and (preferably) a justification
   - each point has a theme and some elaboration
   - the points follow a chronological or cyclical order, or they are in order of importance
   - a simple tense is the main tense (present simple or past simple, as appropriate)
   - general nouns are used more than specific nouns (unless writing about a single person or thing).

3. When you've finished, check your report using the list in Question 2. It is normal to change a piece of writing after the first time you write it. This is called doing multiple drafts. The first report you write is the first draft, the second (better) one is the second draft, and so on.

NUMBERS – PROPERTY AUCTION

Task A | Numbers

PRE-LISTENING PRACTICE

- In sentences, emphasis on the *teen* numbers is usually at the end, whereas emphasis on the *ty* numbers is always at the beginning. That's how you can tell whether the speaker says 15 or 50. The emphasis is underlined for you.
- Fifteen but Fifty

1. Your teacher will read a list of numbers. Write them below.

i.	______	viii.	______	xiv.	______
ii.	______	ix.	______	xv.	______
iii.	______	x.	______	xvi.	______
iv.	______	xi.	______	xvii.	______
v.	______	xii.	______	xviii.	______
vi.	______	xiii.	______	xix.	______
vii.	______			xx.	______

CD 1

2. Write the numbers that each bidder says as you hear them make their bids.

[a] Bidder 11: ______
[b] Bidder 17: ______
[c] Bidder 22: ______
[d] Bidder 17: ______
[e] Bidder 22: ______
[f] Bidder 17: ______
[g] Bidder 30: ______
[h] Bidder 30: 550
[i] John: Number 30 offers Five hundred and fifty thousand dollars. The sun is shining, it was cloudy, but now it's bright. Let's keep this going and get this beautiful home into a new owner's hands today!
[j] John: Ah number 17 Yes! The bid is 550 and you make $__________. Well done.
[k] Bidder 22: ______
[l] Bidder 11: ______
[m] Bidder 17: ______
[n] Bidder 11: ______
[o] Bidder 17: ______
[p] Bidder 22: ______
[q] Bidder 11: ______
[r] Bidder 17: ______
[s] Bidder 11: ______
[t] Bidder 17: ______
[u] Bidder 11: ______

IDENTIFYING STAGES – SPOKEN EXPLANATION

CD 1

5

Task A | A spoken explanation signalling new stages

1. Read the list below of expressions (signals) that indicate stages of spoken explanations. Now, listen to the speaker, and tick the phrases as you hear them.
   - [a] Good morning, students. In this unit so far …
   - [b] Today…
   - [c] Next…
   - [d] After that…
   - [e] You then…
   - [f] Also…
   - [g] To finish…

2. Listen a **second time** and try to write the phrases that follow the expressions (signals). The first one is done for you.
   - [a] Good morning, students. In this unit so far… *we introduced trade in some different ways*
   - [b] We began ______________________________

     ____
   - [c] Next ______________________________

     ____
   - [d] After that ______________________________

     ____
   - [e] You then ______________________________

     ____
   - [f] Also ______________________________

     ____
   - [g] To finish ______________________________

     ____

3. Write the phrases **a** through **g** that match the stages i. through v. below.

   STAGES
   - **i.** Opening: ______________________
   - **ii.** Introduction – Re-cap: ______________
   - **iii.** Definition of terms: ______________
   - **iv.** Preview of what the whole talk is going to be about: ______________
   - **v.** Conclusions drawn: ______________

PAST SIMPLE, USED TO AND PAST PERFECT

Task A | Explanations

1. Examine the following explanations:

   Past simple: expressing a past action that is completed, ie finished.

   Example: I made a profit from my IT shares. I sold them because the company was taken over.

   Used to:

   Example: I used to have green energy shares. (**Unspoken meaning** – *but I no longer do.*)

   Past perfect: expressing a past action that was completed before another past time or event.

   Example: I had ordered those shares before I heard from you. (**Unspoken meaning** – *I wouldn't have ordered the shares if I had heard from you before I did order the shares.*)

2. Underline examples of past simple tense in the *Silk Road* text.

3. Write a paragraph about something you used to have but no longer do. Use all three tenses above.

SENTENCE STRESS, COLLOQUIALISMS AND EXPRESSING OPINIONS

Task A | Practising conversations

In pairs, read the following conversation aloud. Accentuate the underlined words (say them a little louder). Make your voice rise in a question sound where the accents are marked up and down.

WHAT WE SAY	WHAT WE MEAN
A. Hi Phil, how's it goin?	Hi Phil, how are you?
P. Alright	OK
A. You don't sound alright, what's up?	You don't seem to be well, what's the matter?
P. Nah, I'm OK, but I lost some money yesterday.	
A. What do you mean, you lost some money?	
P. On the stock exchange … I had ordered those shares before I knew what I was doing.	
A. So what happened?	
P. Simple, the company went broke.	
A. What? Overnight?	What do you mean? Did the company go broke suddenly?
P. Pretty much.	Yes, that's the way it happened.
A. So you sold?	Thus, you sold your shares?
P. Yep. I sold them. For a lot less than I bought them.	Yes. I sold them. I sold them for a lot less that I bought them for.
A. Bad luck, mate.	That's too bad. I feel sorry.
P. Yeah, bad luck.	
A. Wanta coffee?	Would you like to go to a café and get a coffee together?
P. Sure…	Yes.

Task B | What do you think? Expressing personal opinions

Read the following extracts, then, in pairs, express your personal opinion of each. You will form an opinion, then agree or disagree.

1. IMF and World Bank funding

Since World War II, it has been widely believed that underdeveloped countries cannot become prosperous without billions of dollars from wealthy countries. After 40 years, what is there to show for this strategy? Not much.

Do you agree or disagree?

2. 15–16 April 2005, London – Action for trade justice

25,000 people gathered in Whitehall and Westminster, London, between 15–16 April 2005 for an all-night vigil and protest organised by the World Development Movement and other coalition members of the Trade Justice Movement and Make Poverty History for a global week of action.

From a sold-out club night at The Marquee and a candlelit vigil to WDM's successful, standing-room only, trade justice cinema and a dawn procession, the night sent out a loud and clear message to the UK Government: stop making poor countries open their markets up to unfair trade and respect their right to decide on trade policies that would help end poverty and protect their environment.

The event was part of a global action for trade justice with events and activities in over 70 countries across the world.

Do you think you would have liked to join them?

3. The business environment

A combination of two major changes within the business environment will have dramatic impact on all sectors of the Textile Clothing and Footwear (TCF) Industries. Regardless of where you are in the supply chain, from textile manufacturer, clothing manufacturer, importer, wholesaler, agent, retailer or any other part of this chain your business environment has drastically changed and will continue to change at an even faster rate. The two major changes are government policies and new technologies.

Do you think this is true? If so, why?

FURTHER PRACTICE: READING, FILMS AND FUN

READING

Johan Norberg (2003) *In Defense of Global Capitalism*, Washington DC: Cato Institute.

Doug Bandow and Ian Vásquez (eds) (1993) *Perpetuating Poverty: The World Bank, the IMF, and the Developing World*, Washington DC: Cato Institute.

Susan George (1988) *A Fate Worse than Debt*, London: Penguin Group.

Green Left Weekly, An Australian independent newspaper.

FILMS

There are many films that approach the topic of trade. The following is just a small selection.

The Yes Men, directed by Dan Ollman and Sarah Price. "A comedic documentary which follows *The Yes Men*, a small group of prankster activists, as they gain world-wide notoriety for impersonating the World Trade Organization on television and at business conferences around the world. This dark comic satire highlights the worst aspects of global free trade."

Source: Sujit R. Varma (ND), on Internet Movie Database (http://www.imdb.com/title/tt0379593/plotsummary), accessed 6 August 2006.

The Luckiest Nut In The World, written and directed by Emily James. This film is a whistle-stop tour through everything-you-need-to-know about free trade, a no-nonsense guide to trade in the real world using stories from the international nuts trade.

The Corporation, directed by Mark Achbar and Jennifer Abbott. This film takes an in depth psychological examination of the organisation model through various case studies.

The Gods Must Be Crazy, written and directed by Jamie Uys. This film is a visual delight, a classic and a philosophical, thought provoking wander around a different world. The ending links to trade.

QUESTIONS

FACTUAL ESSAYS (INFORMATION REPORTS, EXPLANATIONS)

1. Explain the term 'trade justice' as it relates to worldwide free trade agreements.
2. Global capitalism appears to be the goal of the developed countries. Explain the rise of global capitalism since WWII.

OPINION ESSAY (ARGUMENTS, DISCUSSIONS)

1. Is free trade assisting all countries who are members of free trade agreements? Discuss.

3 DEMOGRAPHICS

'they who live longest will see most'

BY THE END OF THIS UNIT, YOU SHOULD:

- know more vocabulary for talking generally about societies, people etc ...... Speaking 1: Task B **28**
- be more fluent at talking about societies and people .... Speaking 1: Task B **28**; Language Spotlight 2: Task C **36**; Reading: Task D **30**
- have improved your ability to predict the content of an article from the introduction .... Reading: Task B **29**
- have improved your ability to find meaning from context in a written text .... Reading: Task C **29**
- be able to pronounce many nouns and verbs with the word stress in the correct place .... Reading: Task D **30**
- understand why writers choose to use the passive or active voice .... Language Spotlight 1: Task B **31**
- know the stages to expect when reading an explanation essay .... Writing: Task A **33**
- be able to write a short explanation essay with appropriate staging .... Writing: Task B **33**
- have gained further practice of predicting and brainstorming a topic before listening .... Listening: Task A **34**
- have experienced listening to people with different accents .... Listening: Task B **34**
- have improved your ability to take notes while listening .... Listening: Task B **34**
- be able to recognise and talk about general facts (eg using present simple tense and the zero conditional) and temporary actions happening around now (eg using the present continuous tense) .... Language Spotlight 2: Tasks A, B and C **35–36**
- be able to ask for clarification when you don't understand something .... Speaking 2: Tasks A and B **36**

EMOGRAPHIC n., pl. DEMOGRAPHICS [UNCOUNTABLE AND COUNTABLE]: 1 information about a group such as the people who live in a articular area: *the demographics of a newspaper's readership.* 2 [sing] a part of the population that is considered as a group, especially by advertisers who ant to sell things to that group: *the 21–40 demographic.*

EMOGRAPHY [UNCOUNTABLE]: the study of human populations and the ways in which they change, for example the study of how many births, marriages nd deaths happen in a particular place at a particular time.

BUILDING THE FIELD: INTRODUCTION TO DEMOGRAPHY AND SOCIETY

Task A | Discussion

Look at the pictures. What do you notice about the people and their ages? Are they all from the same cultural background? Can you see similar scenes in your own country? If so, where, and what time of day could you see them? Why?

Task B | Vocabulary

① In pairs, help each other to match the words below to their closest meaning. Use your knowledge, your partner's knowledge (or a dictionary … but try to guess first!).

VOCABULARY

- (the) population (of …) (n)
- retire (vb)
- retirement age (n)
- life expectancy (n)
- birth rate (n)
- infant mortality (n)
- the elderly (n)
- in their early sixties

MEANINGS

- to stop working forever, because of age or health problems
- in many companies, people have to stop working when they reach this
- how many years people live, on average
- the number of children women have, on average (usually number of births per thousand women)
- between around 60 and 64 years old
- the number of deaths of babies under one year old, for every 1000 babies born alive each year
- the number of people who live in a particular place (eg a country)
- a polite word for people who are old. This word can also be used as an adjective.

② Look at the definitions at the bottom of the title page of this unit (page 27) (taken from the *Longman Dictionary of Contemporary English*). What does *21–40* mean in *the 21–40 demographic*?

③ Take turns to tell your partner how the following statistics might have changed in your country over the last 30 years (if this is difficult, think about things your grandparents told you, and news reports, or make an educated guess).

[a] size of families

[b] life expectancy

[c] the number of the elderly

[d] birth rate

[e] infant mortality

[f] retirement age

[g] the age at which couples start families.

PREDICTING; MEANING FROM CONTEXT – AN EXPLANATION ESSAY

Task A | Pre-reading discussion

Discuss the following questions in small groups

① Think of some products that might be advertised

[a] in a woman's magazine

[b] in a sports magazine

[c] in a tabloid newspaper (a tabloid is smaller, and usually but not always less serious than the other type of newspaper, a broadsheet)

[d] on commercial TV at 10 am during school term

[e] in the same situation as [d] but during the school holidays

[f] on TV just after the evening news

[g] on TV after midnight.

2. Think of reasons for these differences.

Task B | Predicting from the introduction

Read the first paragraph only of the essay below, entitled *Market segmentation* and answer the following questions without a dictionary.

1. What do you think *market segmentation* might mean?
2. Why do you think understanding demographics is important for marketing?
3. What do you think the rest of the essay will explain?

Task C | Finding meaning from context

Find words in the text below (*Market segmentation*) that have the same meanings as the following expressions. They are already in the correct order, and the paragraph numbers help you know where to look.

[a] thought about; speculated (para 1)

____

[b] connected with (para 1)

____

[c] features; things that make them different from others (para 2)

____

MARKET SEGMENTATION

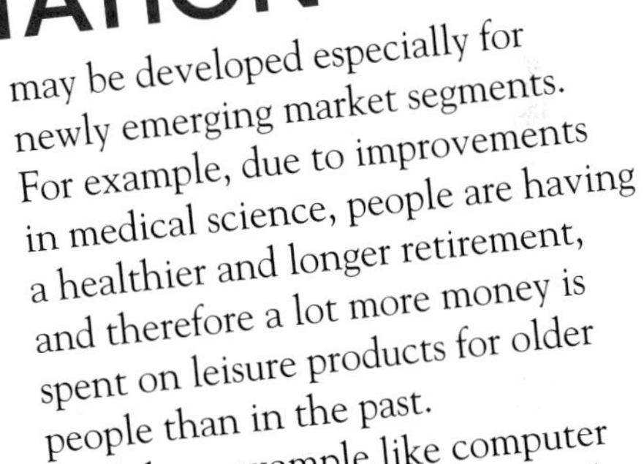

① Have you ever wondered why advertisements for babies' nappies are shown during daytime TV but not usually at night? Or advertisements for beer and wine only in the evenings? The answer is linked to something called market segmentation and is just one of the reasons why an understanding of demographics is important in marketing. So, what exactly is market segmentation, and how is it useful to companies?

② In market segmentation, society is divided into groups, based on such things as age, where they live, sex, socio-economic status (their social class and how rich they are) and whether they have children. A group of people (or cohort) having similar characteristics, for example, women in their 30s and 40s with children and who are living in relatively wealthy neighbourhoods, is known as a market segment or demographic. A market segment could also include a group of people sharing common interests, lifestyle, attitudes etc.

③ The technique of market segmentation is useful to marketers because it helps them to target their marketing to the right group of people. Clearly sales will be higher, for example, if computer games are advertised to young people rather than old people. And different games might be advertised in a magazine for teenagers than in a magazine for young adults. Further, new products may be developed especially for newly emerging market segments. For example, due to improvements in medical science, people are having a healthier and longer retirement, and therefore a lot more money is spent on leisure products for older people than in the past.

④ With an example like computer games, it can be seen easily which ones interest different groups. However, it might be less clear with other products. If, for example, a car company wants to expand into a new country by selling a car it already makes, how does it know which demographic to aim at? Different cultures have different characteristics, so the advertising that works for one market segment in one country might have to be modified in another country.

⑤ The company must do market research, which can show which kind of people are interested in the product and are ready to buy it. Further, different versions of the car, perhaps with different body styles, engine tunings and interior features, might be produced for different demographics, and advertising shown where each demographic is likely to see it.

⑥ The reverse of this process is also common. A company might first do market research to find out what the market wants. Then a product will be designed that fits the results of this research. Different variations of this product may be made to appeal to different demographics.

[d] areas of a town or city (para 2)

____

[e] a part of something (para 2)

____

[f] a way of doing something (para 3)

____

[g] to make bigger (para 4)

____

[h] changed (para 4)

____

[i] the opposite of (para 5)

____

[j] something with small changes (para 5)

____

[k] be interesting (para 5)

____

Task D | Pronunciation – Word stress and shifting stress

1 Listen to your teacher saying the two sentences below. What is the difference in the pronunciation of segments?

- A good marketing plan segments the market.
- A good marketing plan divides the market into segments.

2 Predict where the stress will fall on the highlighted word in each of the following questions by underlining the stressed syllables (don't answer the questions yet).

[a] ***Replay***
- **(i)** Do you like radio stations that have lots of replays?
- **(ii)** Does your favourite radio station replay the same music all the time?

[b] ***Retake***
- **(i)** Did your school have a policy about exam retakes?
- **(ii)** Have you ever had to retake an exam?

[c] ***Export***
- **(i)** What exports is France known for?
- **(ii)** What goods does your country export?

[d] ***Increase***
- **(i)** During this course, has there been an increase in interest in English throughout this class?
- **(ii)** Has your interest in English increased during this course?

[e] ***Record***
- **(i)** Do you record conversations to help with your English learning?
- **(ii)** What other ways are there to keep a record of a conversation?

[f] ***Rebel***
- **(i)** Did you ever rebel against your teachers at school? Or in any other situations?
- **(ii)** Please tell me about the biggest rebel in your high school class.

3 Check the meanings of the words in Question 2 above with a teacher or in your English-English dictionary if necessary. Practise by asking the questions in 2 above with a partner.

Task E | Discussion

Discuss the following points with a partner:

1 How do you think a company might do market research? (Think of several ways – you've probably experienced some!)

2 For the following products, discuss (a) what market segment(s) may be most interested in it, and (b) where/how advertising might reach these market segments. You might be able to think of:

[a] a new design for razors
[b] laptop computers
[c] a new doll to compete with Barbie
[d] a chocolate bar
[e] an English course for people who want to use better English in their office jobs.

PASSIVE VOICE

Task A | Identifying passive voice

1. Find sections of the text on page 29 (*Market segmentation*) that have the same meaning as the following parts of sentences, and write them in the space provided:

[a] *... TV companies show advertisements for nappies during the day but ...*

____

____

____

[b] *Marketing professionals know ... as a market segment ...*

____

____

____

[c] *... if companies advertise computer games to young people ...*

____

____

____

[d] *... we can see easily which ones different age groups will be interested in ...*

____

____

____

What is the difference between sentences [a] to [d] and the sentences in the text?

____

____

____

2. Find other examples in the same text where the writer used the passive voice and circle them.

3. Think about the active version of each of the examples you found in Question 2. With a partner, discuss why you think the passive voice was chosen.

Task B | When is passive voice used?

1. Can you remember (or think of) reasons to use the passive (other than the reasons you looked at in Task A)?

2. Look at examples (a) to (g) below. Match them to the reasons (i) to (viii). There may be more than one reason for each example.

____ **a.** The report will be handed in a little late (cf: I'll hand in the report late)

____ **b.** Surveys are done by the market researchers to find out what the customers think of the product. The results of these are given to the market analysis department.

____ **c.** Society is divided into groups.

____ **d.** The report has been finished (cf: I finished the report)

____ **e.** My mobile phone has been stolen!

____ **f.** It can be seen easily which ones different age groups are interested in (cf: It is easy to see which ones different age groups are interested in).

____ **g.** The murderer was arrested.

The agent is the 'doer' of the action, and is the subject of active clauses, and can sometimes be put after 'by' in passives. Passive voice is often chosen in the following situations:

i. when the agent is unknown
ii. to avoid vague words like 'someone' or 'people' as the subject
iii. when the agent is obvious
iv. when the agent is less important than the action or the object
v. when we don't want to mention the agent (eg to avoid showing who is responsible)
vi. to deliberately make the object more important by bringing it to the front of the sentence
vii. to make the sentence link better with the previous sentence by bringing the object to the front of the sentence
viii. it can sometimes be used to make writing or speaking sound more formal.

Task C | Practice

1. Re-write the paragraphs below, changing the underlined parts of each sentence to the active voice. [a] and [d] have been done as examples.
   - What difference do you feel between the active and passive versions of each? For example, did you find it difficult to choose a subject for the active clause?
   - Does the active voice make the sentence too informal?
   - Does the passive voice help the writer to put the emphasis (first idea in the sentence) on the right idea?

Generations

[a] Three distinct generations are often talked about in marketing circles in Western countries: Baby Boomers, Generation X and Generation Y. Each has different attitudes, so [b] marketing is targeted differently to each generation. But, [c] what is meant by these generational terms, and [d] how is marketing strategy affected by the characteristics of each generation?

To answer the first of these questions, [e] demographic changes over the last 60 years have to be examined. After the second world war, there was a sense of peace and prosperity for the future, and people felt secure and optimistic enough that [f] lots of babies were born, hence the term Baby Boomer. [g] This generation was known for being rebellious during the sixties and seventies, for example [h] many were involved in protests against government policy such as the war in Vietnam. [i] The hippy generation and punks are often included as examples of this rebellious trend, though they by no means represented the whole of the generation. However, [j] the Baby Boomers are generally understood to have made Western society more open minded and accepting of differences. Now, they are taking a more adventurous approach to retirement than their parents, because [k] a longer and healthier retirement is expected.

[l] The members of Generation X were born from around the early sixties to around 1980, and are a very diverse generation, having a very wide range of different attitudes and beliefs. Only a few trends have become clear so far – people of this generation are getting married later, are having fewer children, [m] jobs and careers are changed frequently, and they are more likely to have higher qualifications than any generation before them. The first of Generation Y (born in the fifteen or twenty years since the early eighties) are now becoming adults, and [n] the changes they bring to society will be observed carefully by demographers and marketers.

Examples

[a] People in marketing circles often talk about three distinct generations
– the main point is *three distinct generations*, and passive voice allows this noun phrase to go to the beginning of the sentence/paragraph/text for greater emphasis.

[b] ______________________________

____

[c] ______________________________

____

[d] … how do the characteristics of each generation affect marketing strategy?
– *marketing strategy* is the meaning that the writer wants to emphasise, not the characteristics.

[e] ______________________________

____

[f] ______________________________

____

[g] ______________________________

____

[h] ______________________________

____

[i] ______________________________

____

[j] ______________________________

____

[k] ______________________________

____

[l] ______________________________

____

[m] ______________________________

____

[n] ______________________________

____

2. Discuss the following topics with a partner. Then, write a paragraph to show the ideas you spoke about. Try to use passive voice as much as possible – but remember that passive is generally used more in writing than speaking.

[a] Generations in your own country: How is your generation different from your parents' generation? What big events have influenced birth rates, education, people's expectations, etc?

[b] Products of your country: what well-known products are made there, exported from there, what has been invented, what films were produced/made/filmed there, what art was painted/sculpted etc there?

[c] Your home town and changes in it since you were a child. eg perhaps many fast food restaurants have been opened there (present perfect passive, for changes between the past and now, is most useful for this).

You will get more practice of the passive when you write an explanation essay later in this unit.

STRUCTURE OF AN EXPLANATION ESSAY

Task A | Generic features of an explanation essay

The text titled *Market segmentation* earlier in this unit is an explanation essay. The main purpose of an explanation is to say how or why something happens, or is done. It usually gives facts, not opinions.

1. Read the following table carefully. It shows the stages in explanation essays.

STAGE	SUB-STAGE	PURPOSE
Introduction	General statement	To introduce the topic of the explanation essay, and to define it.
	Preview/scope (essay map)	To show what ideas will be in the body of the essay
Explanations	*for each main idea:*	
	Theme	To introduce the point
	Elaboration	To give further information about the point

Note: the theme is sometimes a sentence. When it is a sentence, it is often called a **topic sentence**.

2. Draw boxes around (or colour) these stages in the *Market segmentation* text earlier in this unit. The introduction has been done for you below as an example. Your teacher will help you if you have trouble.

General statement

Have you ever wondered why advertisements for babies' nappies are shown during day time TV but not usually at night? Or advertisements for beer and wine only in the evenings? The answer is linked to something called market segmentation and is just one of the reasons why an understanding of demographics is important in marketing. So, what exactly is market segmentation, and how is it useful to companies?

Preview/scope: the writer is going to talk in the body of the essay about what market segmentation is, and how companies find it useful.

Task B | Write your own explanation essay

1. Choose one of the topics from Task C, Question 2 of the previous section (or, any other topic you like – but check with your teacher first).

2. Write a plan for your essay, giving (a) the main idea that you are going to explain, and (b) each of the points in your essay.

3. Write a first draft. The point you wrote in part (a) of your essay plan will become the end of the General Statement, and each point in part (b) of your plan should be mentioned in your Preview/Scope, and should also be a Theme/Topic sentence of a paragraph in the body of the essay. Your teacher will look at your first draft during the lesson, and help with any problems.

4. Finish your first draft for homework, and hand it in to your teacher as soon as possible.

5. When you get it back, read the comments carefully. Start writing a second draft.

PREDICTING, NOTE-TAKING AND DIFFERENT ACCENTS – EXPLANATIONS

Task A | Prediction

Next, you are going to listen to some people from different countries talking about the consequences of demographic change in their countries. Below are some of the points they might mention. With a partner, think of some consequences of each.

1. The birth rate is declining and life expectancy is increasing rapidly.
2. People have to pay for their own retirement – the government doesn't provide pensions except for very poor people.
3. The birth rate is very high and infant mortality is falling rapidly.
4. There is a very large movement of people from the countryside to the cities, because the cities are getting richer very quickly but not the countryside.

Task B | Listening and note-taking (different accents)

1 Write the following headings in your notebook, with plenty of space after each to take notes:

CD 1

Speaker 1: Japan
Speaker 2: Russia
Speaker 3: Australia
Speaker 4: China

Listen and make notes about the changes each speaker talks about, and the consequences of the changes.
This recording will be played at least twice.

2 Did the speakers make the same predictions as you did in Task A? Be ready to talk about the differences.

Task C | Discussion

Tell your partner your answers to the following questions about your country:

[a] What demographic changes can you predict in your lifetime?
[b] What kinds of people or organisations need to make predictions about future demographic trend?
[c] Why do they need to make these predictions?
[d] How accurate can these predictions be?

PRESENT CONTINUOUS, PRESENT SIMPLE AND ZERO CONDITIONAL

Task A | Identifying use

1 Listen again to the people talking about the future in their countries. Fill the gaps in the following sentences with the words you hear on the recording.

CD 1

Japan

[a] In Japan, the birth rate ____________
[b] Also, life expectancy ____________ very rapidly …
[c] … the number of old people ____________ all the time.
[d] … if parents ____________ looking after in their old age, **[e]** it ____________ the oldest son's responsibility to do this.
[f] if the old people ____________ to move, **[g]** the tradition ____________
[h] Consequently, the government ____________ more and more to look after the old people
[i] … similar problems ____________ in many countries

Russia

[j] Russia ____________ through some very unusual demographic changes.
[k] … the population ____________ by three quarters of a million people every year.

Australia

[l] If the employee ____________, **[m]** he or she ____________ in some of their own money.

China

[n] The economy in the cities ______________________, but …

[o] If young people ______________________ a choice of staying in a village with few opportunities, or going into the big city where there is the chance of making their fortunes, **[p]** most just ______________________ to the cities.

2 Thinking about the context of the clauses in Question 1([a] to [p]) above:

[a] Which clauses are used for something happening around now, but not true forever (a temporary situation)?

____

[b] Which clauses are used for actions that are happening now but which are probably not temporary (ie happening over a long period of time)?

____

[c] Which clauses are used for points that can happen regularly, again and again?

____

[d] Which clauses are present continuous? Which are present simple?

____

____

[e] In what situations do both clauses of an *if* statement use present simple?

____

____

Task B | Practice

Put the verbs in brackets into the tense that best fits the context.

Many companies nowadays [1] ______________ (notice) a great opportunity, which is to sell to retired people. This demographic [2] ______________ (increase) in size at an enormous rate, because life expectancy [3] ______________ (get) longer but the retirement age [4] ______________ (stay) about the same, thus people [5] ______________ (spend) much longer in retirement. Further, better health treatment [6] ______________ (mean) that retired people are generally more healthy. When people [7] ______________ (have) more free time, they generally [8] ______________ (spend) more money, and the elderly [9] ______________ (be) no exception. The leisure industry [10] ______________ (see) great benefits – if people have more leisure time, companies can expand their business if they [11] ______________ (give) people something to do in this time.

Another booming field is the provision of health care. If people [12] ______________ (live) longer, they [13] ______________ (need) more medical services, home care services and aged care homes, and the number of companies providing these services is increasing.

So, if you [14] ______________ (buy) shares in companies that target the elderly, [15] ______________ (expect) to make a lot of money!

Task C | Personalised practice

1. Think about the answers to the questions below for your own country.
   - Are people living longer in retirement?
   - What do people do in retirement? (eg leisure activities, family activities, voluntary work?)
   - What services are provided for older people in your country? Are they provided by the government, private companies, or both? How much responsibility do families have for looking after old people? How about old people who don't have families?
   - Is there adequate health care for older people?
   - If people live longer in retirement, what consequences occur?
   - What do you think is a good retirement age? Why?
   - When your grandparents have free time, what do they do?

CLARIFICATION

Task A | Expressions for requesting clarification

1. In a conversation, what can you say if you don't understand something? Give as many expressions as you can.

2. In pairs, rewrite each expression below, putting the words in the correct order. They are all requests for clarification.

[a] do mean so, you ...

____

____

[b] mean you what not by sure I'm ...

____

____

[c] understood sure you said I'm when I not you ...

____

____

[d] on a hold minute, catch what about didn't said you I ...

____

____

[e] – please you could say that sorry again? I didn't catch quite afraid I'm it.

____

____

[f] missed about, I sorry that bit ...

____

____

[g] you explain me said about excuse you again could what ...?

____

____

3. Referring to the expressions in Question 2.

[i] Which expression is not so polite (only for close friends)?

____

____

[ii] Which is more suitable for tutorials (more formal situations with a few people)?

____

____

Task B | Practice

Talk about the following with a partner. Your partner will listen and ask for clarification whenever necessary.

1. What is the earliest age people can leave school in your country? (In other words, at what age does compulsory education finish?)
2. Do many people leave at this age? Why/Why not? Is this different from when your parents or grandparents were young?
3. Do people who leave school early have a good chance of finding a job? Why/ Why not?
4. What alternatives to finding a job do people have if they leave school early?
5. In your country, do students who leave school early often go back to studying later in life? (In other words, are there many mature students?)
6. Is youth unemployment in your country high or low? What are the factors in this? If it is high, what can be done to improve the situation?
7. Do people in your country often take time off between school and university to travel overseas or work? (eg a gap year). Or do they travel between university and starting full-time work? What are the benefits and disadvantages of this?

Remember to practise asking for clarification whenever you get a chance!

FURTHER PRACTICE: READING, FILMS AND FUN

READING

There are several articles about demography, demographics, social change and market segmentation on the English version of **Wikipedia**: http://en.wikipedia.org.

The **United Nations** produces a very interesting wall chart showing populations for all the countries in the world. It includes populations in 2005, and predictions for 2015 and 2050. Just go to: **http://www.un.org/esa/population/publications/WPP2004/wpp2004.htm** and click on 'Wall Chart'.

FILMS

Brassed Off, written and directed by Mark Herman. This is a very funny comedy featuring a rarely shown side of British society.

Not One Less, directed by Zhang Yimou. This is a moving story about children, set against the background of some of the demographic issues in China. Use the English subtitles!

QUESTIONS

1. What differences can you see between your lifestyle, and the lifestyle your parents talk about having when they were the same age as you?
2. (For students outside their home countries only.) What differences can you see between the lifestyles of your home country and the country where you are now living?
3. Think of a product that you are interested in (eg sports shoes or cars). How are different varieties of the product designed to appeal to different market segments? For some products, it may be better just to talk about one company's product range; for others, you may have to talk about a variety of products.

4 ENERGY

BY THE END OF THIS UNIT, YOU SHOULD:

'corporations have neither bodies to be punished nor souls to be damned'

ENERGY n., pl. ENERGIES [UNCOUNTABLE AND COUNTABLE]: 1 (habitual) capacity or habit of vigorous activity. 2 the actual exertion of power; operation; activity. 3 power as exerted. 4 ability to produce action or effect. 5 vigour or forcefulness of expression. 6 *Physics.* The capacity for doing work which exists in various forms, as kinetic energy, nuclear energy, etc.; the derived SI unit of energy is the joule.

BUILDING THE FIELD: INTRODUCTION TO THE TOPIC OF ENERGY

Task A | Understanding energy

In groups, examine the pictures.

Each person in your group talks for one minute about one of the pictures. Describe it, or, if you can do more than describe it, say whatever you can about it. You may prepare notes for a minute before you talk.

Task B | Recognising an issue

There are two or more *opinions*, (thoughts, view points or sides) in an argument. These different views are what make it an argument. Arguments are formed around issues. An issue is something that people talk about, write about, discuss. It has to have more than one view point. One side will be for something (in favour or support of it), the other side will be against it.

❶ Read the following statements. Tick 'yes' if you think it's an issue, tick 'no' if it's not an issue.

		YES	NO
[a]	*Most birds have wings.*	❑	❑
[b]	*Spiders have eight legs, dogs have four.*	❑	❑
[c]	*Desks are good for setting up computers.*	❑	❑
[d]	*China's one child policy has been a very good thing in every way.*	❑	❑
[e]	*Music has the power to move people.*	❑	❑
[f]	*Nuclear power is the best and only form of energy for the world in the future.*	❑	❑
[g]	*Children will always turn out badly if they only have one parent.*	❑	❑
[h]	*Sports stars should be allowed to take drugs to make them move faster.*	❑	❑
[i]	*When both people work in a marriage, men should help with housework.*	❑	❑
[j]	*It rains a lot in Cairns, Australia; Calcutta, India, and Hanoi, Vietnam, and in other tropical places.*	❑	❑

❷ If you were correct, explain to a partner how you knew the difference between an issue and a non-issue.

Task C | For or against

Read the following texts concerning the issue of nuclear energy then label them: ***For*** or ***Against***

A________ Nuclear energy on its own seems to work well and many think it is a clean source of power. However, nuclear energy has to be made and when it is made there is always waste. Nuclear waste is poisonous, toxic (very poisonous, deadly) and terribly dangerous. If it leaks, it kills people and in fact, kills all life around it and ruins the environment (the living world around) for hundreds of thousands of years.

B________ Nuclear energy is a clean source of power. Many countries are using it now. Some (people) may argue against it because they worry about the possible leaks of toxic (which means it can kill you) radioactive matter into the air. This only happens if there is an explosion or a leak. But this is rare and there are many ways to stop that from happening. Waste is handled carefully and stored well. It almost never happens.

C________ Nuclear energy comes from mining uranium. Uranium mining produces a sort of waste called tailings. Most of the time, this waste (tailings) is stored in a big hole dug in the ground and then covered with water. If it rains hard or there is ground movement like an earthquake, the water leaks out. This water is contaminated (that means people cannot drink or bathe in the water), and highly radioactive. It destroys every living thing it touches. There is a famous case in Papua New Guinea (the Ok Tedi mine) where an entire river system was ruined by leaking waste from a uranium mine. Villages of people lost their fish, their food, and their life in that place forever.

D________ Nuclear power drives military submarines for the USA, Russia and other countries. These submarines used to carry ballistic nuclear missiles which are powerful weapons that can travel a long distance, fly up into the sky and then back down to earth where they explode, and now submarines carry cruise missiles (these are missiles that fly close to the ground and go for hundreds of miles). There have been a few military nuclear accidents but nuclear powered ships are the best. They are fast and quiet.

E________ Tokai, Ibaraki is the location of a nuclear accident. Physicists used the 5 yen coin to measure the level of poison (neutrons) that went into peoples' houses as far away as 100–550 m from the place (the facility) where the accident happened and took the coins. They could see how much poison was in each coin. Neutrons can be measured to show the levels of radiation (isotopes) that make people sick and die. This radiation is invisible, you cannot see it at all. Did you ever read Superman and see the green kryptonite, a rock, that came from his planet? He only needs to walk near it and he falls down, weakened. In real life, radiation does the same, only people throw up, their skin peels off; they feel horrible pain and die in minutes if the exposure (the time near the source) is high enough. If it is low, women lose their unborn babies, or have babies that are sick or deformed and many people get cancers and die.

A 5 yen coin used to measure levels of poison

Task D | Definitions in context

1. Find the definitions in the texts A–E (in Task C) and write them below. Most of the definitions have parenthesis ( ) around them. Write the definition next to the word it relates to. The first definition from paragraph A is done for you.

   For example: Paragraph A. toxic: (very poisonous, deadly); environment: (the living world around).

PARAGRAPH	WORD	DEFINITION AND 'CLUES OR SIGNALS'
A	toxic	(very poisonous, deadly)
A	environment	(the living world around)
B	toxic	
C	waste	
C	contaminated	
D	ballistic nuclear missiles	
D	cruise missiles	
E	poison	
E	place	
E	levels of radiation	
E	green kryponite	
E	exposure	

2. Explain the photograph of the five yen coin discussed in paragraph E of Task C on the previous page.

3. Look at the graph – Figure 4.1.
   - Explain the graph of Radioactive Materials Release. Use the following passage to help you
   - Use the present tense of the missing verbs.

First radioactive materials are released into the ____________ Then, they go ____________ ways [write a number]. They go into the ____________ From the soil, these radioactive materials move to ____________ and ____________ and they ____________ to animals too. From animals, they ____________ or go into milk and ____________ . Finally, humans ____________ the milk and ____________ the meat. After that, humans absorb the ____________________________ .

4. What do you think about nuclear power and uranium mining?

   Discuss this question with a partner. You can use the texts A–E and the graph below (Figure 4.1) to help you.

5. Are there different opinions in your group or class about nuclear energy? There are different opinions in most countries. Some people are for it and some people are against it. How will you discuss this issue in English? Complete Task E to learn how.

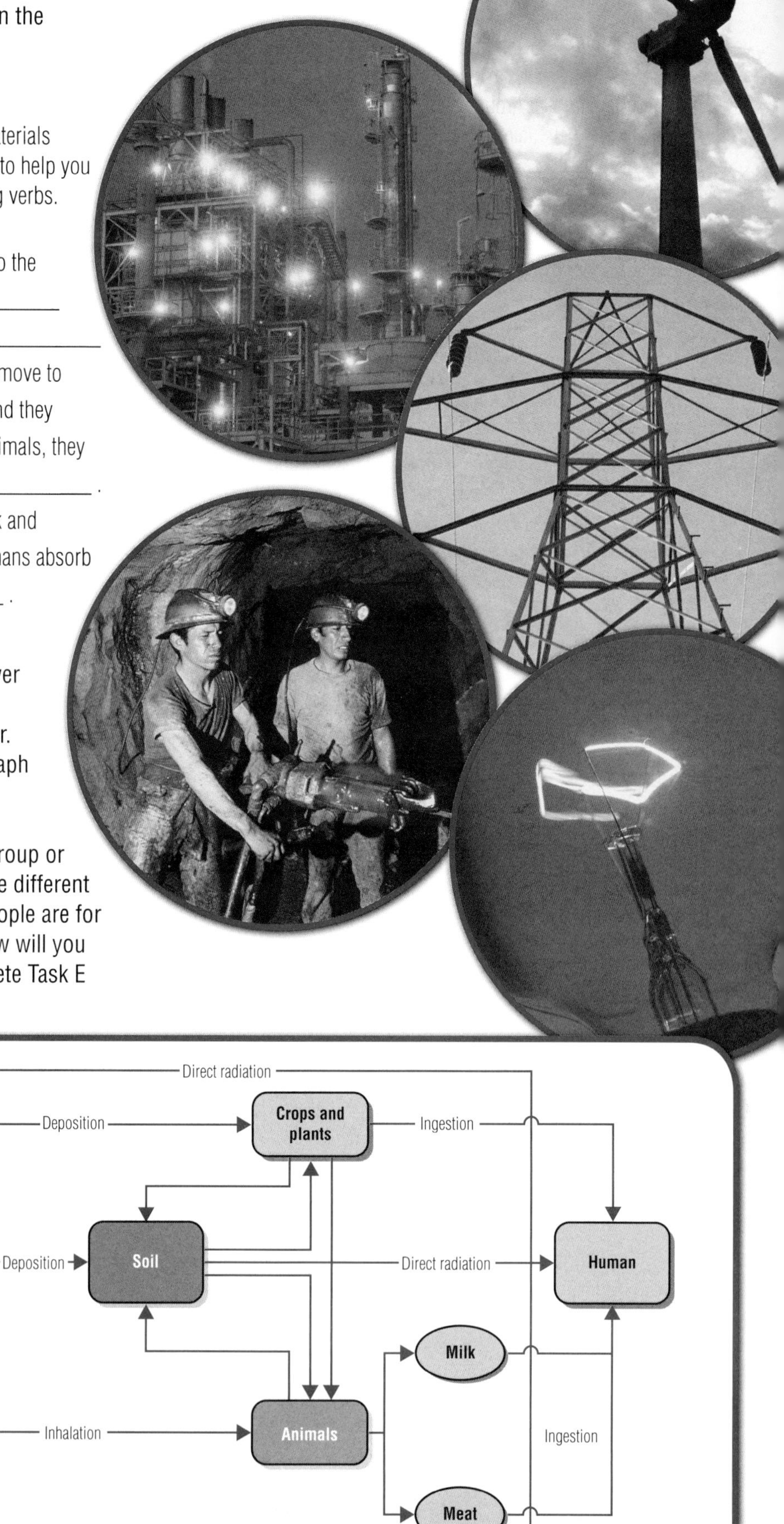

FIGURE 4.1 | Graph of Radioactive Materials Release

Task E | Signposting in speaking/talking about an issue

Prepare a small talk (two minutes) in support of your opinion about nuclear energy. You will be 'for' or 'against' it. You may use the information from Task C, paragraphs A to E plus your own knowledge. Others in your group will listen before arguing with you. Here is how to help listeners understand your talk. Organise it.

Introduction

I think ......
I'd like to say that ......
I want to begin by saying ......
Let's consider ......

Points

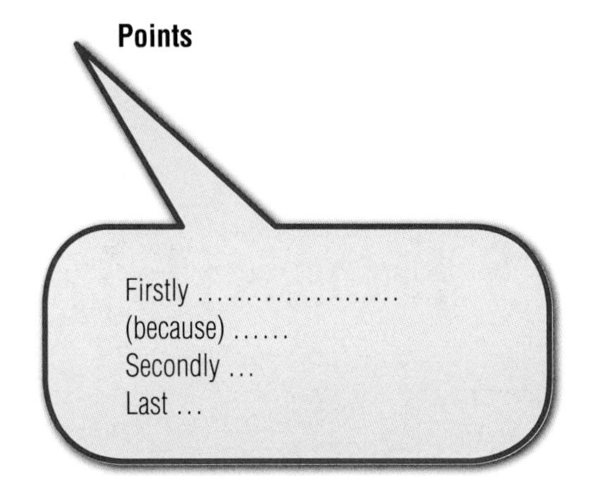

Concluding statement/summary

Therefore ...
Finally ......
To sum up, my reasons for ....
In short ......
So ......

STAGES IN ARGUMENT, DEFINITIONS IN CONTEXT, TOPIC SENTENCES AND LOCATING POINTS IN ARGUMENT

Task A | Staging – The outline, the schema, the map

1. Read the argument *Clean Energy is Possible* on page 44.

2. **Stages** in essays means there is a kind of map that can be followed. Use the stages below to help you *box or underline* the stages in the reading you just completed.
   In an argument you need these **Stages: *Introduction*, *Body*, *Conclusion*** and each of these has staging within them.
   [a] **Introduction**
   - A general statement in the beginning.
   - A definition or definitions of your terms.
   - A preview or scope that lets the reader know what side you will argue.

   [b] **Body paragraphs**
   - Each paragraph needs a main idea. It usually comes first and is called the topic sentence. In an argument, it will support your side.
   - After the topic sentence, you need to write evidence or support for your view.

   [c] **Conclusion**
   - All writing needs to finish and the conclusion is at the end.
   - No new information is introduced.
   - Write a brief summary of what you have been saying in the beginning and body of your argument essay.
   - Make a recommendation or suggestion for the future.

3. Locate definitions for the following words in each paragraph. Write the paragraph number, the sentence number and the sentence. Draw an arrow forward or backwards (as per example 'dirty energies') to the word that tells you a definition is there in the text.

Example

[a] **dirty energies**
Para 1, sentence 2 – There are energy sources that do not cause so much destruction as

oil, coal, nuclear and wood, **which are** *dirty energies.*

Now write on the following:

[b] **clean energy**

____

____

____

Clean energy is possible

1 I'd like to present you with an argument against using energy that ruins our environment and with an argument for using energy that is healthy. There are energy sources that do not cause so much destruction as oil, coal, nuclear and wood, which are dirty energies. Clean energy is energy that uses wind, water or sunshine. It's just that simple. Clean energy is energy that does not pollute our earth as much as dirty energy. Energy that works with nature instead of against nature, energy that doesn't ruin the earth, doesn't pollute the earth as much as what we are using now in the 21st century. A name for this energy is renewable. It's renewable energy. Since renew means to make new again, energy that is renewable can be made over and over again without using up its source.

2 Clean energy is not necessarily perfect. Nothing is perfect. Clean energy does pollute in some ways, for example, wind turbines may kill migrating birds or they may make too much noise when placed near homes. Some say they look ugly and that is eye pollution. Water or hydro energy may ruin land because of dams. The dams flood existing areas and farmers may lose farms. People may have to move from their homes. As for sunshine, that is, solar energy, there do not seem to be any polluting effects. However, dirty energy always pollutes. There are several arguments against that type of energy.

3 Firstly, to define dirty energy, we are looking at wood, coal, oil and nuclear. Wood and coal burning causes a great deal of pollution in the atmosphere. There is no argument to refute that. That is, there is no way to deny that fact. Coal burning is dirty. It is smoky. Oil burning is dirty, too. Oil makes petrol, of course, and cars burn petrol (gasoline). This is also causing pollution in every major city of the world.

4 Next, nuclear power, which starts with uranium mining, is supposed to be clean, but can actually be very dirty. There are three parts to using nuclear power. The first is mining it, the second is processing it and the third is using it in a power station. Nuclear supporters advertise nuclear power as clean energy. Advertising is not always truthful. Nuclear energy is only clean until there is an accident, and accidents happen. In fact, there is no industry that has no accidents. In addition, getting the uranium out of the ground to process into plutonium for nuclear power stations is a very dangerous, risky business for workers. Uranium mining often causes terrible poisoning of people and land. Nuclear power stations, when there are leaks, also cause the same problems: cancer, death, food supplies destroyed.

5 Another argument against nuclear is uranium mining. Uranium is also mined for the purpose of making nuclear weapons. These are weapons that have the power to destroy the entire world and everyone in it. Why mine such a dangerous material? Why not leave it in the ground?

If each country in the world began to use wind, water and sunshine for their power needs, and to drive cars and machinery, even in small quantities, then we would see an improvement in our atmosphere. Soon we would see less smog. Our cities would have clean air and birds instead of filthy air and people wearing masks over their faces.

6 If governments around the world put money into research, we would soon have solar powered cars, solar powered heating, both water and home heating. We could improve wind energy. All technologies improve over time and with research. Look at computers!

7 The question is – why don't governments put money into researching and using clean energy? Why are they continuing to use dirty energy that pollutes our cities, our countries, and our earth? Can you answer that question? We should ask it in the right places and work together for clean energy.

[c] **renewable energy**

[d] **solar energy**

[e] **to refute that**

[f] **nuclear weapons**

4. Locate topic sentences in body paragraphs and write them here.

Para 1

Para 2

Para 3

Para 4

Para 5

Para 6

Para 7

5. Locate supporting statements for the topic sentences in each paragraph.

Para 1

Para 2

Para 3

Para 4

Para 5

Para 6

Para 7

AN ARGUMENT

Task A | Staging in an argument

You read an argument and you located the stages within it. Remember, an argument is either **for** or **against** something.

Use the stages below to write an argument for an educated reader **for** the following topic:

Governments around the world need to spend money on ways to make the air cleaner

Here is some vocabulary to assist you:

> pollution (dirty air from factory emissions, car exhaust fumes, coal and wood burning); government funding; pristine (very clean); respiratory diseases (lung diseases like asthma and cancer); populations; government legislation; and any vocabulary from Reading: Task A (page 43) that might help your argument.

SCHEMA/A MAP/STAGES

INTRODUCTION

Topic sentence: ____________________

Definition of terms: ____________________

Preview or scope: ____________________

BODY PARAGRAPHS

Body paragraph **1**

Topic sentence – the main idea ____________________
Topic sentence explained ____________________
Provide an example or elaborate (say more) OR contrast and compare using only the idea in the topic sentence ____________________

Introduce or lead into next argument for ____________________

Body paragraph **2**

Topic sentence – the main idea ____________________
Topic sentence explained ____________________
Provide an example or elaborate (say more) OR contrast and compare using only the idea in the topic sentence ____________________

Introduce or lead into next argument for ____________________

Body paragraph **3**

Topic sentence – the main idea ____________________
Topic sentence explained ____________________
Provide an example or elaborate (say more) OR contrast and compare using only the idea in the topic sentence ____________________

CONCLUSION

Lead in discourse signal: ____________________
Write a brief summary of what you have been saying in the beginning and body of your argument essay ____________________

Make a recommendation or suggestion for the future. ____________________

VERB FORMS AND FUNCTIONS

Task A | Gerunds and infinitives

*

Gerunds end in *–ing*
gerunds are used only as *nouns*
(and can be modified)
Participles end in *–ing*
participles are used as *adjectives*

*

Infinitives are the base forms of verbs. They usually begin with *to*, eg *to be*, *to go*, *to work*, *to drive*, *to think*, *to love*
Infinitives function as **nouns**, **adjectives** or **adverbs**

1. Underline the *nouns* and/or *noun phrases* in the following sentences and write the function of the gerund. For example:

   Watering and tending a garden can be fun. (*gerund* used as subject)

   (a) Writing is required at all levels of school. ______________________

   (b) My family attended the annual running of the bulls in Spain. ______________________

   (c) The cat's meowing woke me at 4 am, so I got up and opened the door for her. ______________________

   (d) The lazy student finally got motivated and began working. ______________________

   (e) I prefer eating quickly. ______________________

   (f) That baby's loud crying needs attention. ______________________

   (g) Can you think of four sentences using gerunds? ______________________

2. Underline the infinitives and write their function in these sentences.

   (a) To love is to learn. ______________________

   (b) I like to drive carefully. Do you? ______________________

   (c) To think is a process. ______________________

   (d) The process of thinking can be rewarding or it can cause you to go crazy. ______________________

   (e) If you want that computer to work, you'll have to turn it on first. ______________________

   (f) I'm going to see him now. ______________________

   (g) The work to be done cannot be avoided. ______________________

3. Underline the infinitives, participles and gerund phrases in the following text.

> I always believed her to be my friend. I'm afraid I found out differently seeing her at the movies with another guy. To think I was wasting all that time on her for months. I was spending money every day on her as well. I prefer thinking she still likes me but to tell the truth, I'm not so sure. She's avoiding me all the time when seeing me on campus. To me, that means she isn't interested anymore. I'm looking at you and wondering what you're thinking. Are you going to discuss this with me?

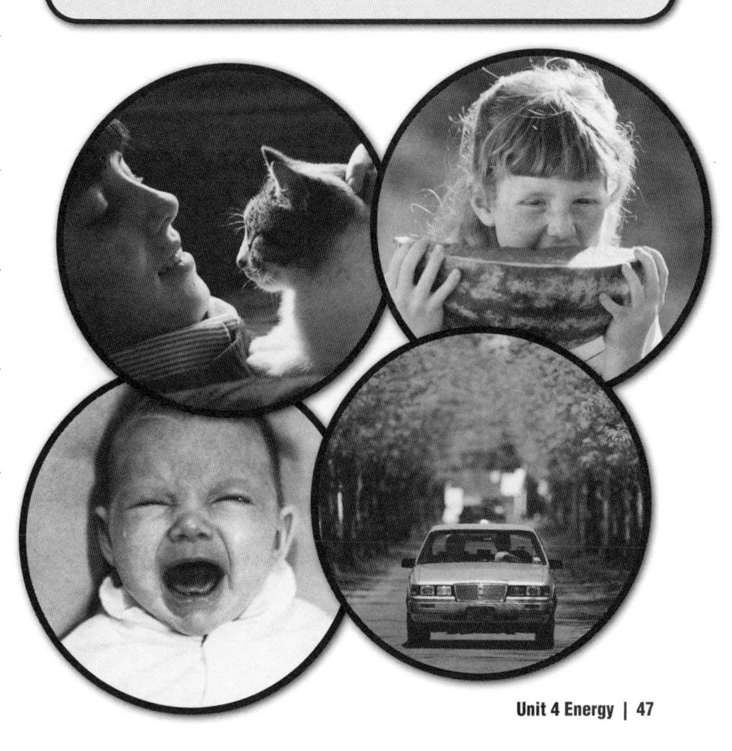

ENERGY TO BURN

Task A | Listening for meaning and content

CD 1 (7)

1. Listen to the dialogue between three friends and answer the following with *true or false*.
   [a] ________ Taki is a musician.
   [b] ________ Jess is wearing a coat.
   [c] ________ Jess thinks Taki is too thin.
   [d] ________ Allen offers a banana, a peach and an apple to Taki.
   [e] ________ Allen has a chicken in his bag.

2. Complete the following:
   [a] You're too thin, that's why you've got no ____________.
   [b] Music – it's pretty high ____________.
   [c] You've obviously got no ____________ and that's why you're ____________.

3. Listen again and write as many forms of 'What...?' as you hear.

4. Write the full sentences that used the 'What' forms (from Question 3).

[a]

[b]

[c]

[d]

[e]

[f]

[g]

[h]

FURTHER PRACTICE: READING, FILMS AND FUN

READING

Suzuki, D. & Dressel, H. (1999) *Naked Ape to Superspecies*. Toronto: Canada: Stoddart Publishing Co.
http://www.zpenergy.com/index.php

FILMS

An Inconvenient Truth: This film is a documentary about how our planet is changing due to huge amounts of carbon dioxide released into the air. It was created by Al Gore who once ran for president of the USA. It is causing a lot of interest and controversy. Hope you get to see it.

Million Dollar Baby: A high energy boxing film with a young woman as the star.

QUESTIONS

ESSAY

1. Research any kind of renewable energy, for example solar or wind, and write an argument in favour of its use.

DISCUSSION

2. Read the true text below and discuss. Do you think it's possible that in the future, the big oil companies will be a thing of the past and cars will run on water and hydrogen? What other kinds of future energy are possible?

1994 Ford Escort gets 100 miles

A scientist named Klein just patented his process of converting H_2O to HHO, producing a gas that combines the atomic power of hydrogen with the chemical stability of water. 'It turns right back to water. In fact, you can see the H_2O running off the sheet metal.' Klein originally designed his water-burning engine for cutting metal. He thought his invention could replace acetylene in welding factories. Then one day as he drove to his laboratory in Clearwater, he thought of another way to burn his HHO gas. 'On a 100 mile trip, we use about four ounces of water.' Klein says his prototype 1994 Ford Escort can travel exclusively on water, though he currently has it rigged to run as a water and gasoline hybrid.

5 COMMUNICATION

'whispered words are heard afar'

BY THE END OF THIS UNIT, YOU SHOULD:

COMMUNICATION n. [UNCOUNTABLE]: the process by which people exchange information or express their thoughts and feelings: *Good communication is vital in a large organisation.* | *Radio was the pilot's only means of communication.*

BUILDING THE FIELD

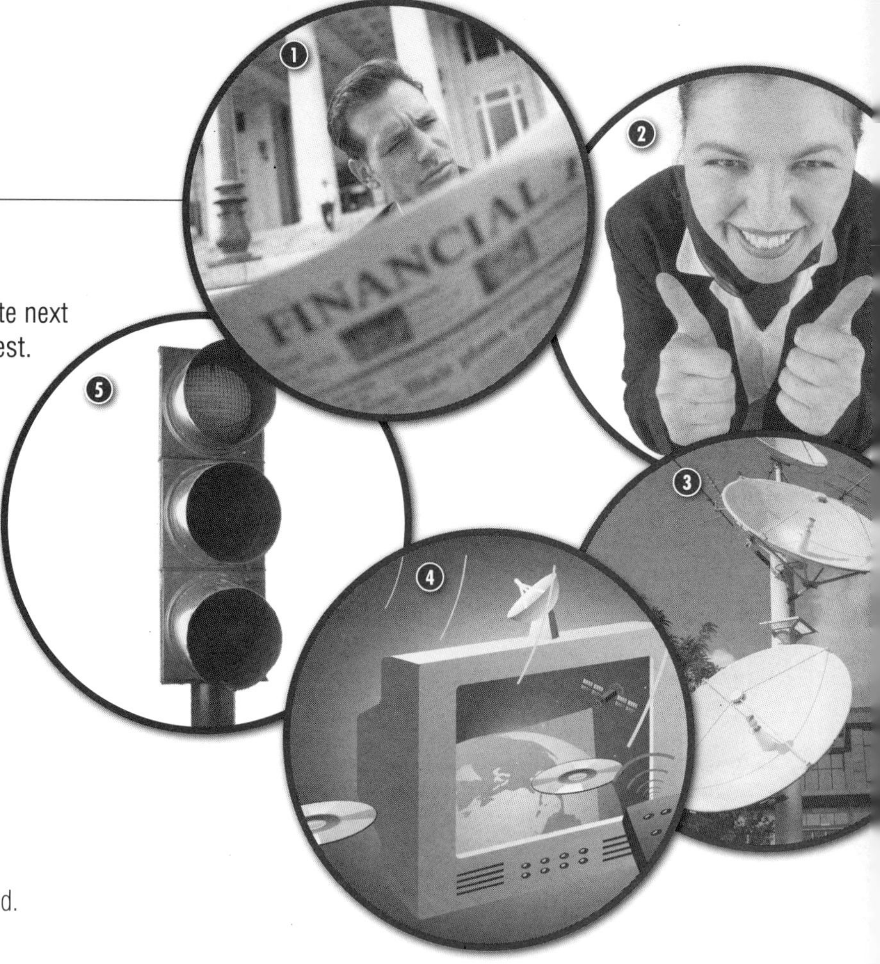

Task A | Types of communication

1. Look at the pictures on the right and write next to each picture the word that matches best.
   - Telecommunications
   - Gestures
   - Visual communication
   - Written communication
   - Mass communication
2. With a partner, think of as many examples as you can for each of the following:
   - Telecommunications
   - Gestures, body language and facial expressions
   - Visual communication
   - Written communication
   - Mass communication
   - Digital communication
   - Communication systems for the disabled.

MAIN IDEAS & SPECIFIC INFORMATION – EXPLANATION ESSAY

Task A | Discussion – Communication and miscommunication

1. Think by yourself about a situation you remember in which communication broke down, that is, someone didn't understand something. Then, in small groups, tell each other:
   - What happened
   - The reasons for the communication breakdown
   - What would have made the situation better?

2. List as many reasons as you can for why communication sometimes doesn't work.

3. What can people do to help communication work well?

Task B | Reading for main ideas

1. Read the text on the next page (*Effective communication!*). In the boxes below, write the number of the paragraph whose main ideas is closest to each of the statements. One answer has been done for you.
   - [ ] Active listening
   - [ ] Good place, good time, good situation
   - [ ] Listening and speaking are equally important
   - [3] Different understandings
   - [ ] Not just words
   - [ ] All areas of life

Address: http://www.unns.edu/fob/cpc/effective.com.html

University of UNNS | Faculty of Business | Centre for Professional Communication

Home | About Us | Mission | Research

EFFECTIVE COMMUNICATION!

1 Many people think that communicating is nothing more than talking a lot and speaking clearly. However, in reality, good communication is far more complicated than that.

2 One of the most important points in good communication is that listening is just as important as speaking. If someone isn't listening, the message is lost just as surely as if it wasn't given in the first place.

3 It is dangerous for a speaker to assume that the listener is thinking the same way they are thinking. Something that is common sense to one person may be illogical to another, especially if they are from a different culture. It's surprisingly common for major communication breakdowns to occur when the listener understands one thing from the speaker's words and the speaker actually wanted to express a very different meaning. Therefore, it is very useful for the listener to check that their understanding is the same as the speaker's, especially in formal discussions such as those during business meetings.

4 Also, communication can be helped considerably if the listener makes an effort to understand the speaker's feelings. It's useful to remember that non-verbal communication such as body language and facial expression is very important in this, although the degree of its importance depends on the situation. Many websites and books say that over 90% of communication is through non-verbal communication. Although this is only partially true – the research that this idea is based on applied only to the communication of emotions and feelings, not facts – it's an important point nevertheless. An example will demonstrate this: if someone tells you that they are interested in a programme they are in the middle of watching on TV but their eyes are looking elsewhere, their facial expression looks bored and their intonation is flat, would you believe their words?

5 In situations where accuracy in communication is important, for example where there might be a possibility of conflict, sometimes the simplest of things can make a big difference. Barriers to good communication are obvious: noisy rooms, frequent interruptions from other people, and situations where one person is concentrating on something else, for example, when driving. Just moving to a different place, closing the door, or waiting until another time to hold the discussion are all things that people often forget, but which can cause a very different result.

6 It may sound as though these techniques are mainly for formal situations such as business meetings and interviews, but in reality they are also useful in every situation in life, whether at a bar, chatting with neighbours, or talking with partners, children and other family members.

7 Many of the skills mentioned above are used in a technique called active listening. This can be used in almost any situation – it is a good idea to try to always be an active listener. There are several parts to this technique. Firstly, an active listener will try to understand from the speaker's point of view, thinking about what there is in the speaker's experience that might affect how something is understood. Also, he or she will watch the facial expressions and body language of the speaker carefully, and try to understand these. The active listener will also give the speaker time to think as well as to talk and, depending on culture, will make eye contact with the speaker. Most importantly, the active listener will check that he or she understands correctly, by paraphrasing what he or she understands that the speaker has said. Benefits of active listening include stronger trust, fewer conflicts and, ultimately, better relationships and thereby greater happiness.

8 In conclusion, there's a lot more to good communication than simply talking at length. Active listening techniques and avoidance of factors that will cause the message to become confused are all things that a good communicator will try to do. Sometimes a quiet person who listens carefully and puts thought into how they express themselves can be a more successful communicator than even an extrovert who doesn't pay attention to the other speakers' ideas, feelings and way of thinking.

University of New North Scotland, Faculty of Business, Centre for Professional Communication

This site is provided as a service to the public by the university

Last updated 14th January 2007

Task C | The five questions for reading any text

Answer the questions below about the text *Effective communication!*

The five questions for any reading

[a] What is it?

____

[b] What is the source?

____

[c] Who is the writer?

____

[d] What purpose does the writer have for writing it?

____

[e] Who is the intended audience?

____

Task D | Reading for detail

1. Scan the text for the following words and phrases.

benefits	barriers
express	technique
extrovert	conflict (two places)
assume	paraphrasing

2. Write the words and phrases from Question 1 next to their closest meanings below. Use the context to find the meaning – don't use a dictionary.

MEANINGS **WORDS**

- communicate ________
- a special or clever way of doing something ________
- say something in different words
- argument ________
- make a guess that something is true ________
- a person who enjoys spending time with other people; usually someone who talks loudly and a lot ________
- advantage, improvement or help that you get from something; something good ________
- a rule, problem, etc that prevents people from doing something, or limits what they can do ________

3. The text below is a summary of the text you just read. Put the words in the box below the text into the gaps.

A good [a] ________________ does much more than just [b] ________________. Listening is also very important, as is avoiding the kind of problems that might stop the message from being [c] ________________in the way the speaker wanted. One such problem is when people make assumptions about what the other is thinking, or assume that something is [d] ________________. To solve this, it is useful for the listener to say what he or she thinks the meaning is, and to ask if this is correct.

Non-verbal communication is also very important, especially when communicating [e] ________________. [f] ________________, and expressions on the face are important for this. It can also help to move to a [g] ________________ place or arrange a better time if the message is important. These techniques are useful in all situations, including [h] ________________ situations.

Active listening includes many of the techniques listed above, and can help to make [i] ________________ stronger. Using active listening can mean that everyone can become a very effective communicator.

informal	communicator	feelings
talk	common sense	relationships
body language	understood	quiet

4. For the following statements, write:

True (**T**) if the statement is confirmed by the text on page 53 (ie exactly the same idea is expressed in the text)
False (**F**) if the statement is contradicted by the text (ie it's the opposite of something said in the text)
Not given (**NG**) if the statement is neither confirmed nor contradicted by the text

[a] Communication is just saying many things clearly. ________
[b] Over 90% of meaning is expressed in ways other than words. ________
[c] Concentrating on other things can be a barrier to communication. ________
[d] Active listeners don't need to paraphrase what the speaker said. ________
[e] Active listening can make people happier.
[f] Active listening is difficult. ________
[g] Introverts are better communicators than extroverts. ________

Task E | Discussion

Talk about the following questions in small groups.

1. Do you already use some of the techniques of active listening?
2. Do you agree that active listening can be used in informal social situations as well as formal situations?
3. Are there situations where active listening might not be so useful?
4. Do you agree that techniques such as active listening can help avoid conflict?
5. 'Hearing is exercise for the ears, but listening is exercise for the brain.' Explain this statement. To what extent do you agree?
6. Can you now add anything to your answers to Questions 1 and 2 in Task A above?

FORMAL AND INFORMAL EMAILS; FORMAL LETTERS

Task A | Reasons for writing emails and letters

1. In pairs, tell each other how often you write:
   [a] informal emails
   [b] formal emails
   [c] formal letters to companies, organisations, etc.

2. Think of as many purposes as you can for writing each of the above.

3. While you are preparing for your college or university course, or during that course, for what reasons might you write formal letters or emails?

Task B | Conventions of emails and letters

1. Look at the following three examples of written communication. Which one is:
   [a] a formal email?
   [b] an informal email?
   [c] a formal letter?

4150 Brookwood Road
Mississauga ON L5C 1B6
Canada
Tel: +1 (905) 828 5459
Email: bwhitehurst@theinternetco.net.ca

Admissions Department
The University Office
University of Newham
Old Elvet
Newham NH1 3HP
UK

22 September 2007

Dear Sir/Madam,

Re: Request for information about BSc Biology (overseas student)

I am writing to you to request information about your courses. I am interested in studying for a BSc in Biology, and I have heard that the course at Newham University is especially good.

Could you therefore please send to the address above any available information about this course? Could you also please send any information that may be relevant to overseas students from Canada?

Thank you very much for your help in this matter,

Yours faithfully

Brendan Whitehurst

Brendan Whitehurst

EXAMPLE 1

From: bwhitehurst@theinternetco.net.ca
To: info@Newham.ac.uk
Subject: Request for information about BSc Biology (overseas student)
Date: Sat, 22nd Sept 2007 17:34:18

Dear Sir/Madam
Could you please send some information about your BSc in Biology, as well as any information you may have for overseas students. I am from Canada.

Could these please be sent to the address below. Alternatively, if the information is available in electronic form, could you please let me know where I can find it, or email it to me.

Thank you for your help with this,

Regards,
Brendan Whitehurst

Brendan Whitehurst
4150 Brookwood Road
Mississauga ON L5C 1B6
Canada
T: +1 (905) 828 5459
E: bwhitehurst@theinternetco.net.ca

EXAMPLE 2

To: curlylurgy@hmail.com
From: bwhitehurst@theinternetco.net.ca
Subject: Info about BSc Biology
Date: Sat, 22nd Sept 2007 17:48:37

Hi Charlene,
How's it going over there in merry old England? Cold, I guess! Hope it isn't raining too much. Are you still your usual self … partying and staying up late?

Anyway, I'm thinking of coming over there myself … I've decided it's biology I want to study … gene therapy and all that kind of thing. Just by coincidence, it seems that Newham is a really good place to study that. So, could you do me a favour? I haven't been able to find much on the internet so far, so could you see what information you can pick up for me?

Anyway, look forward to seeing you when you come home for the hols … let me know how the partying is!!

See ya'
Brendan

EXAMPLE 3

2 Which of the following is true for each kind of correspondence? Mark all that apply (*salutation* is another word for a greeting, eg Dear Sir).

CONVENTIONS	FORMAL LETTER	FORMAL EMAIL	INFORMAL EMAIL
Sender's address and contact details at top right hand corner			
Sender's address and contact details below sender's name, at bottom			
Receiver's address on left, above date, lower than sender's address			
Date below sender's address, above salutation			
Date and time appear automatically			
Topic is on a line after the salutation, starting with *Re:*			
Formal salutation			
Informal salutation			
Paragraphs are used			
First paragraph gives the purpose of the message			
Paragraphs after the first give more detail			
Formal ending			
Informal ending			
Signature included			
Sender's full name at the end			
Sender's given name (only) at the end			
Formal vocabulary (eg *request* instead of *ask for*)			
Contractions (eg *I'm* instead of *I am*)			

3. Write the following next to each expression in the bubbles below:
   - **FL** if it's used in formal letters
   - **FE** if it's used in formal emails
   - **IE** if it's used in informal emails.

   You may write more than one set of letters next to some expressions.

Salutations
Dear Mr Whitehurst
Dear Dr Peter Hallam
Hi Fred

Endings

Best wishes	Take care
Yours sincerely	Love
Yours faithfully	Lots of love
Regards	All the best
Kind regards	Cheers
Catch you later	Thanks
See you	Talk to you soon
See ya'	See you soon

Task C | Write your own correspondence

1. Choose one of the following situations and write a formal letter, a formal email and an informal email for the situation. Try to write in your own words (don't use phrases from the questions).

[a] You would like more information about your future university or college. Write to the admissions department, and to a friend who is already studying there. Ask about:
- your course
- how to apply
- their facilities for free-time activities.

[b] You would like more information about the area around where you will be doing your future course. Write to the tourism authority in that area, and a friend who lives in that area. Ask about:
- tourist attractions in the area
- public transport
- cheap accommodation.

2. When you have finished, use the table you developed in Question 2 of the previous task to check your letter and emails. Then, revise your writing to make sure all the relevant points from the table are covered.

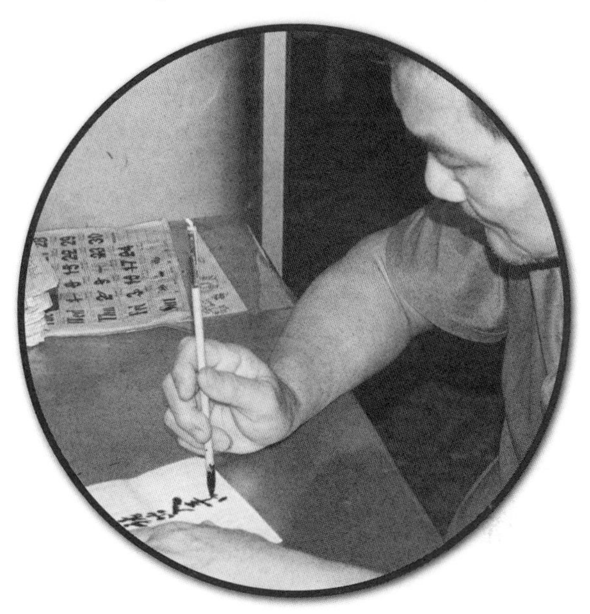

SPECIFIC INFORMATION – TELEPHONE CONVERSATIONS

Task A | Listening for specific information

CD 1 8

Listen to the recording and write the correct words in the gaps in the script that follows.

Leaving a message

(Telephone ringing.)

Receptionist: Hello, Newham University admissions office.
Brendan: Could I speak to [1] _______________ about doing an undergraduate, er, biology degree?
Receptionist: Are you an international student or a local student?
Brendan: I'm from overseas.
Receptionist: Can I put you on [2] _______________ while I see if there's an international student officer available?
Brendan: No problem.

(Telephone music on hold.)

Receptionist: Hello again, er, she doesn't seem to be at her [3] _______________ . Would you like to leave a message on her voicemail?
Brendan: That'll be fine.
Receptionist: I'll just put you [4] _______________ . Her name's Martha.

(Click and change of background hum.)

Martha (recorded voice)**:** This is Martha Billington. I can't [5] _______________ my phone right now. You can leave a message on my voicemail after the tone, or if you press zero you'll get back to [6] _______________ .

(Ding)

Brendan: Ah, hello, it's Brendan Whitehurst here. I'm thinking of [7] _______________ to do a biology degree, and was wondering whether I could pop in and [8] _______________ the department, and perhaps speak with someone. Would you be able to call me [9] _______________ on 07740 942 563, otherwise I'll try again later. Thanks, the number again was 07740 942 563.

Task B | Scanning and finding meaning from context

1. Scan the completed telephone script in Task A above for the phrases in List A below, and underline them.

LIST A

put … on hold
put … through (to)
after the tone
press zero
get back to
call me back
try again (later)

2. Using context, match the words in List A above with the closest meaning in List B below.

LIST B

a sound that means the telephone you are calling to is ringing
push the button with 0 on it
*push the button with * on it*
let you wait (on some phone systems, you listen to music while you are waiting)
call me later
the part of the telephone you pick up
after an electronic sound
push the button with # on it
call the same person again later
a sound that means someone is already using the telephone you are calling
allow you to speak to the person you first spoke with
call someone
ask if someone wants to wait on the line
press buttons on a telephone to call someone
allow you to speak to another person
the part of the telephone with numbers that you press

3. Match the following (List C) with meanings in List B. Some of these don't appear in the recording but are useful. Some items in List B may match with an item in both List A and List C, or two items in List C.

LIST C

after the beep	engaged tone/busy tone
hold the line	receiver
would you mind holding?	handset
press hash	the dial
press star	dial a number
ringing tone	make a call (to …)

4. Read the conversation in Task A again and mark other expressions you think might be useful.

Task C | Listening for specific information

CD 1

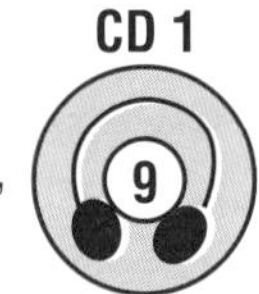

1. You are going to listen to Brendan calling back to speak with Martha. Before listening, predict what he will say.

2. While listening, fill in the following form for the lecturer, just as Martha would be doing during the conversation.

APPOINTMENT REQUEST

Name:
....
Person to see:
....
Day:
....
Time:
....
Purpose:
....
....

❸ Listen again, and fill in the gaps in the following notes taken by Brendan.

Directions

Taxi – about £ ______

______ site ______

Drop off at ______

Follow ______

Go to ______ when arrive

there. ______

Email: ______

______

______

______

Task D | Role plays

In groups of three, practise conversations similar to the ones you heard on the recordings. Try to use as much of the new vocabulary from this section as possible. Two people in each group should practise the conversation, and the third should count the number of new words the other two use. When finished, swap roles.

Which group can use the largest number of new words?

WILL (INSTANT DECISIONS); FIRST CONDITIONALS

Task A | Uses of *will*

CD 1 (9)

❶ Match the following clauses [a] to [d] to the reasons for the use of will in i, ii or iii. The first two sentences are taken from the script on pages 57 to 58; the other two are from the second recording for this Unit (Listening Task C).

______ **[a]** *I'll just put you through*
______ **[b]** *I'll try again later*
______ **[c]** *I'll probably take the train*
______ **[d]** *It'll only be about £3 or so*

i. making a prediction or guess about the future
ii. speaking at about the same time as deciding to do the action ('instant decisions')
iii. no fixed decision made yet

❷ In [c] which word is used together with 'will' to indicate there is no certainty? ______

Task B | Instant decisions

❶ Write responses to the following (make an instant decision).

A: It's hot in here!
B: ______

A: It's so noisy!
B: ______

A: Can I speak with a customer service representative, please?
B: ______

A: I can smell burning – I think there's a fire!
B: ______

A: I think I'm going to drop these books!
B: ______

Task C | Real conditionals – Form and use

1. Look at the following sentences (the first is from the second listening for this unit) and answer the questions below.

[a] If you ask to be dropped off at the library, you shouldn't go too far wrong.

[b] If you call, we might be able to arrange a meeting with a lecturer.

[c] You'll have a better chance of getting university accommodation if you apply early.

[d] If you visit next week, you'll be able to meet some current students.

[e] If you could come to the university this afternoon, you would be able to see the Prime Minister visit, but I guess you're too far away.

For each of the sentences above, is the situation in the *if* clause:

i. certain?
ii. reasonably likely/quite possible?
iii. very unlikely/almost impossible?

(As an example, the sentence [a] matches with situation ii. We can't say the person is certain to ask to be dropped of at the library, so i is not correct. iii is not correct because asking to be dropped of at the library is clearly quite possible.)

2. What is the tense in the *if* clause? Write your answers next to each clause.

3. What is the tense in the main clause? Write your answers next to each clause.

Task D | Real conditionals – Practice

1. Complete these sentences, making them true for yourself.

[a] If it rains at the weekend, ________________________
____

[b] ____
________________________ if our teacher is sick tomorrow.

[c] If my homework is easy this week, ________________
____

[d] If I get really good grades on my course, __________
____

[e] ____
________________________ if I wake up late tomorrow.

[f] If my friend invites me for a coffee this afternoon, ______
____

2. Tell your partner what you would do in the following situations

[a] Your parents decide to visit you.
[b] You have time for extra English study.
[c] You don't enjoy your future college or university course.
[d] You don't understand your lecturer at university or college.
[e] Your mobile phone breaks.

MAKING REQUESTS

Task A | Requests

1. There are several requests in the listenings in this Unit. Look at the recording script for the first call again on pages 57–58, and circle the expressions used for requests. The receptionist also makes an offer. Circle the offer as well.

2. Which of these requests are more polite?

3. Role-play three situations in pairs. Student A should look at page 162, and Student B should look at page 164. On these pages are boxes with the information you need for each situation. In Situation 1, A is the caller – your situation box tells you what you need to find out. B is the person who answers the call – read your situation box to find out what you need to know (it is not in the same order as the questions). You can add your own ideas – but they must not go against the printed instructions. In Situations 2 and 3, the roles are reversed.

FURTHER PRACTICE: READING, FILMS AND FUN

READING

- You can read some interesting ideas about communicating well (including active listening) at: **http://www.mindtools.com/page8.html**
- The Wikipedia article on communication is an interesting place to start exploring this topic. It is at **http://en.wikipedia.org/wiki/Communication**

FILMS

Rain Man, directed by Barry Levinson, starring Dustin Hoffman. Two sons of a millionaire spend time together. One has trouble communicating – but for the first time, the other feels he needs to communicate something very important.

Ace Ventura: Pet Detective, directed by Tom Shadyac; *Ace Ventura: When Nature Calls*, directed by Steve Oedekerk. Both starring Jim Carrey. Comedies about a vet with an amazing ability to communicate with animals.

QUESTIONS

1. Explain some barriers to communication, and say what can be done to stop them.
2. What skills are important for good communication?
3. What are the advantages of mobile phones for everyday life? What are the disadvantages?
4. For people who have lived in at least one country other than their own:

   Do differences in non-verbal communication (eg body language, facial expressions) between cultures cause communication difficulties? Provide examples to show your ideas on this topic.

6 POLITICS

'never discuss politics or religion'

BY THE END OF THIS UNIT, YOU SHOULD:

POLITICS n. [UNCOUNTABLE]: 1 ideas and activities relating to gaining and using power in a country, city, etc.

PREFIXES AND SUFFIXES

Task A | Greek and Latin into English!

Some words have prefixes (at the front of the word) and suffixes (at the end of the word). In English, these prefixes and suffixes are often derived from Latin or Greek words.

Prefixes: Greek into English
olig – small or few
mono – one or single
demo – people, population, common people
bureau – a division of a government department (Latin into English)

Suffixes: Greek into English
archy – rulership
cracy – power

❶ Define the following words without a dictionary but by using your understanding of prefixes and suffixes:

1. *oligarchy* ______________________________

2. *monarchy* ______________________________

3. *democracy* ______________________________

4. *bureaucracy* ______________________________

BUILDING THE FIELD

Task A | Thinking for yourself and talking about it

❶ Look at the photos below. Can you identify anyone?

❷ Read the statistics in the table on the next page. What do you think about the 'War in Iraq'? Are you for war or against it? In other words, do you agree that the war is/was the right thing to do or do you disagree? Do you have an opinion about it? Discuss in groups. Use the phrases in the box below the statistics to help you.

Ⓐ ______________________

Ⓑ ______________________

Ⓒ ______________________

THE HUMAN COST OF OCCUPATION FROM THE BEGINNING OF THE WAR IN IRAQ UNTIL 6 FEB 2006

US military casualties in Iraq

Since war began, 19 Mar 2003	2552 dead
Since 'Mission Accomplished' speech by Bush, 1 May 2003	2115 dead
Since capture of Saddam, 13 Dec 2003	1785 dead
Since US handover to Iraq, 19 June 2004	1386 dead
Since Iraqi election, 31 Jan 2005	816 dead
US wounded (official count)	16,549
Iraqi death toll (est.)	30,000–100,000
Average cost of war per day	US$300 million
Rumsfeld '05 estimate of duration of war	12 years

Source: http//:antiwar.com

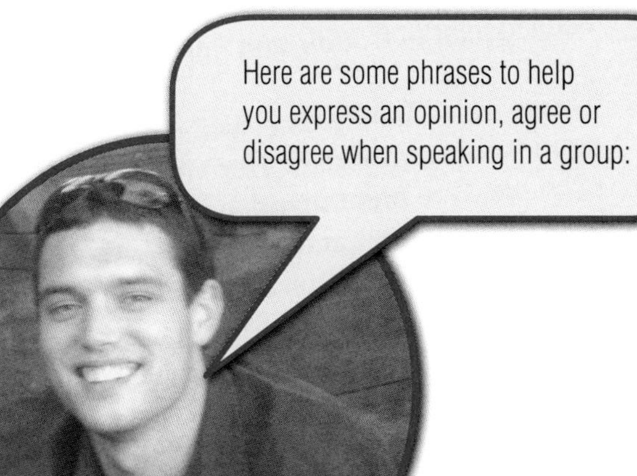

Here are some phrases to help you express an opinion, agree or disagree when speaking in a group:

- *I agree....* (with what someone else said)
- *You're absolutely right, but . . .*
- *Sorry, I just don't agree . . .* (with what someone said)
- *Yes, but . . .* (means you want to speak and don't agree with speaker or want to add something that is different)
- *Well, you could say that, but I think . . .*
- *I think . . .*
- *What do you mean? I don't think . . .*
- *No way . . .*
- *I'm not sure I understand what you mean. I mean . . .*
- *If I may say . . .*

Task B | What is politics?

1. In groups, explain what sort of government is in power in your home country.

2. What do you think 'politics' means?

3. In groups, discuss whether you agree or disagree with the following statement – *People should never talk about politics or religion.*

DISCUSSION ESSAY

Task A | Form and comprehension – Features of individual paragraphs

Read the following discussion that uses the following essay question:

You may have heard the statement: 'People should never talk about politics or religion'. Shorten this statement to 'People should never talk about politics'. Discuss after reading the text on the next page.

DISCUSSING POLITICS AND RELIGION

1 It is often said that people should never discuss politics or religion. It may be because discussions of this nature might begin as pleasant conversations but then become heated arguments and even turn into violent fights. For the same reason, some say that people should never talk about politics. However, 'never' is a difficult word. Perhaps there are times when it is OK and other times when it is not OK to discuss politics.

2 First, what is politics? According to *Longman's Dictionary*, politics is a noun and it means *ideas and activities relating to gaining and using power* in a country (p 1265). Thus, politics involves people – the people who gain power in order to either represent or control the rest of the population. Everyday, we read about politics and see the result of politics, such as political decisions on the television. Every single person's life is affected by politics everyday. Since politics are a huge part of everyone's life, it would be foolish to say you should 'never' talk about politics. However, if politics are discussed, you have to be prepared to take the possible consequences. Following are two consequences that happened when politics was discussed in my country. It is also about my own personal experience. From that, it will be seen that there are times to discuss politics and there are other times when you probably should not.

3 In my country, there was a political figure who caused many discussions between friends about politics. She also caused the news to discuss her and her views and opinions. In both these cases, discussing politics had a negative effect (was bad). This woman was definitely a racist in her views, although she always pretended not to be. My country is a country where most of the population comes from other countries. It is multicultural which means there are many different kinds of people. All these people love their new home while they sometimes speak their own language, eat their favourite foods and follow some customs and religion that is their tradition. Most of the time, people get along together and respect each other while enjoying this country which is a democratic one.

4 This woman became a leader of a little party in our country. This job meant she could speak in public to the press. She spoke badly about others and the media put her face on televisic a lot. Other media around the world seemed to find her interesting too and we heard that she was in newspapers in Japan, China and Indonesia. Her opinions influenced tourists nc to come for a holiday, so discussing politics in the media had a very bad effect. Tourism lost money because visitors changed their minds about visiting this country. Some students of English decided to go to other countries and not come here. She did not represent the majority of people and their thinking but her open discussion of her own personal views caused a lot of trouble and misunderstanding.

5 There are definitely times when discussing politics is inappropriate. Here is another example. One night my friend came over and brought her father and mother too. Her parents came from the same town that this political figure, the woman, came from. They began to talk about her and they said they liked her a lot. They said they agreed with many of her views. I said I did not agree with her and that I didn't like her at all. The father became very angry with me and he and his wife stood up and left quickly. It was embarrassing for everyone. It was quite terrible and my friend and I did not speak for a little while. I wrote her a letter and apologised in the end. If you are the host or hostess for a party and the conversation is getting dangerous, like that example, then maybe it is a good idea to guide the conversation away from the topic of politics.

6 However, discussing politics means you are thinking. It means more than one view can be talked about. A discussion needs more than one point of view, rather like an argument. To discuss politics is to bring out information, opinions and facts. This can be a good thing. Even though people may not change their minds, they may open them a little when they hear discussion.

7 In conclusion, perhaps it is better to 'never say never' rather than say 'never discuss politics'. It is important, however, to choose the time and place if it involves friends or family. A happy social occasion is probably not the best time to discuss important political things. Choose the right time and place and discuss freely so that information can be shared and people have the power of knowledge from your discussions.

This writing follows the form of a discussion in English. Each paragraph has certain features. Match the features described below to the appropriate numbered paragraph(s) in the text.

[a] [insert appropriate para number(s) here] _______ Definition of term with page number from dictionary (cited); explanation of the writer's position (beliefs) so the reader knows what the writer is thinking; restatement of what the essay will be about

[b] _______ *may; might; probably; perhaps* = modality Introductory sentence which restates the topic question sentences explaining how the writer feels about the topic or what the writer believes about the topic question – *Perhaps there are times when it is OK and other times when it is not OK to discuss politics.* This also gives a glimpse of what the preview / scope of the essay will be. The sentence looks like a preview or scope and it does tell a little about what is to come, but the real preview or scope is stated clearly in para 2 when the Introduction formally ends. *From that, it will be seen that there are times to discuss politics and there are other times when you probably should not.*
(*Note, Introductions can be more than one paragraph.)

[c] _______ Background information.

[d] _______ Topic sentence explains that there are times when discussing politics is inappropriate; concrete supporting evidence offered in example using personal anecdote (personal experience).

[e] _______ Topic sentence is about a female political figure; Essay statement is that there was a negative effect from this public discussion on politics; explanation of the country and its people.

[f] _______ Discourse cue: 'In conclusion' signals the conclusion of the paper; brief summary; recommendation.

[g] _______ Topic sentence further clarifies the 'woman' from para 3 concrete supporting evidence that the media discussion around this woman's politics had a negative effect.

[h] _______ Discourse cue: 'however' posits the other side of the discussion; concrete evidence in opinion form that discussing politics has good sides as well as bad.

Task B | Understanding

This task is intended to help comprehension and expand your vocabulary. Answer the following questions by circling the correct letter.

1. The country mentioned in the text is:
   - [a] democratic
   - [b] autocratic
   - [c] communist
   - [d] a dictatorship

2. The writer likes the woman politician mentioned in para 3.
   - [a] true
   - [b] false

3. According to the text, an example of when discussing politics is negative is:
   - [a] at the movies
   - [b] with relatives
   - [c] at a dinner party
   - [d] at the beach

4. A multicultural country means:
   - [a] a country which has racism
   - [b] a country where people eat their favourite foods
   - [c] a country where most of the population came from somewhere else
   - [d] a country which is a democracy

5. In the conclusion, the writer says:
   - [a] you should never discuss politics
   - [b] you should only discuss politics with your best friends
   - [c] you should only discuss politics with your family
   - [d] you should make your own decision when to discuss politics

6. When the writer says, *'Even though people may not change their minds, they may open them a little when they hear discussion'*, she means:
   - [a] you should never discuss politics
   - [b] discussions help people to learn more
   - [c] having an open mind is a good thing
   - [d] people change their minds after a discussion

7. 'Never say never' means:
   - [a] you should never discuss politics
   - [b] always say never
   - [c] keep an open mind
   - [d] never say always

8. In para 2, last line *From that, it will be seen . . .* 'From that' refers to:
   - [a] two consequences
   - [b] political decisions
   - [c] politics are a huge part of everyone's life
   - [d] television

9. *Point of view* means:
   - [a] a stick for pointing
   - [b] beautiful scenery
   - [c] an opinion or belief
   - [d] a sharp object

10. In a discussion:
   - [a] you need only one point of view
   - [b] you need ten points of view
   - [c] you need four points of view
   - [d] you need more than one point of view.

DISCUSSION GENRE

Task A | Map or schema of discussion essay

1. Examine the reading – *Discussion essay: People should never talk about politics* – and draw the following stages on it.

Introduction
- First sentence restates the topic question.
- Positions the reader as to what the writer thinks.

Definition stage
- Definition stage appears here.
- Defining terms can let the reader know more about the writer's intention.

Preview/scope stage
- Indicates what the writer is going to write about in the rest of the essay.

Body
- Paragraphs *for* the topic question. Include support information. (Information that makes the reader know what you mean. This information must directly relate to the argument *for*.)
- Paragraphs *against* the topic question. Include support information. (Information that makes the reader know what you mean. This information must directly relate to the argument *against*.)

Conclusion
- Sentence to allow the reader to know you are finishing up.
- Summary.
- Recommendation.

TALKING ABOUT FUTURE PREDICTIONS (GOING TO), MODALITY (PROBABILITY), PRESENT SIMPLE TENSE

*** YOU CAN EXPRESS FUTURE BY USING THE PRESENT CONTINUOUS – *I'M.......ING*; BUT YOU CAN ALSO USE TO BE + GOING TO 'INTENTIONS'. FOR EXAMPLE:**
- ***I'M GOING TO LOSE WEIGHT!***
- ***REALLY! I'M GOING TO TRY TO GAIN SOME, MYSELF.***
- ***YOU'RE BOTH SILLY, I'M GOING TO STAND FOR GOVERNMENT AND FORGET ALL ABOUT WEIGHT!***

Task A | Future predictions – *Going to*

1. Write five sentences talking about things you're *going to* try to do in the future.

____

____

____

____

____

2. Complete the following dialogue:

Jess: *What are you doing tonight?*
Sveti: *Well, I haven't really decided yet. But, I think I'm ____________ the movies.*
Jess: *What do ya' want to see?*
Sveti: *Again, I haven't decided yet.*
Jess: *Well, that's a coincidence, because I'm ____________ go.*
Sveti: *Do you know what you're ____________ see?*
Jess: *Yep! I'm ____________ see a foreign film at the Independent.*
Sveti: *Sounds pretty good to me. I'm ____________ come with you. Alright?*
Jess: *Yes, of course, that's fine. We're ____________ have a good time.*

Task B | Modality – *Probably* or *possibly*

When you write or speak, it is important to make sure the discussion can be carried out by more than one person. This means you must leave it 'open'. If you write or say something like this – *'Divorce is very bad for all families'* – you have closed the door on discussion. What about writing or saying – *In many cases, divorce may be bad for families* – Can you see that there is room now for a 'however'? *In many cases, divorce may be bad for families, however, there are cases where divorce is beneficial. For example . . .* etc. You now have a discussion and that came about by adding modality: words that express possibility rather than absolute certainty, eg *might, may, could, maybe, perhaps, sometimes, probably, at times, possibly*, and so forth.

Examine the two sets of five sentences below in Questions 1 and 3. Question 1 uses *to be* or *to have.*

I am ....ing (to come) coming	*They have ....ed (to succeed) succeeded*
You are ...ing? (to go) going	*He has .....ed (to try) tried*

1 Complete the following:

[a] I am .... (to think).
I'm .... (think).

[b] She is .... (to think).
She's .... (think).

[c] He is .... (to think).
He's .... (think).

[d] They are .... (to think).
They're .... (think).

[e] We are .... (to think).
We're .... (think).

2 What happened to the main verb *think*?

____

____

3 In the sentences below, the main verbs are *go, apply, try* and *come.*

[a] *I might go; he might go; she might go; they might go*
[b] *I may apply; we may apply; she may try; she may not try*
[c] *I could come; she could come; he could come*
[d] *I could try; we could try*
[e] *they could change; she could do it; he could show up.*

Did anything happen to these verbs in the above sentences?

____

____

*

***MIGHT, MAY, COULD* – USE THESE WORDS TO EXPRESS POSSIBILITY, IE 'MAYBE', AND REMEMBER NOT TO CHANGE THE TENSE OF THE MAIN VERB WHEN YOU USE THEM**

4 In pairs, read the dialogue. When finished reading the dialogue write the answers in the gaps in the text.

Al: *I _________ have a party next week and I _________ invite you, if you're lucky.*
Max: *Well, that's nice of you and I just _________ come along, if you ask me nicely.*
Al: *What do you think I should buy for food and drink?*
Max: *Hmmmm, depends on who's coming. You _________ buy a lot of different things to suit a lot of different tastes.*
Al: *Yeah, and I _________ be a millionaire, too.*
Max: *HAH! You _________ have to stay within your budget then.*
Al: *Yeah, but I _________ lash out and really go crazy with this one. I love having parties. I _________ try and do an extra shift and get more money.*
Max: *I _________ put a little cash in too, mate.*
Al: *You're a good friend, you know.*

Task C | Present simple tense

Present simple is used to express: routines or habits; when something is true and it will remain true (facts); when things stay the same over a long period of time.

1 Underline each example of the present simple tense in the following texts:

Present simple tense

[a] *For routines or habits* – Sylvia washes her hair everyday. She sets her alarm for 7, gets up and washes her hair in the shower. Then, she brushes her teeth, makes a cup of tea, drinks it and heads for the university library. She almost never varies this pattern. It's her habit.

[b] *When something is true and it will remain true. It is always true* – The clock strikes midnight every twenty-four hours. That's a fact. It's also a fact that a match burns when you light it, sand makes glass, and in winter I see my breath. Another fact that lends itself to the present simple is that birth and death happens to everyone.

[c] *Things that stay the same over a long period of time* – Rory Lee goes to accountancy classes. He's been going for two years and he has to keep going another two years. He goes with his room-mate just about every day. He attends each class, never misses a lecture and remembers his laptop as well.

2. Write a paragraph using the present simple tense to talk about your own habits.

____

____

____

____

____

____

____

____

3. Read the following text below and
   - **a.** underline the *present simple* tense
   - **b.** double underline all forms (tenses) using *going to*, and
   - **c.** broken line any words you think show *probability*. Probability means 'maybe' or 'it's possible that'.

> My uncle runs for the local Green Earth Party every year. He's going to do so again this year and may do so next year too, if he loses again. One day, he might win. We hope he does. I mean, he could win. He just needs a few more votes. We vote for him. We always vote for him. His wife, my aunt, goes to the polls, casts her vote and walks away. Each time she does it, she hopes this will be the year he may win.

AGREEING AND DISAGREEING

Task A | Discussion – Future of government

This is a critical thinking task to activate the language you have been taught in this Unit. Consider the following question.

Do you think there will be a world government one day? Something like the United Nations but not controlled by one, large, industrialised country? Rather, it might be organised as a proper League of Nations or democratic world group that would work together to make the whole world a better place. Do you think it's possible? Do you think there will be other planets discovered and governments to run those planets in space?

1. In pairs, look at the following terms, some of which appeared at the beginning of this Unit. They are terms to help you agree or disagree in a discussion. From the Language Spotlight in this Unit, use the present simple tense and also modality language. Discuss the question above.

> ***Agreement***
> *I agree; You're right; I think so too; Good idea; Good point; I know; Exactly; You're telling me; I suppose so; I guess so; That sounds great*
>
> ***Disagreement***
> *No, it isn't; That's not right; That's not necessarily true; I really can't accept that; No, I don't accept that; I see your point, but; No way; You can't be serious.*
>
> *Source: Longman Dictionary of Contemporary English,* pp 983, 984.

MINI-LECTURE, GOVERNMENT AND POLITICS, NOTE-TAKING FROM LISTENING

Task A | Importance markers: intonation, stress, emphasis

CD 1

The purpose of the recording is to focus your listening on the spoken cues so that you learn to recognise those parts in a text that are important to note.

- You already have a copy of the text of the talk and so you can take notes while listening for extra points that the lecturer brings in.
- In order to take notes when listening, you need to know what is important and what is not.
- Not everything a speaker says is meant to be written down.
- You need to recognise certain words or phrases that guide you.
- You also need to know the purpose of those words or phrases.

1. Place a tick in Column B next to the following markers each time you hear one in the talk.

COLUMN A	COLUMN B ☑	COLUMN C – Purpose
Today's talk is about		
that is		
define		
so		
we are concerned with . . .		
Government is about . . .		
I'll give you . . .		
Now then . . .		
This type of . . . . . . is		
This form of . . . . . . is		
Think (used as imperative, directed at listeners . . .)		
. . . . . . means		
then this . . . . . . is		
A third type . . . . . . is		
There is		
A second type . . . . . . is		

2. Now you need to add the purpose/function of the language in Column C from the following list, using the number of the purpose below.

1. To explain the order of something.
2. To define – to offer a definition.
3. To tell the listener to focus or pay attention.
4. To signal a result or conclusion the speaker has reached, *eg thus*
5. To explain what the talk is about.

3. Listen for the following intonation and stress in the talk. Match the words and sentences from Group A by placing the number next to the letter in Group B.

GROUP A

1. louder – volume increases in voice
2. softer – volume drops in voice
3. upwards in the voice
4. downwards in the voice
5. less confident or a little insecure in voice

GROUP B

A. ______ Because it adds emphasis
B. ______ Because it is important
C. ______ Because it is less important
D. ______ Because it is an aside – not really important at all.

FURTHER PRACTICE: READING, FILMS AND FUN

READING

Booktopia Political Science:
http://booktopia.com.au/books/political-science/0/

Xing Lujian, *Rhetoric in Ancient China, Fifth to Third Century BCE: A Comparison with Classical Greek Rhetoric*, Uni of South Carolina Press.

FILMS

The Yes Men: A modern documentary that combines humour and fact to expose the way corporate power rules the world.

Crash: A look at racist issues and politics in America.

Bowling for Columbine: A satirical documentary about a sad event. Michael Moore, writer and film maker, produced this film as a political comment on what makes the sort of country that produces high school massacres.

QUESTIONS

1. What sort of government is in your home country? Describe the current government and explain how it came to power.

2. Politics in England and the Western world are linked to Greece and Rome. Research early politics in one of these countries and discuss how it relates to present day democracy.

7 MEDIA

'remember to distrust'

BY THE END OF THIS UNIT, YOU SHOULD:

MEDIA n., pl. [UNCOUNTABLE]: all the organisations, such as television, radio, and newspapers, that provide news and information for the public, or the people who do this work.

BUILDING THE FIELD

Task A | The range of media

1. In small groups, list as many different types of media as you can (eg magazines ...).

____

____

____

____

2. For each type of media, list as many different kinds of that media as you can (eg sports magazines, news magazines . . .).

____

____

____

____

3. Which would you call *mass media*? Which would you call *specialist publications*?

4. Which are the most interesting? Why? Which do you read or watch regularly? Why?

IDENTIFYING TEXT TYPE; COHESION – ADVICE AND INSTRUCTIONAL TEXTS

Task A | Identifying text type

Where do the following three texts (Texts 1, 2 and 3) come from? How did you know?

- text book
- magazine
- newspaper
- instruction book for something in the house
- student essay
- government information leaflet

TEXT 1

HOW TO BECOME A FILM STAR

1 Everyone wants to become a film star – the glamour of Hollywood, the fame, the money, the excited fans and mixing with the most talked-about people in the world – wouldn't that be 5 wonderful! We know that's not easy, but, if you follow these tips, you just might get your photo on the front pages of the celebrity magazines!

The first thing is to make sure you're in the right place – it's no good trying to hit the big time in the 10 north of Scotland where there are no producers to meet or casting directors to give you a job. You're much better off going to southern California where all the action is.

And when you're there, do all you can to meet the 15 right people. Go to as many parties as you can, get your hair cut at the same places as the stars, do whatever you can to find out what's going on, and talk, talk, talk. Get eye-catching business cards printed, give them out to everyone you meet, and 20 above all, make as many contacts as you can.

Looks are also very important. Make yourself as beautiful or handsome as possible. Any money you spend in this area is a good investment – Hollywood just doesn't want to employ average-looking actors. 25 Almost everyone will need cosmetic surgery to fit into the Hollywood ideal of perfect looks.

You will need to present yourself well. Get professional photographs made – they have to be the best quality they can be. Of course, it's 30 important to dress well, just like any other job … but you have to be even more careful in this image-conscious field by paying attention to fashion.

All of this will help you to get an agent. An agent 35 can help by introducing you to the right people at the right time … but there are thousands of people all wanting the services of one of these people, so you'll have to use the contacts you've made to help you with this. And make lots of copies of 40 your photograph, and mail them together with a carefully-written, exciting-sounding letter to every agent in the phone book.

And don't forget to check the newspapers – there are sometimes adverts for extras and assistant staff 45 members on the film crews. Get as much experience as possible, and take every opportunity to spend time with those important casting directors!

It's also useful to make sure your acting skills are good. Do whatever classes you can, practise 50 whenever you can … the more of this you do, the better.

Regarding personal qualities, the most important points are persistence – keep on trying every day, and patience – it can take a few years before your 55 name is known to enough people.

Good luck! Of course there are other ways – become famous on TV or as a singer first, for example, but these require more than one talent and are far more difficult!

60 **Agnes Daydrew, staff writer**

75 New Celebrity Magazine, March 2007

TEXT 2

DVD instructions for use

1. Make sure your Philsoniba DVD player is connected as instructed in the *Instructions for set up* section (see previous).
2. Press the power switch to switch on the DVD player.
3. Press the eject button. The DVD tray will open.
4. Put a DVD in the tray, with the printed side facing up.
5. Close the DVD tray by pushing it in, or by pressing the eject button once again.
6. On your TV, select either the AV1 or AV2 channel.
7. By now, a menu should have appeared on your TV screen. Use the arrow keys to select 'Scene 1', then press 'OK'.
8. Press the play button. You will now be able to watch the movie.
9. You can move to the next scene by pushing the fast forward button. Similarly you can pause by pressing pause, and rewind by pressing the rewind button.
10. To pause the picture simply press pause.

TEXT 3

ADVERTISING AND CHILDREN: GOOD OR BAD?

1 There has been a dramatic increase in the number of overweight children in recent years, leading to many health problems that usually affect older people. To improve the health of children, it is important to find out the reasons for this increase. Many factors have been put forward, but it is becoming more and more clear that one of the most important is the increased consumption of junk
5 food by children. For example, recent research (Hydermann, 2006) has shown that it was junk food consumption, not a reduction in exercise, that has led to an increase in childhood obesity in at least one country. There are many arguments against this from the food companies, of course, but in this essay it will be shown that there is more and more evidence that a reduction in the exposure of children to junk food advertising will mean an improvement in their health later in life.

Task B | Meaning behind the words

1. Look again at Text 1. Is the text formal or informal? How do you know?

____

____

____

2. What does the text say that shows the writer of Text 1 was trying to be funny?

____

____

____

Task C | The five questions for any text

Answer the questions below about Text 1: *How to become a film star.*

[a] What is it?

____

____

[b] What is the source?

____

____

[c] Who is the writer?

____

____

[d] What purpose does the writer have for writing it?

[e] Who is the intended audience?

[e] all of **this** (line 34):

[f] **this** (line 50):

Task D | Cohesion

1. Look back at Text 1 (*How to become a film star*) and write what each of these words refers to:
   - [a] **that** (line 4): becoming a film star, star – the glamour of Hollywood, the fame, the money, the excited fans and mixing with the most talked-about people in the world
   - [b] **there** (line 14):
   - [c] **them** (line 19):
   - [d] **this** area (line 23):

2. Students should complete the following sentences taken from Text 1:
   - [a] **better off** (line 12) means better off than
   - [b] **even more careful** (line 31) means even more careful than
   - [c] **far more difficult** (line 59) means far more difficult than

LANGUAGE SPOTLIGHT

LONGER NOUN GROUPS

Task A | What is nominalisation?

1. Look again at Text 3 in the Reading section at page 76 (*Advertising and children*). Mark the groups of words that have the same meaning as those in the following list. (The first has been done for you):
   - [a] the number of overweight children has increased dramatically
     a dramatic increase in the number of overweight children (line1)
   - [b] children are eating more junk food
   - [c] exercising less
   - [d] childhood obesity is increasing
   - [e] the food companies argue against this
   - [f] showing less advertising of junk food to children
   - [g] they will become healthier later in life

To help you:

eating = consuming (vb); consumption (n)
junk food = food that is mostly fat and sugar – it isn't healthy
very fat = obese (adj); obesity (n)
less = reduce (vb); a reduction (n)
show = expose (vb); exposure (n)

2. In the table below, write words from [a] to [g] in Question 1. Write them next to words with the same meaning from Text 3. One of them has been done for you as an example. Then, in the sentences at the bottom of each column of the table, circle the correct word.

TEXT 3 (academic)	QUESTION 1 (less formal)
[a] increase (n)	
[b] the increased consumption of ...	eating more
[c] a reduction in exercise	
[d] an increase	
[e] arguments	
[f] a reduction in the exposure of ... to ... advertising	
[g] an improvement in the health	
The main words here are mostly nouns / verbs / adjectives	**The main words here are mostly nouns / verbs / adjectives**

In which column do the words and expressions sound more informal and conversational? ____________________

____

Task B | Understanding nominalisations

Convert the following nominalisations into clauses with verbs. The first has been done for you as an example.

[a] his desire for fame

➔ He wants to be famous

[b] the danger of traffic accidents

➔ Traffic ____________________

[c] instructions on the use of DVD players

➔ How to ____________________

[d] a drop in mobile phone use

➔ People ____________________

[e] a decrease in the amount of exercise in children

➔ Children ____________________

[f] a gradual increase in the amount of advertising

➔ Companies ____________________

[g] a halt to the introduction of new products

➔ New products ____________________

[h] a lack of improvement in the quality of mobile phone service

➔ mobile phone companies ____________________

____

To help you:

halt = stop | gradual = slow | desire = want strongly

Task C | Giving instructions

1. Look again at Text 2 from the Reading section (*DVD instructions for use*, page 76), and answer the following questions for all the numbered instructions except for the ones numbered 7, 9 and 10:
   [a] For each sentence, can you see a subject?
   [b] What form of the verb is used?

This kind of sentence in Text 2 is called the *imperative* and is used for instructions. However, be careful only to use imperatives:
- in formal writing, eg notices, forms, instructions
- with people who are much younger than you, or more junior than you – and even then, be very careful!
- with people you know very well, in relaxed situations.

Don't use the imperative:
- with strangers
- with people at a similar level or higher in a company
- in any other situation where you aren't sure about what is polite or not.

In these situations, there are other expressions you can use (see next question).

❷ Text 1 (*How to become a film star*) also gives instructions, but does so in a more polite, gentle way.

[a] Circle all the other instructions/advice in that text, except imperatives.

[b] Put the instructions you found in [a] in the table below, in columns according to the headings. The first two have been done as examples.

[c] What is the most common verb form? ______________________

[d] Underline the imperatives in Text 1. Why do you think they don't sound as direct as they do in Text 2?

____

SENTENCE STARTER	INFINITIVE OR GERUND	REST OF SENTENCE
The first thing is	to make sure	you're in the right place
it's no good trying	to hit	the big time in the north of Scotland

Task D | Practising giving instructions

Give instructions to your partner on how to do one of the following tasks. Your partner will mime it exactly as you say it. Take turns.

- use a television
- use a camera
- start a car and drive it
- cook something.

PROCEDURAL GENRE

Note: There are a wide variety of procedural texts (such as recipes, company procedures and games instructions). Only one is used here – an advice article. Your teacher may tell you about others.

Task A | Stages in an advice article

In previous units, you looked at how introductions often have at least two stages: General Statement and Preview/Scope. You also looked at expressions that start different stages of paragraphs or essays.

❶ In Text 1 on page 75, draw a box around the General Statement and the Preview/Scope.

❷ Double underline words that signal new stages in Text 1.

❸ List any other expressions you can think of to begin a new stage or paragraph.

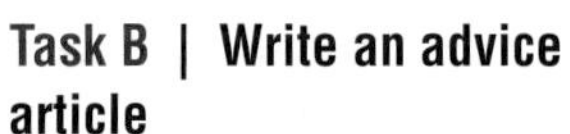

Task B | Write an advice article

Choose from one of the following topics. Write an advice article, paying attention to:

- Choice of grammar and expression for instructions/advice (see previous section, Language Spotlight)
- Stages
- Expressions that start different stages.

Topics to choose from

- How to choose a language college
- How to find an apartment/house to rent
- How to become very good at playing video games
- How to look fashionable
- Your own idea!

NOTE-TAKING – LECTURE ABOUT MEDIA REPORTS

Task A | Opinions in the media

1. Imagine a newspaper is owned by a political party. The newspaper never says anything bad about its owner, but says lots of good things about it. How would you describe the opinions of this newspaper?
   - [a] neutral
   - [b] biased
   - [c] impartial

2. Think of a few newspapers in your country. With other students:
   - [a] list as many sections of those newspapers as you can.
   - [b] decide which sections give opinions.
   - [c] discuss whose opinions they give – the government's, the owners', or the journalists'.
   - [d] discuss whether the newspapers sometimes show bias.

3. Do you ever read newspapers online? What is the difference between the online and print version? What features are provided online that cannot be provided in print? What are the advantages of printed newspapers compared with online news?

Task B | Listening and note-taking

In this section, you will listen to part of a lecture in a Diploma of Media Studies course.

1. Read the notes on the next page made by a student in the lecture. Check any vocabulary you don't know, first with a partner (note: some words are abbreviated, eg *mrktng for marketing*, and other common abbreviations are used, for example cf = compared with).

CD 1 (11)

2. Follow the notes as you listen. Tick off or mark the ideas as you hear them. Three items in the notes are wrong – correct them. You can also add your own notes.

3. These questions focus on the layout of the notes:
   - [a] Which ideas are on the left hand side of the page – main ideas or supporting ideas?
   - [b] Which ideas are on the right hand side of the page?
   - [c] What is the advantage of this format when looking at notes quickly?

CD 1

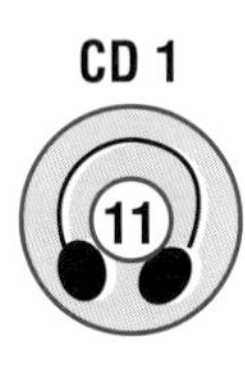

4. Listen to the rest of the recording and complete the notes. Use the space provided in the boxed notes below. Try to use similar formatting.

5. Compare your notes with those of another student.

Media Interpretation subject 14th Feb

Lecture 2 – dealing critically with the media

Signs of bias:
- argmnt mostly one-sided
- show only owner's opinion
  (more later ...)

Types of texts
- news, features, editorials, adverts
- news
- features
  - longer
  - focus on two major issues
  - cover all sides
    (just one side = sign of bias)
- editorials
  - one sided, give opinion
  - useful – predict bias: clues – pub's viewpoint
    - smtms all jrnlsts must follow pub's viewpoint
    - smtms not necessary to follow
      - more freedom
- adverts

Electronic media
- whole new can of worms
- only small media companies here
  - content: same as print, + blogs, + discussion forums
  - blogs – like adverts, maybe biased
  - discussion forums
    - anyone can say anything
    - but, moderator may be censoring
    - maybe info false (eg pple don't say who really are)

TV & radio
- wider range of content ⇒ be aware! more techniques for bias
- eg drama: choice of consequences of actions

Adverts
- smtms disguised
- smtms look like articles but written by sales/mktng pple
  ⇒ biased, aim to sell
- shopping programs
  - sponsored by companies
  - only +ve, no rival products, ⇒ easy to find bias
  - really: long adverts
- product placement (⇒ assignment!!)

HOW TO SYSTEMATICALLY RECOGNISE BIAS

Task C | Discussion

Discuss the following questions in small groups:

1. Do newspapers in your country have editorials? Letters pages?
2. Do newspapers in your country usually follow the government's ideas, or do they often have different opinions?
3. Do you prefer reading the news online, or in newspapers? Or, do you prefer to watch the news on the television?
4. Do you have shopping programs like those described in the lecture in your country?
5. Is it possible for media to be completely neutral, that is, to have no bias at all?

LISTENING TO AND FOLLOWING INSTRUCTIONS – MAKING A FILM

Task A | Making a film

Next you are going to listen to a talk about how to make a film. First, discuss the following questions about film making:

1. Have you been involved in making a film before? Or would you like to make a film?
2. Have you ever seen a program about how a film was made?
3. What do you know about:
   - the steps in making a film?
   - the roles of people who help to make a film (eg camera operator)?
   - the equipment needed to make a film?

Task B | Order of stages

1. Read the following. Try to guess which order they happen in.

- ☐ add special effects
- ☐ choose locations
- ☐ write screenplay
- ☐ editing
- ☐ start filming
- ☐ decide story/plot
- ☐ choose actors
- ☐ get permission to use locations

CD 1 (12)

2. Now, listen to the recording and check that you have put the steps in the correct sequence. Write 1 next to the first step you hear, 2 next to the second, etc.

CD 1 (12)

Task C | Listening for specific information

Listen again. Complete the following with no more than three words from the listening for each.

1. A screenplay is more difficult to write than a novel because feelings can't ______________________
2. In a film, the feeling has to come from the character's words, the music or the ______________________
3. The person in charge during filming is ______________________ ______________________
4. Make sure you have permission to ______________________ ______________________
5. During filming, there isn't much time for discussion because of ______________________ of everyone's time, equipment hire, etc.
6. Post production work can be very ______________________ ______________________
7. The purpose of editing is to make sure the final version of the film is well ______________________

SURVEY – PREFERENCES AROUND MEDIA CHOICES

Task A | Discussion

Later in this section, you will conduct a survey about people's choices of media. To start you thinking about this topic, discuss these questions in groups or with a partner.

1. Which forms of media are the most popular nowadays?
2. How about five years ago? Ten years ago? Twenty years ago? Has much changed?
3. Some people say that DVDs and Internet downloads of movies will mean the death of the cinema. Do you agree? Why?
4. People also say that the Internet will take over from television. Do you agree? What are your reasons?
5. What other changes (if any) do you expect in media use in the next five or ten years?

Task B | Survey

1. In groups, choose a question about media use that you can research with a survey. For example:
   - Is the Internet taking over from TV?
   - Are DVDs taking over from cinemas?
   - What do people use the Internet for the most, browsing, Internet chat or emailing?

   Or – better – make up your own question to research.
2. In your groups, choose at least five questions for the survey.
3. Conduct the survey.
4. When you have finished, help each other to draw conclusions from the answers.
5. Prepare a short talk (2–3 minutes) about the results and present it to the class.

FURTHER PRACTICE: READING, FILMS AND FUN

READING

- For some of the celebrity magazines mentioned earlier, look at **http://www.hellomagazine.com/**, **http://www.ok-magazine.com/**
- For some very different opinions on the media, look at **http://www.adbusters.org/home/**

FILMS

The Truman Show, directed by Peter Weir, starring Jim Carrey. This film is about a man who lives for television – but doesn't know it!

Shattered Glass, directed by Billy Ray, starring Hayden Christensen. This film tells the story of a newspaper reporter who makes up his own stories.

Also, many films have a 'making of' documentary, showing how the film is made. These would follow on nicely from the second listening of this Unit. As you probably know, you can often find them as an extra track on the DVD of the movie.

QUESTIONS

1. Some people say TV is bad for children because it discourages them from having exercise and from communicating with other children. However, others say it stimulates the mind and gives children knowledge of the world. Overall, is TV good or bad for children? Give reasons.
2. Should TV companies be stopped from showing violent programs in case children watch them? What should be the limits (if any)? Give reasons for your answer.
3. Should journalists be free to write about views that are different from the opinion of the owner of the publication?
4. Some people say that a journalist's main responsibility is to tell the truth. Others say that journalists should help their newspaper or TV station make a profit by making the news sound more dramatic than it really is, so that more people listen to the news programs or buy the newspaper. Which of these views do you agree with?
5. The media should be stopped from giving opinions against the government. Do you agree with this opinion? Give reasons.

8 ART

'there are pictures in poems and poems in pictures'

BY THE END OF THIS UNIT, YOU SHOULD:

ART n. [UNCOUNTABLE]: 1 the use of painting, drawing, sculpture to represent things or express ideas: *an example of Indian art \ contemporary/modern art the Museum of Modern Art → ART FORM, FINE ART, PERFORMANCE ART.* 2 pl., objects that are produced by art, such as paintings, drawings etc: an *art exhibition \ an art critic \ an arts and crafts fair \ The exhibition features 175 works of art.*

BUILDING THE FIELD

Task A | Discussion and vocabulary

In small groups, tell each other as much as you can in answer to the following questions:

1. What do you think of when you hear the word 'art'?
2. When do you think art began?
3. What kind of art do you like?
4. Do you have a favourite piece of art you have seen or know about?
5. Examine the photographs in Pictures 1 to 7
6. What's a 'griffin'? Do you know? You can find it in the dictionary and there's a photo of one painted over 4000 years ago on a palace wall on the island of Crete in Picture 7.

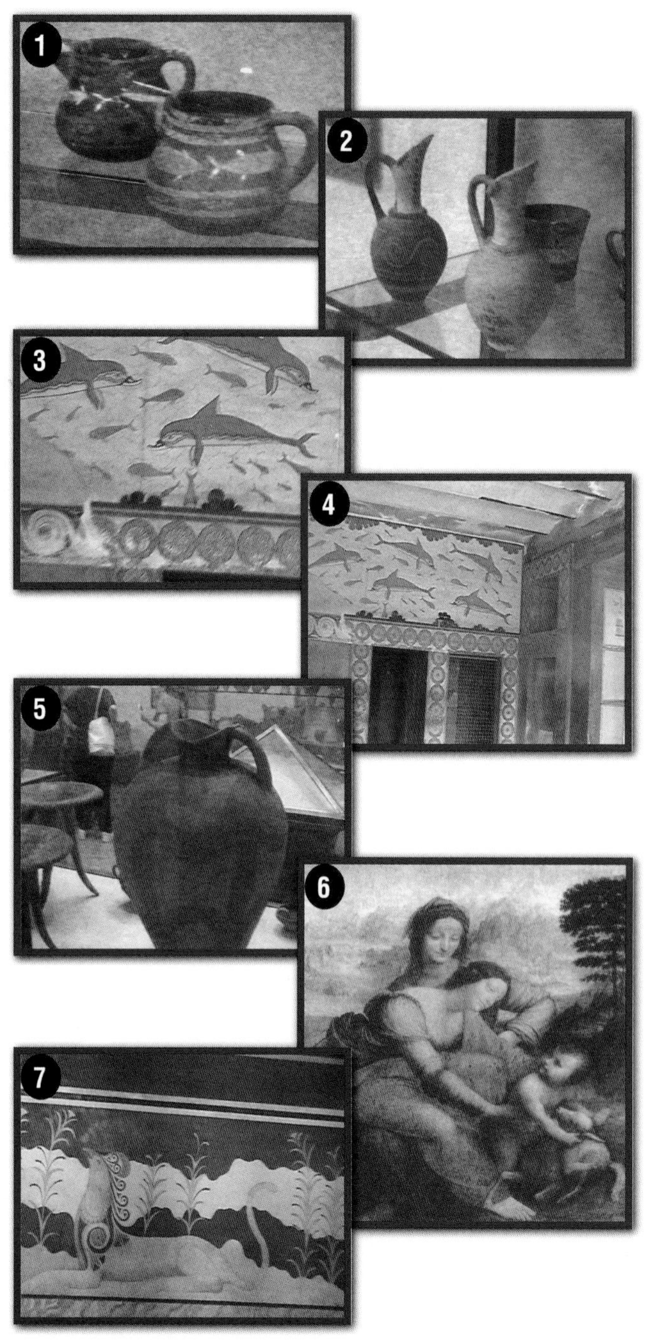

VOCABULARY

Read the extract below and try to match the following words to their definitions using the knowledge you gained from the reading.

words

ceramic | artisan | afterlife
casting | motif | oil paint
ritual

Text

Artisans, or skilled craftspersons, work very hard. Some create objects made from clay and once they have glazed them, these objects become beautiful ceramics. Another thing artisans do is casting. It's dangerous, in a way, because hot liquid metal can be pretty difficult to handle.

I like oil painting myself. I've even tried it. I enjoy mixing the pigment to get just the right colour. When not painting, I also often study a motif within a work of art for hours. One motif I have seen repeated is that of figures carrying wine or other offerings to a central place, like a temple, for example. Often these are wall paintings, or they are embroidered on cloth or tapestry. Sometimes, they are carved in relief out of stone. There is a lot of meaning there and I think they help people with the afterlife, after they die.

Task B | More vocabulary fun

Complete the crossword by using the vocabulary you've learned in this Unit.

				1		2						
										3		
								4				
					5							
6												
		7			8							
9												
	10											

ACROSS

1. A piece of pottery usually ancient.
3. Said by the director of a film to tell people to stop acting, filming.
5. Someone who made or invented a particular thing. Creation/something that has been created.
9. Someone who produces art, especially paintings or drawings.
10. Something you say, write, or do that shows what you think or feel.

DOWN

2. To look at something and think how impressive or beautiful it is.
3. Shade, hint, hue.
4. A model of the human body, used for showing clothes in shop windows.
6. A plan or suggestion.
7. The use of painting, drawing, sculpture to represent things or express ideas.
8. An object hand shaped from clay.

A REVIEW

Task A | The five questions for reading any text

① The reading below is a review of Van Gogh's painting, 'Irises'. It is called 'Looking at Art'. Scan the review then answer the questions below.

[a] What is it?

____

____

[b] What is the source?

____

____

[c] Who is the writer?

____

____

[d] What purpose does the writer have for writing it?

____

____

[e] Who is the intended audience?

____

____

② Read the review about Vincent Van Gogh's painting, *Irises*. Then answer the questions that follow the review.

LOOKING AT ART

By Charlene C. Rose

'FLOWER POWER'

It may seem odd to you, my readers, that I have just seen Vincent Van Gogh's painting 'Irises' for the first time. By this, I mean the first time on canvas and the real thing. Of course, I saw it many times in books and as a print. But, last week, while in Europe, I visited an art gallery that displayed his works. 'Irises' hung on the wall and as I passed by it, I stopped in amazement. I found it absolutely amazing. It is a wonderful work of art. It is a beautiful work of art.

There is an astonishing amount of energy in this painting. It seems to jump off the canvas as the deep purple flowers gather in their French garden setting. Lines create a feeling of movement and the irises look like they are bobbing about on their long stems. The leaves twist and turn reaching for sun and look like they are dancing.

Van Gogh is probably the most famous of and well-known of European artists of the period. He was born in Holland in 1853 and like many of that era, he loved nature and art. The middle and last half of the 19th century was a time for the Romantics who adored nature and praised it through their poetry and painting.

This painting was done in 1889 and during that time, many artists were interested in the art of Japan. 'Irises' may be influenced by Japanese wood blocks. It is known that Van Gogh collected them. Look at the thick, dark lines around the edges of the stems and leaves. They are like dark outlines. Also, the way he has arranged the picture like a flat screen is Japanese in style.

As well as irises, there are other flowers in the picture. At the left and moving away to the back out of the painting are marigolds. They are orange and make a beautiful contrast to the deep purple of the irises in the foreground. In front of the marigolds and left of the centre in the painting is one, lone, white iris. What does it mean?

I. How does the reviewer describe *Irises* in the first paragraph?

II. Does she like the painting?

III. How do you know she likes the painting?

IV. Make a list of the words the reviewer uses throughout the review to describe the actual work of art. Use the adjectives and the nouns together.

V. Do you think there are a lot of adjectives in this article?

VI. If you answered 'yes' to Question V, why do you think there are a lot of adjectives?

VII. Who painted the painting?

VIII. What year was the painting done?

IX. What country's art may have influenced Van Gogh?

X. What did Van Gogh collect?

XI. Which era in history admired nature and the environment?

XII. Do you agree with the reviewer's opinion of the painting?

XIII. Why do you think the lone white iris is in the painting?

3. Match the nouns in the list below by drawing a line to their meanings.

NOUNS	MEANINGS
his works	front
canvas	the material artists paint upon
in amazement	the artist's paintings or other art
a print	with surprise
foreground	a printed copy of a painting or drawing
astonishing amount	surprising quantity, surprising level of energy

4. Now match the verbs by drawing a line to their meanings.

VERBS	MEANINGS
bobbing about	change direction
twist	say or think good things about a person or thing
turn	move about in a spiral way, turn from the waist
praise	moving up and down, like a cork in water

REPORTED SPEECH

Task A | Reporting direct speech

When we talk to each other, sometimes we need to tell or report what someone else has said. Look at this example –

A. *'Did Tina say she's (she is) coming to the party?'*
B. *'Yes, she said she was.'*

Look at what changed in the two simple sentences. *Tina* – the noun/name changed to the pronoun 'she'. The verb – present simple tense 'is (she's)'– changed to the past tense 'was'. This is the key to reported statements. There are other changes, but practise this one first. Present simple tense verbs become past simple tense.

Change the sentences in the list below into reported speech. The first one is done for you.

[a] **Aarron**: 'I think blue mobile phone covers are the best.' (Note: there are two verbs to change in this one.)
Aarron said (that) ______________________________

____

____

____

[b] **Gina**: 'I'm going to Hawaii for a holiday this June.'
Gina said (that)______________________________

____

____

____

[c] **Aarron**: 'Well, I'm as tired as a dead snake.'
Aarron said (that) ______________________________

____

____

____

[d] **Gina**: 'I think Hawaii is a wonderful place.' (Note: there are two verbs to change in this one.)
Gina said (that)______________________________

____

____

____

Task B | Verb tense changes when reporting speech

In the previous task, you practised changing simple present tense to simple past tense. This task discusses how to report speech where the person you are reporting speaks in the past tense. For example, *'I gave mother a present'.* What will you say?

PAST SIMPLE > BECOMES PAST PERFECT
'I gave mother a present'. He said he had given a present to mother. (or) He said he had given mother a present.

PRESENT PERFECT > ALSO BECOMES PAST PERFECT
'We have completed our projects', the students told the lecturer.
The students (or they) told the lecturer (that) they had completed their projects.

PRESENT CONTINUOUS > BECOMES PAST CONTINUOUS
'I'm working at a restaurant while I'm studying for my exams.'
She said she's been working at a restaurant while she's been studying for her exams.

*

MODALS: PRESENT MODALS LIKE *CAN* AND *MAY* CHANGE TENSE TOO. BUT PAST MODALS LIKE *COULD* AND *WOULD* DO NOT CHANGE.
CAN > COULD
MAY > MIGHT
SHALL > SHOULD
WILL > WOULD

❶ Complete the following by changing the verb tense:

[a] 'I'm surprised she managed to get a ticket to Hawaii in June.'
He said ______________________________

____

[b] 'I wished I had booked earlier.'
She said ______________________________

____

[c] 'I wish you'd (you had) booked earlier, too.'
He said ______________________________

____

[d] 'My flight leaves at 4 in the morning.'
She said ______________________________

____

[e] 'I hope it's going to be really good weather that day.'
He said ______________________________

____

[f] 'I'm sure it will be.'
She said ______________________________

____

[g] 'I know you're going to have a fabulous time, no matter what.'
He said ______________________________

____

[h] 'I think you're very sweet and I'm going to miss you a lot.'
She said ______________________________

____

[i] 'So does that mean you'll go out with me when you get back?'
He asked ______________________________

____

[j] 'You'll just have to wait and see, won't you?'
She said ______________________________

____

AN ARTICLE

Task A | Another view of art – Art as technology

1. Quickly examine the reading below and answer the five questions that go with every reading.

[a] What is it?

____

____

[b] What is the source?

____

____

[c] Who is the writer?

____

____

[d] What purpose does the writer have for writing it?

____

____

[e] Who is the intended audience?

____

____

ART AS TECHNOLOGY

by Winnifred Smith-Cox

1 **1** Mobile phones are so popular in present day life that one wonders how we ever lived without them. Not only are they a communication tool, but for many young 5 people, they are a fashion item. They are decorated very artistically. Recently, mobile phones have gone way beyond being just a telephone and SMS (send message service) tool. Now, they are a camera, a music 10 listening device, a radio, a mini television, and an internet service! It seems that mobile phones are essential and their uses quite wide. They could be called (no pun intended) a complete communication tool.

15 **2** As for fashion, there is no doubt that both males and females enjoy the look and feel of their little phones. Boys sometimes chain them to their pants and personalise them with screen savers. These screen savers 20 might be a sporting achievement of their own or a photograph of a pretty friend. Girls like to add small jewels and things that dangle or jingle off theirs. Fashions come and go. Flip screens are popular sometimes 25 and then it's the bigger screen in a smaller phone that wins the day.

3 There is, however, one thing that most people may not realise. There are two billion, yes, two billion mobile phones a year 30 that are thrown away. Two billion a year are discarded. Mobile phones are currently made of metal and plastic that does not break down in the soil nor can they safely be burned. Because of this, they become 35 what is called 'land fill'. That is, junk that takes up space in the earth.

4 Most people want to know what they might be able to do in order to reduce all this junk. A company has designed mobile phones 40 that are biodegradable. That means they will deteriorate or kind of fall apart in a good way in the earth. They have a computer board with computer chips that are made of soy beans! Not only that, they 45 have biodegradable disposable cases. This seems a very modern and good invention that combines art with technology. Science is art in a way and design is always art.

5 So ... a mobile phone made from soy beans 50 that does everything that mobile phones made from metal and plastic do. I know I'll be keeping an eye out for an advertisement in the future that tells me I could purchase a phone that is biodegradable! I hope you will 55 too.

Extract from *Go Green Thinkers!* Jan 2007.

2 Answer the following questions about the text.

I. What does no pun intended mean in para 1?

____

____

II. Why does the writer say *mobile phones have gone way beyond being a telephone and SMS tool?*

____

____

III. Who enjoys mobile phones more – boys or girls?

____

____

IV. Describe two types of screens on mobiles.

____

____

V. How many phones are thrown away each year?

____

____

VI. What does the writer say can be done about the problem of metal and plastic going into the earth?

____

____

VII. What natural product makes computer chips for these phones?

____

____

VIII. What is the advantage of the outside casing in these phones?

____

____

IX. What does dangle or jingle mean?

____

____

X. List two ways people 'personalise' their mobile phones.

____

____

Task B | Scanning

1. Create your own work of art using the letters in your name. You can make as many names as you like. You have to scan in this task. **Scan** means to look for one thing while moving your eyes over text. Don't read – scan and search.

INSTRUCTIONS

- From a magazine or newspaper, scan quickly and look for the letters that spell your name. You can add those of your friends or family later.
- When you find a letter, tear or cut it out and lay it on a clean piece of paper.
- Arrange the letters to spell your name.
- Make it artistic by the way you cut out the shapes around the letters and by the way you arrange the letters next to one another.
- If you have paste, stick them down.

OPINIONS

Task A | Thinking about opinions

1. What would your opinion be on the four questions below?
   - **[a]** What television shows do you like?
   - **[b]** Write or tell a partner what you like about them.
   - **[c]** Have you watched a show or movie that you didn't like? Explain what you didn't like.
   - **[d]** Note how you are expressing your opinion. Are you able to say more than just 'I like' or 'I don't like'?

2. **Circle** any of the following phrases which you think ***introduces or expresses an opinion***:
   - **[a]** They arrived last night.; I thought . . .; I mean . . .; then they . . .; Frankly, I was rather offended . . .
   - **[b]** Yes, that's right; Well, as far as I'm concerned . . .; I hear what you're saying . . .
   - **[c]** but . . .; it's also quite funny . . .; that's pretty boring . . .; it's very weak . . .
   - **[d]** it's interesting . . .; I do like . . .; Come here.; I'm not sure I . . .; Who is he? . . .

REVIEW, OPINIONS, TAG QUESTIONS

Task A | Locating opinions, summarising

CD 1

Listen to the dialogue between two television reviewers. The show is something like a movie review program but they are discussing a new television program.

1. Which summary *best* describes Christine's opinions of the show?
   - **[a]** She thinks it is an excellent program and would recommend others to view it.
   - **[b]** She thinks it is weak in places but that it's entertaining and funny at times.
   - **[c]** She thinks it is a terrible program that ought to be banned from TV.
   - **[d]** She thinks it is the best thing on television.

2. Which summary *best* describes Oliver's opinions of the show?
   - **[a]** He thinks it is a good program and that many viewers would enjoy watching it.
   - **[b]** He thinks it is a waste of time to watch reality television, including this program.
   - **[c]** He thinks it is a good example of boring television but still likes the show.
   - **[d]** He thinks it is an entertaining and fun program with an interesting format.

TAG QUESTIONS

Task A | Practise speaking

In pairs, read the dialogue extract from the Listening in this unit. It's between two reviewers and they are talking about a TV program called *The Country Cousin.* If you are reading Oliver's part, make sure your voice falls on the tag question. The voice does not rise (go up) because he is only looking for agreement. He is fairly certain of the answer. His voice goes down because he already knows the answer.

Oliver: Yeah, a bit of a waste of energy, if you ask me. And they can't ask direct questions, can they? Like to each other about family or something.
Christine: No, they can't. No direct questions are allowed.
Oliver: And they aren't allowed to talk in private, with no people around, are they?
Christine: No, they aren't.
Oliver: Also, they don't mention mutual relations or family members that could give it away, do they?
Christine: No, they don't, Oliver. They just have to live a normal life and work it all out.

Task B | Voice down tag questions

VOICE DOWN TAGS
In pairs, drop your voice at the end of each question. The questioner is quite certain of the answer and is seeking agreement. You need to answer yes or no and change the verb form.
For example:

1. 'You're wearing that dress tonight, aren't you?'
   Yes, I am.
2. 'You were born in Los Angeles, California, weren't you?'
   Yes, I was.

The *yes* or *no* must agree with the verb as a positive or negative.
NEVER – ~~Yes, I won't; No, I am; Yes, I'm not.~~

3. 'You're coming with us now, aren't you?'

   ____

4. 'He's late now, isn't he?'

   ____

5. 'I just knew Marcus would win. He did, didn't he?'

   ____

6. 'There's politics in everything, isn't there?'

   ____

7. 'Is that your new computer? (normal question) Wow! It's state of the art, isn't it?'

   ____

8. 'You won't be home until very late, will you?'

   ____

Task C | Voice up tag questions

VOICE UP TAGS
In pairs, raise your voice at the end of each question. The questioner is not as certain of the answer.

For example:

1. 'You're not wearing that dress tonight, are you?'
   Yes, I am. (going to wear the dress) OR *No, I'm not. (going to wear the dress)*
   NEVER – ~~*Yes, I'm not*~~. **NOR** ~~*No, I am.*~~ The *yes* or *no* must agree with the verb as a positive or negative.
2. 'You can't afford *that* car, can you?'

   ____

3. 'You *do* still want to come, *don't you*?'

   ____

4. 'I think Kiki studied hard. She won the award for best student, *didn't she*?'

   ____

5. 'Why didn't *Marge* win? She studied hard, *didn't she*?'

   ____

6. 'I know she did and I can't understand why she didn't win. *Can you*?' (understand why she didn't win)

   ____

7. 'You're still playing football, *aren't you*?'

   ____

8. 'They're still coming to the game, *aren't they*?'

   ____

9. 'We're still in love, *aren't we*?'

   ____

10. 'They will help us, *won't they*?'

   ____

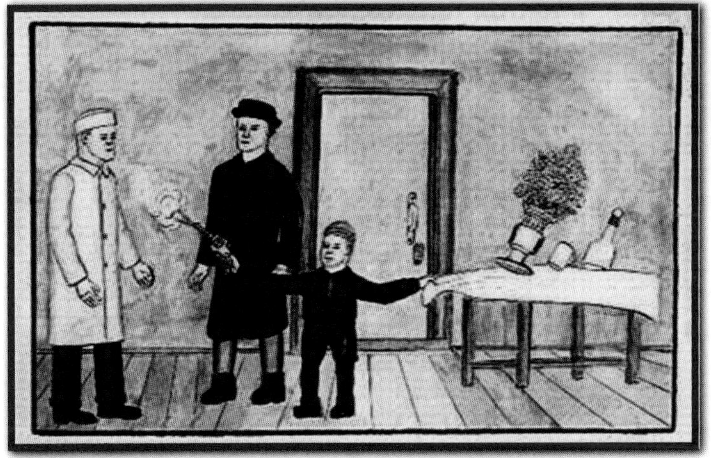

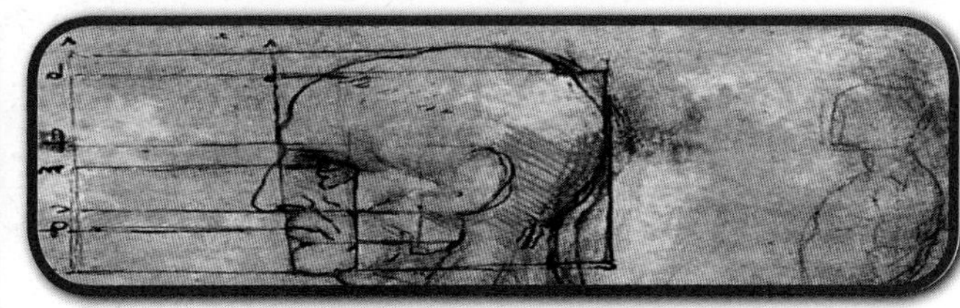

YOUR OWN REVIEW

Task A | Writing a review

Using your knowledge from this Unit and any previous knowledge you have, choose a work of art and write a review of it. Your teacher may show you a work of art and ask you to review that. Remember to use adjectives to express your opinion and to describe the work using the present tense. If you discuss its history, then move to the simple past tense.

Here's a short model paragraph to help you with tense and the stages. Underline the verbs and note how many are present and present continuous. Then write your own review.

Movie review model paragraph

Name of movie: *Blood and Guts*

Description of movie or thing being reviewed: it is a very long movie and very violent. The acting is pretty good and the actors seem happy doing what they're doing.

Comparison to same thing: Like most horror movies, the characters wander into very dark rooms, separate from each other and wait to die. It's pretty sad. There's a lot of screaming and a fair bit of grunting that goes on when people are being stabbed to death. But, compared to something like *Chainsaw Massacre*, it's tame.

Opinion and recommendation: I like horror so it amused me but if you don't, then don't go see it.

FURTHER PRACTICE: READING, FILMS AND FUN

READING

Flanigan, R. (2001) *Gould's Book of Fish*, N.Y.: Grove Press.

Shedd, Julia A. (1896) *Famous Painters and Paintings*, Boston: Haughton, Mifflin and Co.

FILMS

The Movie Show, ABC television (Australia).

Frida, directed by Julie Taymor, starring Selma Hayek. A confronting movie about the wife of famous artist in Spain. Frida suffered a horrific bus accident and was severely injured. She was a beautiful woman and painted in ways that reflected her own mutilation and suffering.

Camille Claudel, French with subtitles. About a young sculptor who was the lover of Auguste Rodin.

Sister Wendy's American Collection, DVD. A nun reviews and informs about art.

QUESTIONS

1. Write a report about the folk art of your own country.
2. Write a review about a movie you saw recently.
3. Discuss the question – *Is art a waste of time?*

9 ARCHITECTURE

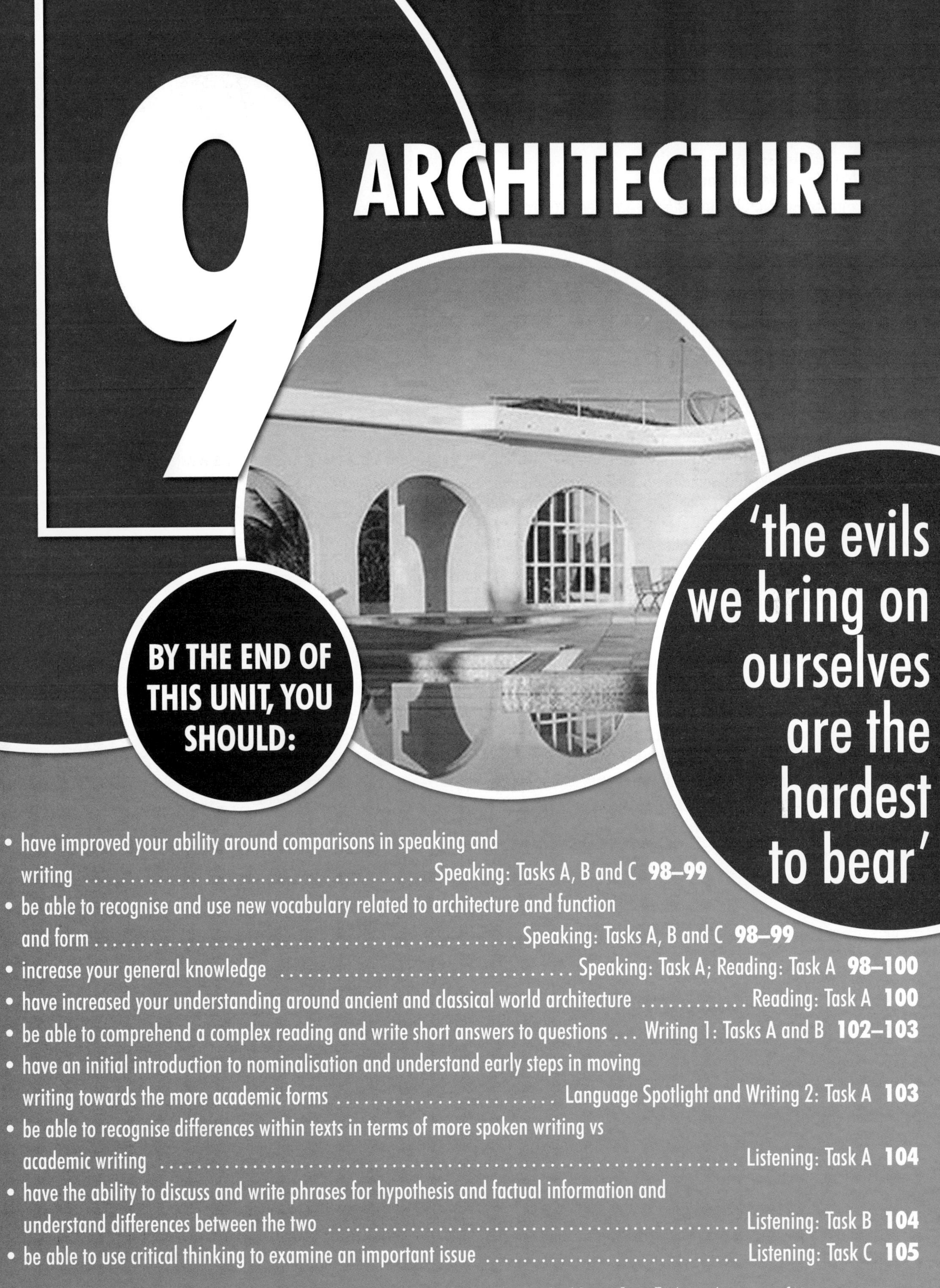

'the evils we bring on ourselves are the hardest to bear'

BY THE END OF THIS UNIT, YOU SHOULD:

- have improved your ability around comparisons in speaking and writing .... Speaking: Tasks A, B and C **98–99**
- be able to recognise and use new vocabulary related to architecture and function and form .... Speaking: Tasks A, B and C **98–99**
- increase your general knowledge .... Speaking: Task A; Reading: Task A **98–100**
- have increased your understanding around ancient and classical world architecture .... Reading: Task A **100**
- be able to comprehend a complex reading and write short answers to questions ... Writing 1: Tasks A and B **102–103**
- have an initial introduction to nominalisation and understand early steps in moving writing towards the more academic forms .... Language Spotlight and Writing 2: Task A **103**
- be able to recognise differences within texts in terms of more spoken writing vs academic writing .... Listening: Task A **104**
- have the ability to discuss and write phrases for hypothesis and factual information and understand differences between the two .... Listening: Task B **104**
- be able to use critical thinking to examine an important issue .... Listening: Task C **105**

ARCHITECTURE n. [UNCOUNTABLE]: 1 the style and design of a building or buildings: [+of] *the architecture of Venice.* 2 the art and practice of planning and designing buildings: *He studied architecture at university.* 3 the structure of something: *the architecture of DNA.* 4 *technical* the structure of a computer system and the way it works.

ARCHITECT n., pl. ARCHITECTS [UNCOUNTABLE AND COUNTABLE]: 1 someone whose job is to design buildings.

SPEAKING

BUILDING THE FIELD

Task A | Compare and contrast

1. Examine the pictures of different architecture around the world. Discuss any similarities and differences you see.

____

____

____

____

____

____

____

____

____

____

2. Explain your idea of a perfect city. Talk about traffic – Where would cars, buses and the like be allowed? Talk about people and where they would walk – Would you create places for them next to water (bays, ponds, lakes, rivers, oceans)? Where would the tallest buildings be placed? Can you draw a sketch of your perfect town?

1 Wat Thailand

2 Notre Dame stadium

3 Sydney Opera House

4 University of Scotland

5 Jenners shopping building

6 Castle

7 Nagoya housing and commerce

8 Stratford Shakespeare theatre

9 Tokyo Cathedral

10 Architect housing

Task B | Function (What's it for?)

Match the following types of buildings to the photographs in Task A and discuss how they are used.

[a] Religious ______________________

[b] Housing ______________________

[c] Housing and commerce areas ______________________

[d] Sport ______________________

[e] Government ______________________

[f] Theatre, entertainment ______________________

[g] Education ______________________

[h] Retail, business ______________________

[i] What other uses for buildings can you think of?

____

[j] Identify the following shapes by matching the name from the list below with the picture:
dome; hexagon; square; circle; rectangle; oval; octagon; ovoid

______________________ ______________________

______________________ ______________________

______________________ ______________________

______________________ ______________________

Task C | Comparisons

Adjectives for contrasting and comparing:
similar to; different from; taller than; shorter than; more open; pleasing; more…than

Linking devices for contrasting and comparing:
whereas the other one is; but; on the contrary; though; on the other hand; however

1. Underline both the *adjectives* and *linking devices* in the paragraph below;

The Eiffel Tower is an interesting and tall building located in Paris. It is considered beautiful. However, there are other towers that I think are far more interesting and far more beautiful. For example, the one in Beijing; it is taller than the Eiffel Tower. Whereas the first one is meant for people, the other is meant as a landmark.

2. Compare a place of worship you know about with an office building. Write some differences based upon:
   - what the buildings look like
   - what the buildings are used for.

____

____

____

____

____

____

____

____

____

____

BROADENING GENERAL KNOWLEDGE

Task A | Classical and ancient architecture around the world

1. You should read the text '*Architecture around the world*', looking for content and learning new vocabulary while you are reading.

2. Personal pronouns are underlined **only** in the first paragraph of your book. For this question, you are to underline all the other personal pronouns you find in paras 2, 3 and 4 of the reading.

ARCHITECTURE AROUND THE WORLD

1

Architecture is something that exists in every country in the world. World architecture represents the past, the present and the future. Buildings that manage to survive from the past tell people in the present a great deal of information about the people who used them. They show how people lived, shopped, worshipped and carried out *commerce* with the rest of the world. Who built those buildings, and why they were built or *designed* the way they were, is another important part of architecture. Generally, there are two main approaches to the *examination of architecture* and history.

2

The first approach is to *link* buildings to great men or women who designed them. So a history of buildings would be about the architects. A second approach is to link buildings to the *technical status* of the *era*. In other words, building design is really about what materials were at hand and what sort of workers you had to help carry out your plan.

3

Architecture is a form of art. It is about the style and design of buildings. It is an art *that considers* practical things like providing shelter for humans. Sometimes, it seems the shelter they made could be for dead people as much as for living ones. The pyramids of Egypt are an amazing example of architecture yet they were designed only for the dead. This tells us something about the people of that time. Were they more concerned with the afterlife than the present one? 3000 to 1500 BC is a very long time ago.

4

India has excavations at Harappa and Mohenjo-Daro of large cities. They were from a grid system and had main boulevards running right across the city. The shape of the cities was rectangular. There were many small buildings surrounding a court and they seemed similar to early Egyptian architecture in their function. These cities were *citadels*. Sadly, they lasted but 1500 years and evidence (in the form of skeletons) suggests they were invaded and their civilization ended.

5

In the lifetime of Mohammed (d. 632) there is an early major work of Moslem architecture. It is the Ka'ba at Mekka. However, it is the Dome of the Rock, located in Jerusalem which is probably of greatest importance

commerce – trade

designed – created or made to

examination of architecture – looking at many things about architecture

link – connection between two or more things

technical status – how advanced people were with technology

era – a period of time

that considers – that thinks about

citadels – forts, a building meant for protection from outsiders

to architecture. It was begun in 643 and it still exists. It is said to be the site from which Mohammed made his night journey to heaven. It has a golden dome set over an *octagonal rotunda*. It has a well with a small *domed cupola*. Fresh water is always part of Middle Eastern architecture. 35

gonal rotunda – round e building having t angles and eight s with a dome

ed cupola – a rounded r-like structure on top roof

reflect most things about a culture – tell you about the people and their ways of living

6

Buildings and other architecture have the ability to *reflect most things about a culture*. The Great Wall of China is an *architectural wonder*. It goes across Northern China for some 4,000 miles. It is said to be the largest man-made structure in the world and was started around 200 BC. It is not about housing, because the wall was built for protection from the *nomads*. 40

architectural wonder – something beautiful and unusual built by people

nomads – people who move from place to place/ sometimes in the desert

7

It is interesting to note that the word for 'city' and 'wall' was the same in early China: *ch'eng*. Most parts of a city were walled and any palace had many walled *enclosures*. A city wall made of *rammed earth* was found and dated as early as the 11th century BC. 45

losures – spaces ed to the outside

med earth – dirt nded down hard and t

ch'eng – city and wall

8

The oldest brick building in China is a *Pagoda*: The Pagoda of the Sung Yueh temple, Mt Sung, Honan. This shows religion was very important just as it was in other parts of the world.

oda – a sacred lding, usually tall and ped like a pyramid or er

9

In Japan, natural forces affected their early architecture. Japan has many natural forces to worry about. There are earthquakes and fierce storms coming in from the Pacific. As islands, these things affect them in a serious way. This fact means that they often chose to build from stone (for castles) and wood, timber and bamboo. Designs have been kept and certain buildings built over again exactly as they were before, for example, *Shinto shrines*. Japanese gardens are a beautiful, unusual and important part of their design. 50 55

nto shrines – Shinto tive religion of Japan) ine (a place of religion ere special objects or nains are kept)

10

In Greece, in their ancient and classical period, there is the *temple of Olympian Zeus*. It was begun in 174 BC. The kind of building was called Corinthian and we still call the supports or pillars you see right up to now as Corinthian. They are an example of 'classical' design in the West. 60

temple of Olympian Zeus – Zeus was the main Greek god who ruled the heavens. Olympus is a mountain in north-eastern Greece. The Olympic Games are held in honour of Zeus and began in 776 BC.

11

In the West, architecture moves across major periods such as *Medieval*, *Gothic*, *Renaissance* and into the modern period. But that is another reading!

thic – in architecture ers to a style started in ance in the 12th century. inted arches, high ildings, rib vaulting ide.

Medieval – a period of time that is the Middle Ages – 700 to 1500 AD.

Renaissance – a new birth – in history; new birth or revival of art and learning in Europe during the 14th, 15th and 16th centuries. Moved out of the Medieval period into the Renaissance.

SHORT ANSWERS

Task A | Comprehension

In this section, you locate the answers to the questions within the Reading *Architecture around the world*. When writing your answer, please write a complete sentence. For example,

1. Which country had the earliest found architecture in this text?
   Answer: The country that had the earliest found architecture was India.

Note: you change the question form 'which' by replacing it with 'that'. Word order changes as well. You repeat the question stem or core and then provide the answer.

Answer the following questions:

1. Which country had the earliest found architecture in this text? (this one has been done for you above)
2. Which country built a wall about 4,000 miles long?
3. What was the name of the long wall built across China?
4. What is the name for classical supports or pillars of Western origin?
5. What does weather have to do with architecture? Give an example.
6. Which is the earliest work of Moslem architecture?
7. Name two examples of religious buildings.
8. What was the function of early cities beyond just living in them? In other words, for what other purpose were they designed?
9. How did cities protect themselves?
10. Why would modern people think the early Egyptians were very interested in the dead and the afterlife?
11. Who was Zeus?
12. Are there some countries that have no architecture?

Task B | Finding the main ideas

1. Match the various paragraphs with the countries described within them. Write the number of the paragraph next to the name of the country.

[a] __________ Jerusalem

[b] __________ China

[c] __________ Greece

[d] __________ Egypt

[e] __________ India

[f] __________ The West

2. In the spaces below write the name of each type of architecture described in the paragraphs above. Begin with Jerusalem.

[a] Jerusalem ______________________

[b] China ______________________

[c] Greece ______________________

[d] Egypt ______________________

[e] India ______________________

[f] The West ______________________

LANGUAGE SPOTLIGHT | WRITING 2 — NOMINALS AND NOMINALISATION (NOUNS)

Task A | Writing – Refer to *Architecture around the world*

1. You are working to move your writing away from sounding 'spoken'. You want your writing to become academic and acceptable to an educated audience. One step towards this is to remove the personal pronouns from the writing. Personal pronouns are substitutes for people. For example, *I*, *we*, *you*, *she*, *they*. Add to this list:

____

____

____

2. In the Reading section (Task A) you underlined the personal pronouns in paragraphs 2, 3 and 4 the reading. Remove these personals and try to rewrite the three paragraphs. You can change word order and you may have to change tenses at times. Your teacher will guide you in this work.

Paragraph 2

____

Paragraph 3

____

Paragraph 4

____

DIFFERENTIATING BETWEEN HYPOTHESIS AND FACT

Task A | Pre-listening

1. Examine the following two sets of phrases – Sets A and B in the lists – and answer the questions below.

SET A

I think that ...
It's quite possible that ...
In the future, it may happen that ...
I don't think that ...
Probably, ...
I predict that ...
To me ...
Trends show that ...
We could see ...
It may be that ...
Maybe, ...

SET B

We cannot (can't) predict ...
It will be (It'll be) ...
It's going to be ...
This is going to be ...
That is (That's) going to be ...
It's about ...
It is not (It isn't) about ...
In the not too distant future, we will see (we'll see) ...
What will (What'll) happen is ...

Can you explain the differences between the two sets of phrases? Which set (A or B):

[a] ___ is more certain?

[b] ___ is going to talk about facts?

[c] ___ is more about speculation (guessing)?

[d] ___ is about hypothesising (guessing)?

[e] ___ would you use to state a fact?

[f] ___ would you use to talk about a future trend that might happen?

2. Now, choose a sentence or phrase from the sets which matches the different functions outlined in [a] to [f] above.

[a] ______________________

____

[b] ______________________

____

[c] ______________________

____

[d] ______________________

____

[e] ______________________

____

[f] ______________________

____

3. Complete the sentences using a phrase from either Set A or B. The first one is done for you.

[a] .... dogs make good companions.
I think that dogs make good companions.

[b] .... that the population is ageing in many countries.

[c] .... a very cold night.

[d] .... hotter weather and global warming. Some think we're seeing it now.

[e] If a train goes too fast for the tracks, ... it will fly right off them.

[f] .... true.

[g] We .... the time of our own death.

[h] She'll .... come to our wedding.

[i] He'll .... come as well.

[j] It .... rain, but then again, it may not.

Task B | Listening for *certainty* versus *speculation* CD 1

1. Listen to the interview and place a tick next to one of the phrases in the table that follows each time you hear it. Listen carefully for phrases from Set B in the previous task that introduce facts. Notice that the past is in the table, not just future.

14

It will be ... (It'll be)	It's going to be ... It was ...	It's not about ... It was not about ...	In the not too distant future ... In the past, we ...	We will see ... (We'll see) We saw ...	What will happen is ... What happened was ...
I think	... is ...	It's possible that	I predict that We can't predict	I saw	It may happen that ...

2. Listen a second time and try to note down the facts you heard.

[a] ______

[b] ______

[c] ______

[d] ______

3. Is there more speculation and prediction in the text or are there more facts?

______

______

______

Task C | Thinking about the listening; value judgment

In pairs, think back to the listening and discuss the issues.

1. Was the worker right about the problems with the foundations and steel girders used in the construction?

______

______

2. How do you know? (from Question 1)

______

______

3. How did Mark (the boss) treat the workman's concerns? ie What did he say to him?

______

______

4. How many times did the workman mention he was worried about the strength of the building?

______

______

5. What did the worker predict would happen to the steel girders in the building?

______

______

6. What did the boss answer the second time, when the workman told him how worried he was?

______

______

7. What could the boss have done? Or what might the boss have done?

______

______

8. What did the weather man predict in the weather report?

______

______

9. What sorts of storms were predicted?

______

______

10. What was going to happen to the roads?

______

______

11. What happened to the airport?

______

______

12. Is there anything else the worker could have done?

______

______

FURTHER PRACTICE: READING, FILMS AND FUN

READING

Phaidon Atlas of Contemporary World Architecture, Phaidon Press. (824 pages. The Atlas includes entries on 1052 buildings built over the last six years by 656 architects in 75 countries. The text is accompanied by 62 maps and 7000 illustrations. The book comes in its own clear plastic carrying case, and is a foot and a half tall and weighs 18 pounds.)

architecture.about.com/cs/greatbuildings/f/worldstallest.htm
en.wikipedia.org/wiki/History_of_architecture

FILMS

Spiderman 1 and *Spiderman 2*: Here we see action, adventure and architecture galore! Beautiful graphics are devised for the cityscapes where Spiderman hurls himself from building to building saving the world from crime.

Howl's Moving Castle: Another wonderful film by Japanese artist and director Hayao Miyazaki of 'Spirited Away' fame. Miyazaki makes his central themes work within an actual moving castle that looks a little like a junk heap with magical rooms inside.

QUESTIONS

1. Choose a famous architect for yourself or choose one from the following list. Then do some research and write a report about both the architect and his or her work: Frank Lloyd Wright, Avlar Aalto, Gaudi, Vladimir Tatlin.

2. Research the tallest buildings in the world and describe them. Compare and contrast them, discussing their similarities and differences.

3. Explain the function of your favourite building. What does it look like?

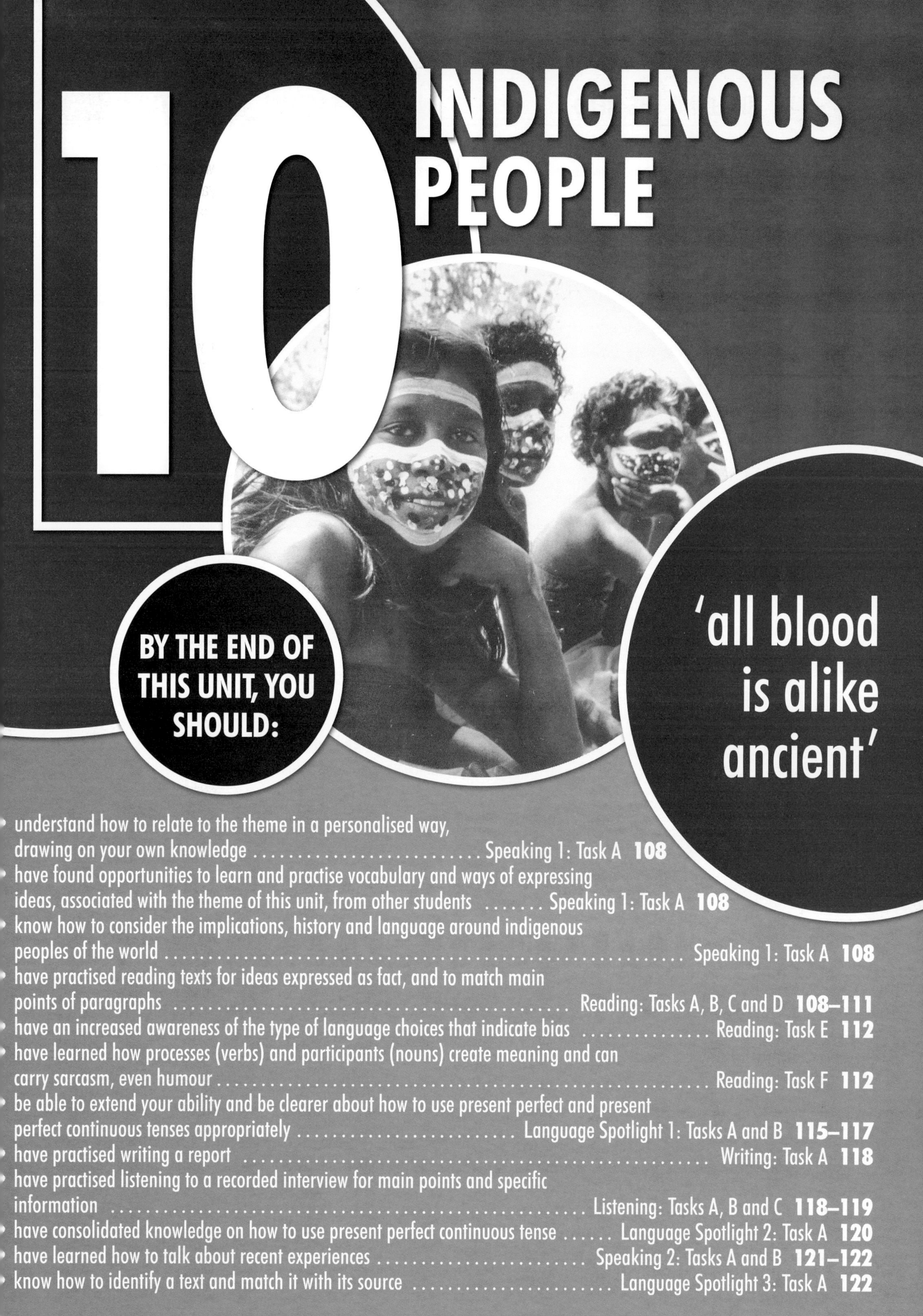

10 INDIGENOUS PEOPLE

'all blood is alike ancient'

BY THE END OF THIS UNIT, YOU SHOULD:

NDIGENOUS PEOPLE: indigenous people or things have always been in the place where they are, rather than being brought here from somewhere else.

BUILDING THE FIELD

Task A | Discussion – What do you know about Aboriginal people?

In small groups (mixed nationality if possible), tell each other as much as you can in answer to the following questions. Which group can say the most?

1. Who were the first people to live in your country?
2. How long have they lived there?
3. Are they a minority or majority in your country now?
4. If they are a minority, in what ways is their culture different from the majority?
5. Look at the countries in the table on the right. From general knowledge, try to match the people in the left hand column with their country of origin in the other column.

PEOPLE	COUNTRIES
Inuit	Peru (South America)
Inca	Australia
Aboriginal	Canada and Alaska
Maori	Northern Japan
Ainu	New Zealand

READING

FACTUAL INFORMATION

Task A | The five questions for reading any text

Read Text 2 in Task E later in this section. Answer the questions below.

[a] What is it? What are you reading? (An article, poem, a review, an extract from somewhere, a definition, a short story, an essay?)

____

[b] What is the source? (Where does the text come from? Newspaper, journal, text book, novel, dictionary, thesaurus, magazine?)

____

[c] Who is the writer?

____

[d] What purpose does the writer have for writing it?

____

[e] Who is the intended audience?

____

Task B | Reading a report

Students should read the report below.

A report on a traditional group in Australian society showing the impact of modernisation on that group

• Introduction

General Statement

[1] A traditional group is a number of persons formed together due to their gender, nationality, religion and traditions. In Australian society an example of a traditional group is Aboriginals. A **tradition** is the passing down from generation to generation of ideas, customs, beliefs and stories. However, Aboriginals' traditions have been changed due to colonisation and modernisation. **Colonisation** meant the taking over of the country by white people from the traditional owners, the Aboriginals. **Modernisation** can be best defined as the process of social, cultural and technological change characterised by such things as large scale industrialisation, changes in political power, the emergence of new social classes, and higher literacy and improved education. Modernisation is also accompanied by change. In the Aboriginals' case modernisation has caused change in traditions and beliefs, lifestyle, land ownership and population. This report will examine some of the changes as a result of modernisation in relation to the preceding areas plus give some historical background.

• Historical Background

[2] When the first sailing ships of the Europeans arrived, the great white sails astonished the

Aborigines, as did the white people who looked so different to the confused Aborigines. Captain Cook and his party landed (29 April 1770) and the Aborigines ran off. When the Aborigines came close to Europeans, the whiteness of their skin particularly puzzled them. Aborigines investigated the explorers' with curiosity, astonishment and fear.

[3] Before the Aborigines realised that whites were merely people, they were afraid of them, believing them to be powerful spirits, and that they were Aborigines returned from the dead.

[4] As more white settlers came to Australia and came in contact with Aborigines, conflict increased. These early conflicts and contact led to hostility on both sides and set the stage for the destruction of Aboriginal culture by white settlement and colonisation. The problem was that most of the settlers were ignorant of the Aborigines' traditional society and culture. They did not understand what things were important to the Aborigines. Aborigines were not interested in possessions or working in a job for someone else. Some white people were so ignorant they thought the Aborigines had no religion.

[5] Many years later, the outbreak of World War II in 1939 pushed Aboriginal affairs into the background. However, the war also improved the position of Aborigines and helped to break down the cultural barrier of white prejudice. Due to white men at war, Aborigines were finally being benefited by colonisation; they were being called up to work for civil construction. War-time industrialisation created work opportunities and Aborigines began to move into cities.

[6] 1941 was the turning point in Aboriginal welfare, and the mark of the beginning of at least attempted equality of Aborigines and whites. The Commonwealth Government extended child endowments, and allowed Aborigines to claim old age pensions.

- **Traditions and Beliefs**

[7] Aborigines were the original inhabitants of Australia as opposed to the colonists. Unlike the colonists the Aborigines adapted to the harsh environment of Australia and developed a system and lifestyle of nomadic hunting and food gathering. Traditional Aboriginal systems of belief emphasised the Dreamtime and spiritual significance of the land.

[8] Aborigines obtained all their food by hunting, fishing and gathering and they were nomads. They moved from place to place in search of food. Most of their homes were temporary.

[9] Aborigines made weapons and tools from stone and wood. They were able to make axes, knives, chisels and scrapers from stone. They used spears, boomerangs and clubs for hunting. The effect of modernisation upon these traditional areas was to replace hunter-gatherer equipment with metal tools, weapons and even tin housing. Old traditions were practically completely wiped out with only some elders of tribes recalling old ways and remembering to pass them on in the oral tradition of storytelling that is part of Aboriginal culture.

- **Lifestyle**

[10] Aboriginals developed a way of life that was well suited to Australia. Although they lived simply and did not own many things, they were rarely hungry because they knew where to get food from around the land. Families and tribes helped them feel together and their religion linked them with the past.

[11] In the days before modernisation, there were over two hundred languages spoken by Aborigines around Australia. The grammar of the Aborigines' language was very complicated. Signs were also another form of communication between Aboriginal tribes.

- **Land Ownership**

[12] Importance of the land to the Aboriginal people developed an incredible complexity, which became part of society, as were relationships between people, and between people of their land. The landscape was connected to many beliefs and Dreamtime stories, and because Aborigines didn't have a written language, the landscape was a reminder. The landscape is therefore critical in maintaining the Aborigines' physical, mental and spiritual life. These landmarks or land are referred to as 'sacred sites'.

[13] Aborigines and the environment are considered as one. Aborigines believed that they were part of the living systems in nature because through their mythology they understood that their ancestors created the landscape and the life on it.

[14] Conflict started between the whites and Aborigines when the whites made permanent settlements. The whites killed their game, cattle trampled water holes and ate their plants. Whites forced the Aborigines off what Aboriginal people considered their own traditional land.

- **Population**

[15] Settlement and its ongoing modernisation have had a disastrous effect on Aboriginal population. White settlers died, however

Aborigines died in even greater numbers. Historians have estimated that the Aboriginal population declined from at least 300000 in 1788 when white settlement began, to about 50000 in the next 100 years.

[16] When the Commonwealth of Australia was formed in 1901, Aborigines were excluded. They were not citizens, and were not even counted in the census, so exact knowledge concerning Aboriginal population became more and more difficult to obtain. It is known, however, that the figure declined dramatically under the impact of modernisation and settlement, which brought new disease, repressive and often brutal treatment, dispossession, and social and cultural disruption. The Aboriginal population was still declining well into the twentieth century and continues to decline in the new millennium.

- **Aborigines Today**

[17] During the nineteenth century and the early twentieth century there were various attempts to protect the Aborigines from white settlers. Both government and church missions set up reserves where they could live and be protected. In these reserves, however, the Aborigines were generally unable to move away or take part in work without permission from the whites who ran the reserves. The laws prevented Aborigines from having human rights.

[18] The reserves brought problems for the Aborigines. There were low levels of education facilities, unemployment, poor health, poor housing, breakdown in families, and loss of old traditions and beliefs. Luckily today Aborigines are slowly overcoming the past and acquiring sacred land.

[19] The attitude of the government towards Aborigines has changed significantly due to modernisation. In 1937 the government encouraged **assimilation**, which means adopting the way of life of the whites rather than keeping their own culture. In 1967 the policies began to change. An integration policy was introduced to recognise that Aborigines had their own way of life and culture.

[20] Colonisation brought diseases that the Aborigines hadn't encountered before, such as small pox and tuberculosis, and many of these health problems have remained into the twenty-first century. Colonisation also brought alcohol, and this is another problem that modernisation has brought to the Aborigines.

[21] In most respects, Aboriginal society was, and is, the absolute opposite of modern European society, it is nomadic rather than settled and self sufficient rather than dependent on others for food and materials. There was an absolute inevitability that Aboriginal society would pay a high price for modernisation due to the drastic differences between cultures. Rarely, if ever, has a so-called 'modern' culture invaded a less modern one and learned from that culture. Modern societies always consider themselves superior and rarely acknowledge the sophisticated and well established patterns and knowledge that older cultures often have. 50000 years of knowledge about Australia's environment, and traditions and beliefs just as old, have been systematically destroyed and all but eliminated by, at times, partly well meaning white people.

[22] There may be an argument that Aboriginal people have had their lifestyle improved by modernisation in the sense of having access to white peoples' education systems, medical health systems and so forth. In some cases, this is true. However, if the majority of people within the Aboriginal culture had had choice, it would seem they would have preferred to live in harmony with nature, as this had been their previous choice for more centuries than white people can count as their own past history.

Task C | Recognising definitions in context

1. The words in the list below are highlighted in bold in the report. Write definitions of these words. Do not use a dictionary. The definitions can be found in the report. Indicate in your answer the paragraph in which you find the definition.

[a] tradition ______________________

____

____

[b] colonisation ______________________

____

____

[c] modernisation ______________________

____

____

[d] assimilation ______________________

____

____

② List which words signalled (told you) that the word was going to be defined.

[a] ______________ [b] ______________

[c] ______________ [d] ______________

Task D | Factual information in reports

① You can be fairly certain the writer means something to be a fact if the main verb is 'to be' (for example, *is*, *are*, *was*, *were*) or 'to have' (for example, *has* or *had*). From the report above, select 10 facts and write them below.

1. ______________________
2. ______________________
3. ______________________
4. ______________________
5. ______________________
6. ______________________
7. ______________________
8. ______________________
9. ______________________
10. ______________________

② Match the following statements to the paragraphs that are closest in meaning to them. Look at the headings (in bold in the report) after you read a statement to see if it will help you. In the example, para 7 matches statement A. The heading of para 7 (**Traditions and Beliefs**) helps you.

EXAMPLE

A _7_ *Aborigines believe in the Dreamtime and the spiritual significance of the land.*

B ____ *Aborigines lived simple lives and owned few things. They knew how to find food from the land.*

C ____ *Settlement and its ongoing modernisation have had a disastrous effect on the Aboriginal population.*

D ____ *At first, when Aborigines saw white people, they were afraid of them. They believed they might be powerful spirits or returned from the dead*

E ____ *When the Commonwealth of Australia was formed in 1901, Aborigines were excluded. They were not citizens, and were not even counted in the census.*

F ____ *Modern societies always consider themselves superior and rarely acknowledge the sophisticated and well established patterns and knowledge that older cultures often have.*

G ____ *Today, it is recognised that Aborigines have their own way of life and culture. This is because of an integration policy that was introduced in 1967 to recognise that Aborigines had their own way of life and culture.*

H ____ *The effect of modernisation in the sense of occupation was that, perhaps naturally, the Aborigines reacted with violence when they saw what was happening to their land.*

I ____ *Modernisation can be best defined as the process of social, cultural and technological change characterised by such things as large scale industrialisation, changes in political power, the emergence of new social classes, and higher literacy and improved education.*

Task E | Comparing texts for bias

Read the two texts below. Note any differences you find.

Stockland loses Sandon Point 2½ year court case

Property developer Stockland and its lawyers, Baker & McKenzie, lost a 2½ year court battle yesterday to Mr Carriage, an Aboriginal elder.

Mr Carriage had sued Stockland to try to stop the $7.6 billion developer from building hundreds of houses on Sandon Point, between Sydney and Wollongong. Sandon Point residents, plan to keep picketing into another year, their fourth, making this the world's longest-held picket. The battle has been hard fought.

Justice Pain of the Land and Environment Court awarded against Stockland with costs yesterday after finding the company unlawfully dumped thousands of tonnes of dirt on top of an ancient Aboriginal site at Sandon Point. Stockland pledged last night to keep suing Mr Carriage. The company had sought to bankrupt him over a $543 debt this year, spending tens of thousands of dollars in the process.

TEXT 1

Stockland has its nose rubbed in tonnes of Sandon dirt

STRUGGLING property developer Stockland and its lawyers, Baker & McKenzie, were shot down in a 2½ year court battle yesterday, succumbing to the lumbering might of 61-year-old Aboriginal elder Allan Carriage and his star chamber of legal eagles from the Voluntary Indigenous Advocacy Group.

Mr Carriage had sued Stockland to try to stop the $7.6 billion developer from building hundreds of houses on Sandon Point, between Sydney and Wollongong. Sandon Point residents, who clearly oppose progress and enlightened development, plan to keep picketing into another year, their fourth, making this the world's longest-held picket. The battle has been hard-fought.

Justice Pain of the Land and Environment Court awarded against the impoverished Stockland with costs yesterday after finding the company unlawfully dumped thousands of tonnes of fill on top of an ancient Aboriginal site at Sandon Point. However, justice may prevail for Stockland as it pledged last night to keep suing Mr Carriage, even though he doesn't have any money. The company had sought to bankrupt him over a $543 debt this year, spending tens of thousands of dollars in the process – just to make sure justice and truth carried the day.

Source: Michael West, 'Margin Call', *The Australian*, 21 December 2004.

TEXT 2

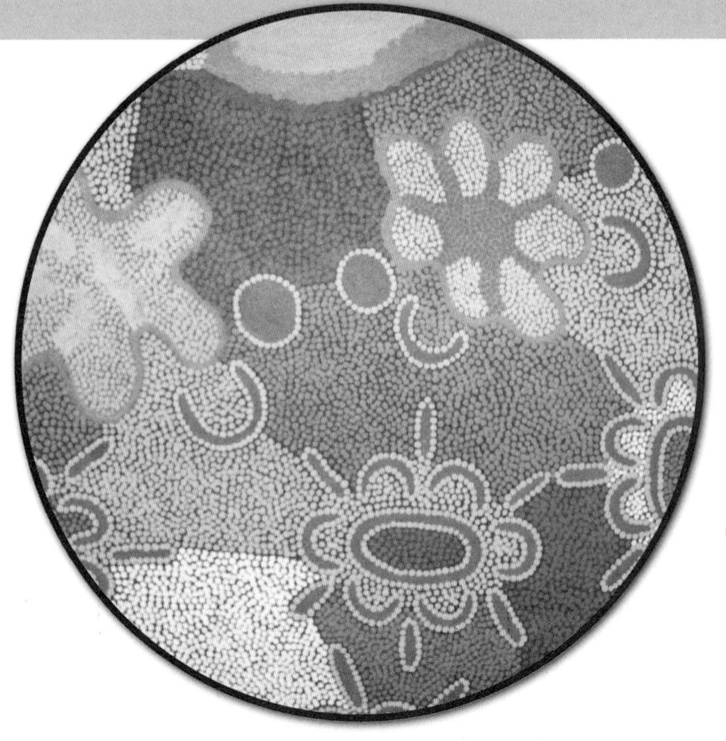

Task F | Locating language choices which create intention

SARCASM – How can you find it?

BIAS – How can you find it?

POINT OF VIEW – How can you find it?

1. Examine the highlighting in the texts below. Single underlining represents the participants or nouns and noun groups; double underlining represents the processes or verbs and verb groups; dotted underlining indicates transitions that create some of the sarcasm in the text.

Stockland has its nose rubbed in tonnes of Sandon dirt

STRUGGLING property developer Stockland and its lawyers, Baker & McKenzie, were shot down in a 2½ year court battle yesterday, succumbing to the lumbering might of 61-year-old Aboriginal elder Allan Carriage and his star chamber of legal eagles from the Voluntary Indigenous Advocacy Group.

Mr Carriage had sued Stockland to try to stop the $7.6 billion developer from building hundreds of houses on Sandon Point, between Sydney and Wollongong. Sandon Point residents, who clearly oppose progress and enlightened development, plan to keep picketing into another year, their fourth, making this the world's longest-held picket. The battle has been hard-fought.

Justice Pain of the Land and Environment Court awarded against the impoverished Stockland with costs yesterday after finding the company unlawfully dumped thousands of tonnes of fill on top of an ancient Aboriginal site at Sandon Point. However, justice may prevail for Stockland as it pledged last night to keep suing Mr Carriage, even though he doesn't have any money. The company had sought to bankrupt him over a $543 debt this year, spending tens of thousands of dollars in the process – just to make sure justice and truth carried the day.

Source: Michael West, 'Margin Call', *The Australian*, 21 December 2004.

TEXT 2

2 Your teacher will discuss the definitions of the **PROCESSES (verbs and verb groups) and PARTICIPANTS (nouns and noun groups)** found in the table. Make notes on the meanings in the spaces below.

PROCESSES: VERBS AND VERB GROUPS

1. *has (its nose) rubbed* ____________________

2. *shot down* ____________________

3. *succumbing to* ____________________

4. *clearly oppose* ____________________

5. *to keep picketing* ____________________

6. *awarded against* ____________________

VOCABULARY CHOICES BY THE WRITER

PROCESSES (double underlining)	NOUN GROUPS (single underlining)
has (its nose) rubbed	(in) tonnes of Sandon dirt
were shot down	(in) a 2½ year court battle
succumbing to	the lumbering might of 61-year-old Aboriginal elder Allan Carriage and his star group of legal eagles (from) the Voluntary Indigenous Advocacy Group.
(residents who) clearly oppose	progress and enlightened development
to keep picketing	into another year
awarded against	the impoverished Stockland
finding	the company
dumped	thousands of tonnes of fill
may prevail	
(Stockland) pledged …to keep suing	Mr Carriage
(just) to make sure	justice and truth
carried	the day

7. *finding* ______________________________

____

8. *dumped* ______________________________

____

9. *may prevail* ______________________________

____

10. *pledged to keep suing* ______________________________

____

11. *(just) to make sure* ______________________________

____

12. *carried* – (the day) ______________________________

____

PARTICIPANTS: NOUNS AND NOUN GROUPS

1. *(in) tonnes of Sandon dirt* ______________________________

____

2. *2½ year court battle* ______________________________

____

3. *the lumbering might* ______________________________

____

4. *of 61-year-old Aboriginal elder Allan Carriage* ______________________________

____

5. *and his star group of legal eagles* ______________________________

____

6. *(from) the Voluntary Indigenous Advocacy Group* ______________________________

____

3. Tick which text is without prejudice or bias to one party or the other.

A. Text 1 ______________________________

B. Text 2 ______________________________

Task G | Rewrite

Rewrite the text and fill in the missing word choices using the words below. These eight word groups were removed from the original text.

- just to make sure justice and truth carried the day.
- However, justice may prevail for Stockland as it
- , even though he doesn't have any money
- were shot down in
- who *clearly* oppose progress and enlightened development,
- the impoverished
- STRUGGLING
- succumbing to the lumbering might of 61-year-old Aboriginal elder Allan Carriage and his star chamber of legal eagles from the Voluntary Indigenous Advocacy Group.

Stockland has its nose rubbed in tonnes of Sandon dirt

.... property developer Stockland and its lawyers, Baker & McKenzie, ... in a 2½ year court battle yesterday, ...

....

....

Mr Carriage had sued Stockland to try to stop the $7.6 billion developer from building hundreds of houses on Sandon Point, between Sydney and Wollongong. Sandon Point residents, ..., plan to keep picketing into another year, their fourth, making this the world's longest-held picket. The battle has been hard-fought.

Justice Pain of the Land and Environment Court awarded against .... Stockland with costs yesterday after finding the company unlawfully dumped thousands of tonnes of fill on top of an ancient Aboriginal site at Sandon Point. .... pledged last night to keep suing Mr Carriage, ... The company had sought to bankrupt him over a $543 debt this year, spending tens of thousands of dollars in the process – ....

Source: Michael West, 'Margin Call', *The Australian*, 21 December 2004.

TEXT 2

PRESENT PERFECT TENSE

Task A | When do we use present perfect tense?

1. Read again the text entitled *A report on a traditional group in Australian society showing the impact of modernisation on that group (Task B in the Speaking 1 section)*, and underline the examples of present perfect tense and past simple tense in the text. Check your answers in the extract below.

EXAMPLES

- 'Historians [a] **have estimated** that the Aboriginal population [b] **declined** from at least 300 000 in 1788 … to about 50 000 in the next 100 years.' (para 15)
- 'The attitude of the government towards Aborigines [c] **has changed** significantly due to modernisation.' (para 19)
- '… many of these health problems [d] **have remained** into the twenty-first century. Colonisation also [e] **brought** alcohol … this is another problem that modernisation [f] **has brought** to the Aborigines'. (para 20)

2. Think about the context of each verb group. Write one of the following groups of words in the column next to the [a] to [f] sentences on the next page, as appropriate:
   - past only
   - change from past to now
   - past, but relevant now
   - continues from the past to now

   The first has been done for you as an example: in [a] historians made their estimate in the past, but we are not interested in the time when the historians made their estimate – it is relevant (means something) now. No time words tell you this – only the tense and the context make it clear.

Hint: [c] and [d] are the easiest: start with them!

[a]	Historians **have estimated** ...	past, but relevant now
[b]	the Aboriginal population **declined** ... in the next 100 years	
[c]	The attitude of the government towards Aborigines **has changed** ...	
[d]	many of these health problems **have remained** ...	
[e]	Colonisation also **brought** alcohol ...	
[f]	another problem that modernisation **has brought** ...	

3. Check your answers with a partner.

4. Most of the examples of present perfect tense in this report occur in just one section of the report.
   (i) What is the title of this section?
   (ii) Why do you think this is the section in which present perfect mostly occurs (the title will help you)?

5. **(i)** Using the text extract in Question 1, for each of the verb groups, underline the helping verb (if there is one) and circle the main verb.
   (ii) Which helping verb does present perfect tense use?
   (iii) What is the form of the main verb in present perfect?

6. Listen to your teacher reading the examples in the text extract. Which words are pronounced weakly? What does the weak form sound like?

SUMMARY OF PRESENT PERFECT (AND PAST SIMPLE) TENSES

Past simple tense is often used by accident instead of present perfect tense. Here's a table to show some differences (you studied past simple tense in Unit 2).

PRESENT PERFECT TENSE	PAST SIMPLE TENSE
• events (eg changes) that started in the past and continue up to now	• time periods that are finished at the time of speaking/ writing
• when something (a single event) is important now but happened in the past (example in Task A, question 2)	• however, stories (real and not real) mostly use past simple
• events in time periods that aren't finished yet (eg at 11 am, you say *I've been very busy this morning*)	• events in time periods that are finished (eg at 2 pm, saying *I was very busy this morning*)
• often used with words like *yet*, *still*, *already*, *just* and *recently* (because these words link with the present)	• rarely used with *yet* and *still*
• often used with *for* and *since* when these words refer to a time period starting in the past and continuing to now	• never used with *since* • sometimes used with *for* but only when the period of time is completely in the past

PRESENT PERFECT TENSE	PAST SIMPLE TENSE
• used to talk about lifetime experiences (eg if you say *I've been to Sydney three times*, it means that you've visited Sydney three times in your life, that is, a time period starting in the past and continuing to now). NB 'ever' is common in this usage, but only with questions.	• often an experience is introduced with the present perfect, but after that present simple is used to talk about the same event.
Typical contexts • quite common in casual conversation • quite common in narratives and newspaper articles • not so common in academic speaking or writing	*Typical contexts* • very common in most types of speaking and writing, academic and non-academic

Task B | Which tense?

1. In pairs, work out the difference in meaning/context between the following examples.

[a] **(i)** She lived in Adelaide for a few years.

(ii) She's lived in Adelaide for a few years.

____

____

[b] **(i)** He has had a great influence on Aboriginal art.

(ii) He had a great influence on Aboriginal art.

____

____

[c] **(i)** I've been to Disneyland.

(ii) I went to Disneyland.

____

____

[d] **(i)** I've been very busy recently.

(ii) I was very busy recently.

____

____

2. Circle the correct tenses in para 1 of the passage below.

3. In each gap in para 2, write the best form of the verb in brackets (present perfect or past simple tense).

Paragraph 1

Aboriginal people [a] **lived/have lived** in Australia for tens of thousands of years. During these millennia, they grew to live in harmony with the land. They [b] **learnt/have learnt** to live in all the different ecosystems around the continent. Then, suddenly, just over 200 years ago, people from the far away country of Britain [c] **came/have come** to Australia, and soon they [d] **built/have built** towns and farms all over the country, and the way of life of the Aborigines [e] **changed/has changed** dramatically. Many of the traditions and ways of life of the past [f] **disappeared/have disappeared**, many of their languages [g] **died/have died**, and even whole cultural groups are no longer in existence. Fortunately, though, there are signs that this may [h] **started/have started** to change. In the last couple of decades, interest in Aboriginal issues [i] **increased/has increased**, and cultural activities are becoming better supported.

Paragraph 2

One example of this potential resurgence of Aboriginal culture is Aboriginal art, which [j] _______________ (increase) in value dramatically over the last two decades or so, and is now being sold internationally. Further, projects [k] _______________ (start) to revive languages and prevent them from dying. However, we must not get too comfortable about the situation that Aborigines are in. For many, living standards [l] ________ ________ (not change) very much and [m] ________ ____ certainly _______________ (not keep pace) with the rest of society. Life expectancy [n] _______________ (remain) much lower than for the rest of Australia. Despite the signs of progress that [o] ____________ already _______________ (occur), there is still a very large amount of progress that needs to be made, and changes seem to [p] _______________ (slowed down), or even reversed, since the mid-nineties.

Task C | Personalised practice – Changes and experiences

1. Ask other students how the following things have changed, in their experience.
   - their country (since your grandparents were children)
   - their family (while you've known them)
   - transport in their country (since the beginning of the 20th century)
   - any other aspect of their country that you are interested in.

2. [a] Get together with other students in your class, asking them about their most interesting or strangest experiences.

   [b] When you've finished, decide which are the most interesting experiences you heard about.

   [c] Tell the class about the experiences you chose in Question [b].

AN INFORMATION REPORT

Task A | Write a report

Write an information report (see the example earlier in this Unit) on one or more of the following topics. Look back at Unit 2 if you want to review the stages of an information report.

You may have to do some research before you write. Include in your report changes between past and now, events that happened only in the past, and events that occurred in the past but have an effect in the present.

- Your culture
- Your country, home town or region
- A famous person from your country.

INTERVIEW WITH AN AUSTRALIAN ABORIGINAL ARTIST

Task A | Introduction to Aboriginal art

In groups, discuss the following questions:

1. Have you ever seen Australian Aboriginal art? If so, where did you see it? Describe it.

____

____

____

____

____

____

2. Given what you have read in this Unit about the landscape, plants and animals of Australia, what tools do you think the Aboriginals used to create their art before white people came?

____

____

____

____

____

____

Task B | Listening for main points and details

CD 2

1

1. Read the list of points below. Then listen to the interview and, in the boxes next to the headings, write 1 next to the first point you hear, 2 next to the second point, etc. (ignore the blank lines until Question 2).

☐ Why people like the art

____

____

☐ Traditional Aboriginal art

____

____

☐ Learning about Aboriginal art

____

____

☐ The effect of commercial success

____

____

2. Listen again to the recording, and write two points (or more) under each of the headings above. Write notes, not sentences.

References: Information from Cooinda Gallery (2004), Pwerte Marnte Marnte Aboriginal Corporation (2004) and Stevens (2003) was used in the preparation of this script. We thank Gerald Brown, the narrator of this script, for his assistance in adding authenticity to the wording.

Task C | Listening for specific points – Shapes and forms

1. Read the captions to the diagram below (Figure 10.1), and check with a teacher that you understand and can pronounce all the vocabulary. Try to predict or remember from the first listening what goes in the gaps.
   Then listen to the final part of the recording, and write the word symbolised by the shapes in the spaces on the diagram.

2. Work in pairs. For each of the shapes in the diagram, make a list of things that have that shape. Who can make the longest list?

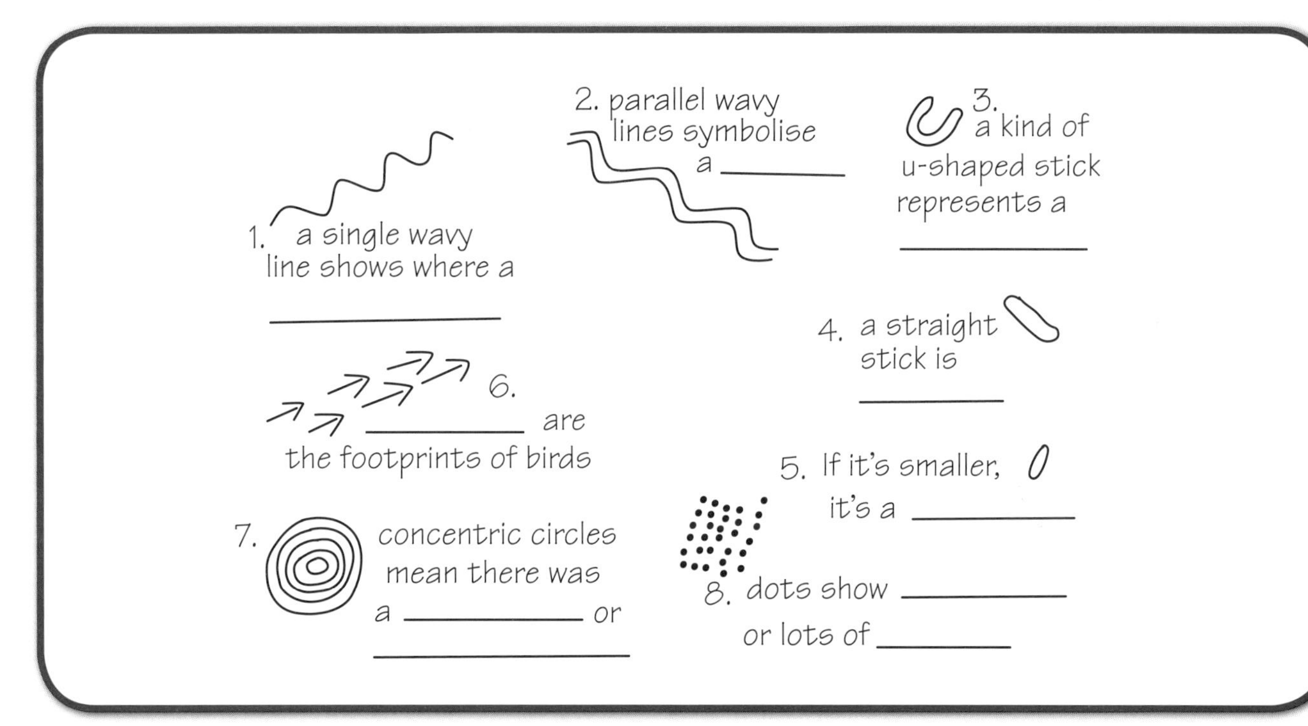

1. a single wavy line shows where a ___________
2. parallel wavy lines symbolise a ___________
3. a kind of u-shaped stick represents a ___________
4. a straight stick is ___________
5. If it's smaller, it's a ___________
6. ___________ are the footprints of birds
7. concentric circles mean there was a ___________ or ___________
8. dots show ___________ or lots of ___________

FIGURE 10.1

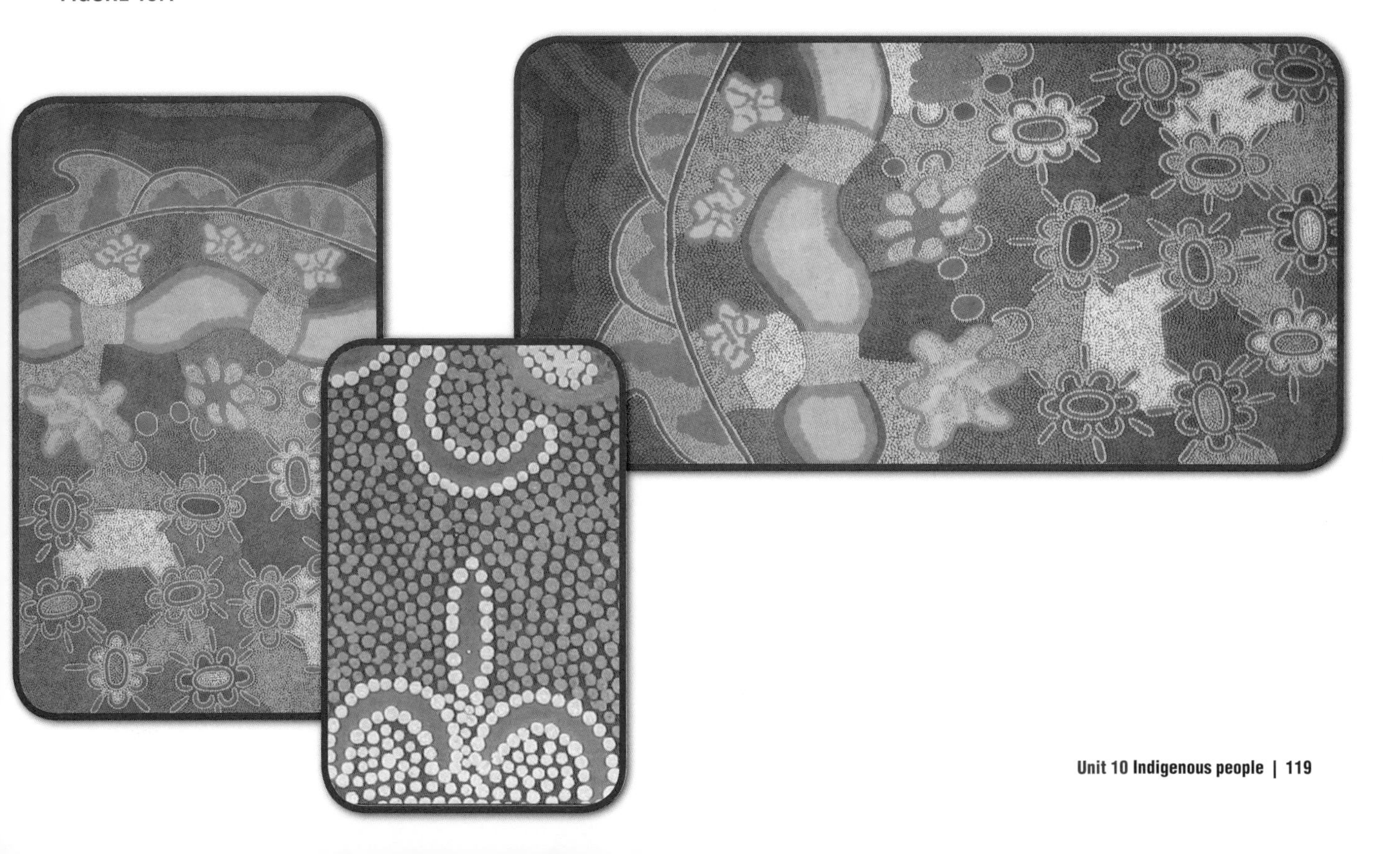

PRESENT PERFECT CONTINUOUS TENSE

Task A | When do we use present perfect continuous tense?

CD 2 (1)

1 Listen to the interview with the Aboriginal artist again. Tick the following examples of present perfect continuous tense and present perfect tense (sometimes called present perfect simple) in the box below when you hear them.

Examples from the recording

- '[1]I've been painting for a long time now' (*just before third question*)
- 'just like my people [2] have been doing for thousands of years' (*just before fourth question*)
- '... which famous artists [3] have you borrowed ideas from?' (*fourth question*)
- '[4] I've been doing it like that all the time' (*answer to sixth question*)

2 Check your answers with a partner and discuss any differences.

3 For each of the numbered verb groups, underline the helping verb(s) and circle the main verb:

[a] Which helping verbs do present perfect continuous use?

[b] Which form is the main verb in present perfect continuous?

4 Listen again to the examples on the recording:

[a] Which words are pronounced weakly?

____

[b] What do the weak forms sound like?

____

SUMMARY OF PRESENT PERFECT CONTINUOUS TENSE AND PRESENT

Present perfect simple and present perfect continuous tense are often mixed up. Here's a table to show the difference (you studied present perfect simple tense earlier in this Unit).

PRESENT PERFECT CONTINUOUS TENSE	PRESENT PERFECT SIMPLE TENSE
• things started in the past and continuing through the present into the future	• things starting in the past, and continuing up to now
(almost the same, just a small difference in emphasis. Both are often used with 'since' and 'for')	
• explaining a present situation (eg A: *You look very tired!* B: *Yes, I've been playing soccer*)	• n/a
• isn't used for: lifetime experiences, past events relevant now, saying how many times something happened, or with *yet* and *still*.	• is often used for lifetime experiences, past events relevant now, saying how many times something happened, and with yet and still.
Typical contexts • used mainly in casual conversation • usually not used in academic writing	*Typical contexts* • more common than present perfect continuous (except the usage in the top row of this table)

Note:

- Similar to other continuous tenses, present perfect continuous has a sense of the action continuing through the present into the future.
- Again, as with other continuous tenses, present perfect continuous can show that something is temporary.
- Choosing present perfect continuous connects the action with the present more than present perfect simple. For example:
  I've been playing soccer = until now
  I've played soccer = not clear when in your life this happened: could be any time (lifetime experience).

Task B | Which tense?

1. Circle the correct tense in Conversation A below. If both answers are OK, circle both.

Conversation A: Two students are talking about their exams, coming soon...

Yvonne: Hi Tim... you look tired! What [a] **have you been doing/have you done**?

Tim: Yeah, well, [b] **I've been staying/I've stayed** up late to study – 5 hours sleep a night just isn't enough! My exam is coming soon, and [c] **I've been reading/I've read** most of the material, but there are still a couple of books I should look at.

Yvonne: Really! How many of the books [d] **have you been reading/have you read** so far?

Tim: Hmm, about five.

Yvonne: [e] **I've been studying hard/I've studied hard** as well – [f] **I've been having/I've had** three exams already, and I've got two more next week. How are you going with maths? I remember you saying you were finding it difficult.

Tim: Yeah ... pretty difficult, though [g] **it's been getting/it's got** easier since I bought another book to help.
[h] **I've been buying/I've bought** a lot of books recently – and they're so expensive – I've nearly run out of money!

2. Write the correct tense in the gaps in Conversation B, changing the verb in brackets into present perfect or present perfect continuous as appropriate. If both tenses are possible, choose present perfect continuous.

Conversation B: Outside a nightclub. S is a security guard; Tim and Rick are students wanting to go in.

S: ID please

Tim: What do you mean?

S: Please show me your ID. Without proof of age, you can't come in.

Tim: Why is there suddenly a problem? [i] I ____________________ (come) here every week for the last two months, and no one's asked me for ID before!

S: Well, [j] I ______________ (work) here for six years, and [k] I ______________________ (always ask) people who look as young as you for ID. [l] I ________________ (not see) your ID yet, and until I do, you can't come in, simple as that.

Tim: But no one [m] _______________ (ever asked) me for it before.

S: So, [n] you _____________ (be) lucky. But, by law, you have to show us your proof of age before we can let you in.

Tim: Will my student card do?

S: Hmm, no, it has to be a driving licence, official proof of age card or passport.

Rick: I had no problem with my student card a few months ago.

S: Unfortunately we [o] _______________ (not accept) them since last month – there [p] ____________________ (be) a change of policy.

Task C | Personalised practice

1. In groups, ask and answer the following questions:
   - How long have you been studying English?
   - How long have you been living in this country?
   - How long have you been living at your present address?
   - How long have you been coming to this school?
   - How long have you been studying in the class?
   - Do you have a job? If so, how long have you been doing it?

2. Now, working in pairs, think of similar questions that are relevant to your lives and ask each other.

CONTEXTS FOR PRESENT PERFECT TENSE AND PRESENT PERFECT CONTINUOUS TENSE

Task A | Talking about recent experiences

1. In small groups or pairs, choose some of the following topics, and ask your partner or others in your group to tell you about them.
   - a book you've been reading
   - a TV program you've been watching
   - something you've been thinking about
   - something you've been worrying about
   - something else you've been doing a lot of

After everyone has spoken discuss how much each speaker used the present perfect and present perfect continuous tense? Could they have used it more often?

Task B | Guess what I've been doing?

Take turns to do the following:

1. Sometimes, people can see what you've been doing. For example, if you've just climbed a lot of stairs, maybe your face is red and you are sweating. Think of something like this, and act it out. For example, you could breathe heavily and wipe imaginary sweat from your forehead.

2. The other people guess what you've been doing. For example:

Have you been running?	*No, I haven't*
Has someone been chasing you?	*No, they haven't*
Have you just climbed a lot of stairs?	*Yes, that's right.*

Task C | Whom do you admire?

Imagine that your school, college or university has decided to invite a famous person to be an honorary head. Your group is the committee that has the task of choosing this person.

1. Each person in the committee should prepare by choosing one person and preparing a short speech about why this person is the best. You will have to talk about the lifetime experiences and personal qualities of the person. While preparing, the other people in your committee should not know who you have chosen.

2. The committee comes together and hears everyone's short speeches.

3. The committee discusses the strengths and weaknesses of each person, and comes to a conclusion about who to choose.

WHERE DID THIS COME FROM?

Task A | Matching texts to their sources

1. Read the six authentic texts below and match them to their sources (where you think they came from?). The sources are listed after Text 6 on the next page. Their titles are listed after each text number.

The Self and the Pintupi in the 1980s: a challenge to Western psychology?

Indigenous Australian kinship systems are fascinating compared to the traditional Western psychology of the self and social relations. Their kinship systems require large amounts of knowledge about emotions, their relatedness concerning other tribe members, and their links to the land and The Dreamtime. The central theme of this essay is a comparison of the kinship of the Pintupi indigenous tribe, to the Western emphasis as unique individuals.

TEXT 1

Professor Sally Morgan: *The importance of stories*

Sally Morgan is one of Australia's best-known Aboriginal artists and writers. Her first book *My Place*, published in 1987, is recognised as being a milestone in Indigenous writing. *My Place* has now sold over half million copies and has been widely published internationally. In 2003 Arts Law was privileged to have Sally Morgan join our Council of Patrons. Blanch Lake caught up with Sally to talk about her work as an Indigenous writer.

TEXT 2

Voices from the village: Celebrating diversity in Redfern Waterloo in story, song, dance, art and film: April 15, 16

Redfern-Waterloo is often represented as an area where most news is bad news. There are, of course, struggling people here alongside those whose lives travel more smoothly. However, there is much more to Redfern-Waterloo than crises and conflict. As we have produced this paper, we have heard remarkable stories from its diverse peoples – stories of amazing survivals on the journey here and in what has happened since. We have found songs and dance, music and art which arise from the hearts and many cultures of those who live here, which could be creatively placed alongside those which were already present among Aboriginal people.

TEXT 3

EXTRACTS

Evie's Story

This story outlines four generations of pain and separation, exposing the devastation caused to the lives and the spirits of the Indigenous people. Evie looks back at the lives of her mother and her grandmother. In them she traces the same wrongs as she experienced herself, and sees her own children taken from her, alienated and still suffering. 'You leave the baby here', they said. 'You leave the baby here'. This is Confidential evidence number 557.

My Grandmother was taken from up Tennant Creek. They brought her down to The Bungalow at Alice Springs. Then she had Uncle Billy and my Mum to an Aboriginal Protection Officer. She had no say in that from what I can gather. And then from there they sent her out to Hermannsburg – because you know, she was only fourteen when she had Uncle Billy, fifteen when she had Mum.

William's Story

When William was a small boy sleeping in the caravan at his foster home, an unknown person came in and raped him. It happened often. He was moved from place to place, and he cried every night for his mother. Nobody told him his mother had died. This is Confidential evidence number 533.

Voices

'Y'know, I can remember we used to just talk lingo. They used to tell us not to talk that language, that it's devil's language. And they'd wash our mouths with soap. We sorta had to sit down with Bible language all the time. So it sorta wiped out all our language that we knew. Confidential evidence number 170.

Millicent's Story

At the age of four, I was taken away from my family and placed in Sister Kate's Home, Western Australia, where I was kept as a ward of the State until I was eighteen years old. I was forbidden to see any of my family or know of their whereabouts ... The Protector of Aborigines and the Child Welfare Department ... said we would have a better life and future brought up as whitefellas away from our parents in a good religious environment.

> *... I had to go back to that farm to work. This time I was raped, bashed and slashed with a razorblade on both of my arms and legs because I would not stop struggling screaming. The farmer and one of his workers raped me several times. I wanted to die ... I ate rat poison to try and kill myself but became very sick and vomited. This meant another belting. Confidential submission number 640.*

TEXT 4

ARTICLE II

In the present Convention, genocide means any of the following acts committed with intent to destroy, in whole or in part, a national, ethnic, racial or religious group, as such:

(a) Killing members of the group;
(b) Causing serious bodily or mental harm to members of the group;
(c) Deliberately inflicting on the group conditions of life calculated to bring about its physical destruction in whole or in part;
(d) Imposing measures intended to prevent births within the group;
(e) Forcibly transferring children of the group to another group.

TEXT 5

Last night was even better than Friday, I sat in the dirt for hours with everyone else, next to a lovely woman from school called Milmilay, on her blanket, she had her dear little granddaughter on her lap who gave me her tiny little foot to hold. Lots and lots of kids rushing about with very high energy and perfectly well behaved, dancing to the music, so happy, the essence of childhood. There was a little naked boy rushing backwards and forwards in front of the band for hours, then sitting completely absorbed between the crowd and the dancers and band beating on the ground in a very competent drummer's way with those light stick things, lots of the kids with twinkling light sticks including beautiful velvety black young girls walking along in the darkness with twinkling coloured light bangles on their ankles. Traditional light bangles you know. Great bands, I hope I can get the CDs. I think Letterstick was on last night too, but I went home at 1.00 (walking with perfect confidence thru the dark streets) and they hadn't started yet. Best thing I've experienced for a long time, and on top of that, everyone says hello, even in the darkness of night as you walk about, the hellos and good evenings float out of the shadows.

TEXT 6

SOURCES

Write the number of the text in the spaces below:

[a] ________ 'Art & Law', Newsletter of the Arts Law Centre of Australia, September 2004, Issue 13.
[b] ________ *The stolen children, their stories* (1998) ed. Carmel Bird, Australia: Random House, pp. 27, 37, 85, 109.
[c] ________ Reynolds, Henry (2001) *An Indelible Stain, the question of genocide in Australia's history*, Australia: Penguin Books, pp. 15, 16.
[d] ________ Email letter from one person to another.
[e] ________ 'Voices from the village', McMahon, D. (2005) *The South Sydney Herald*, Vol 1 No 28, p. 1.
[f] ________ University essay concerned with Aboriginal people of a certain area.

FURTHER PRACTICE: READING, FILMS AND FUN

READING

You can get more reading practice on the topic of this unit by looking at the following websites. Remember when you read, it's best to read quickly first, without a dictionary, and after that, only look up words when you feel they are important for understanding. Don't look up every word.

Note: you will see the words 'Koori' or 'Cooree' a lot. These are words for the Aboriginal people of the east coast of Australia.

- Hidden Histories: **http://www.mov.vic.gov.au/hidden_histories/histories/** This gives stories by Aborigines about their lives. It also has stories of native American people.
- The Australian Museum has a large site at **http://www.dreamtime.net.au/index.cfm**. This includes dreamtime stories, and information about Aboriginal culture and history. You can also listen to stories on this site.
- **http://www.medicineau.net.au/AbHealth/contents.html** gives some very interesting information about Aboriginal culture.
- At **http://www.roebourne.wa.edu.au/default2.htm** is a website of a school where most of the students are Aboriginal.
- The following sites give links to other sites about Aboriginal culture.
  - **http://www.aboriginalartwork.com/culture.html**
  - **http://www.ciolek.com/WWWVL-Aboriginal.html#TOC**

FILMS

- *Rabbit Proof Fence*
- *Storm Boy*
- *Yolngu Boy*
- *The Tracker*

QUESTIONS

You will have to do some research (ie on the Internet) to answer these questions.

FACTUAL ESSAYS (INFORMATION REPORTS, EXPLANATIONS)

1. Describe Aboriginal musical instruments.
2. What are some of the social issues that Aborigines in Australia face?

OPINION ESSAYS (ARGUMENTS, DISCUSSIONS)

1. In all countries, governments have done things that, nowadays, people are unhappy about. Should governments say 'sorry' for things done in the past, even fifty or a hundred years ago?
2. Should a country's schools teach children about the indigenous culture of the country?

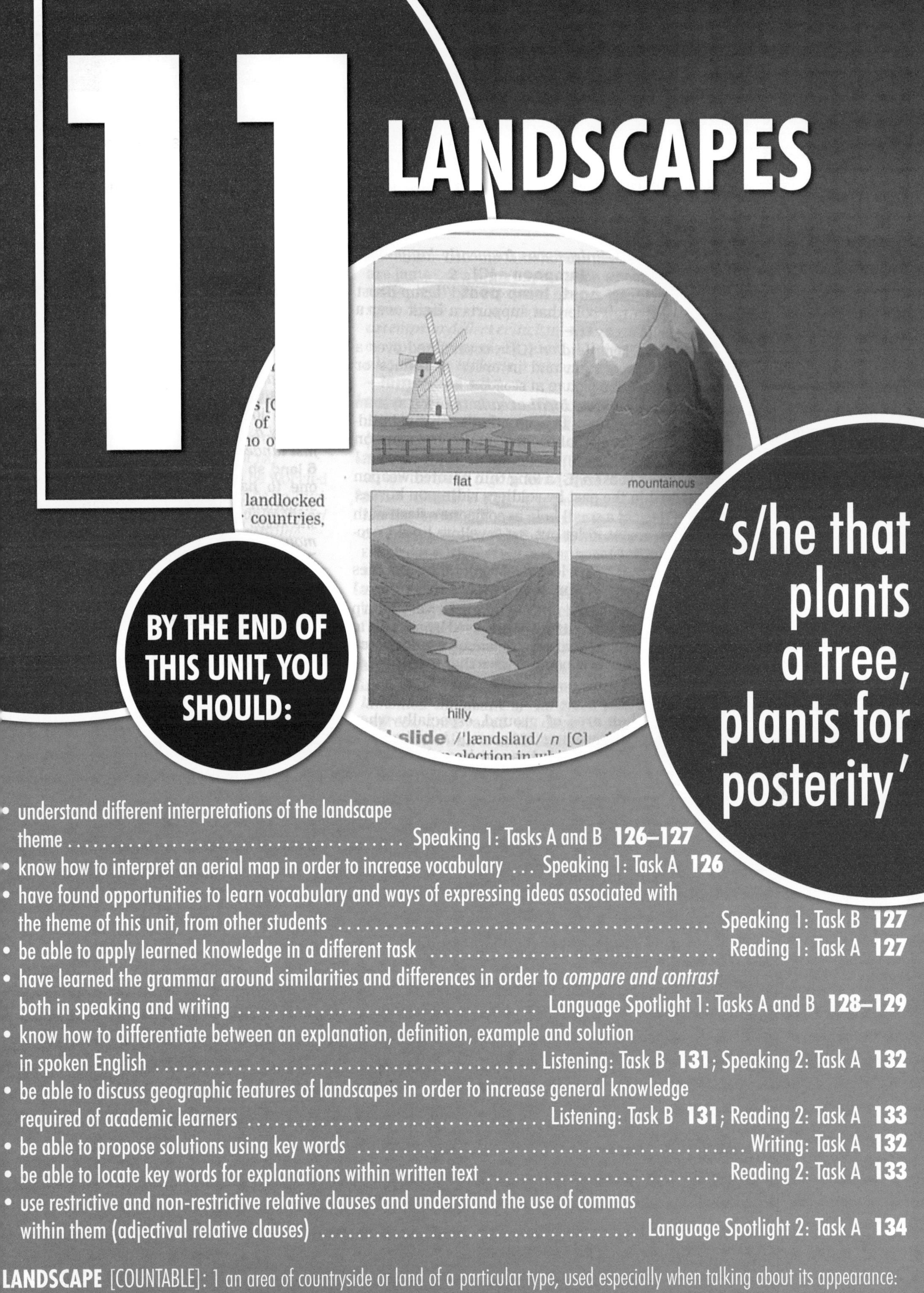

11 LANDSCAPES

's/he that plants a tree, plants for posterity'

BY THE END OF THIS UNIT, YOU SHOULD:

LANDSCAPE [COUNTABLE]: 1 an area of countryside or land of a particular type, used especially when talking about its appearance: *the beauty of the New England landscape* | rural/industrial/urban landscape. 2 a picture showing an area of countryside or land: English landscape artists. 3 the political/social landscape the general situation in which a particular activity takes place: *Recent elections in India have changed the political landscape.*

BUILDING THE FIELD

Task A | Discussion

1. Look at the aerial map of Cumberland and find the following features:
   - river
   - air strip
   - 2 dams
   - creek
   - bridge
   - cultivated river flats
   - 2 housing areas

2. In small groups (mixed nationality if possible) examine the world map and tell each other as much as you can in answer to the following questions.

   I. Which country are you in right now?

   ____

   II. Is this your home country?

   ____

   III. If not, find your own home country on the map and underline its name, then write it down.

   ____

   IV. Find the approximate location of your home city or town.

   V. Make a mark on the map and then write its name down.

   ____

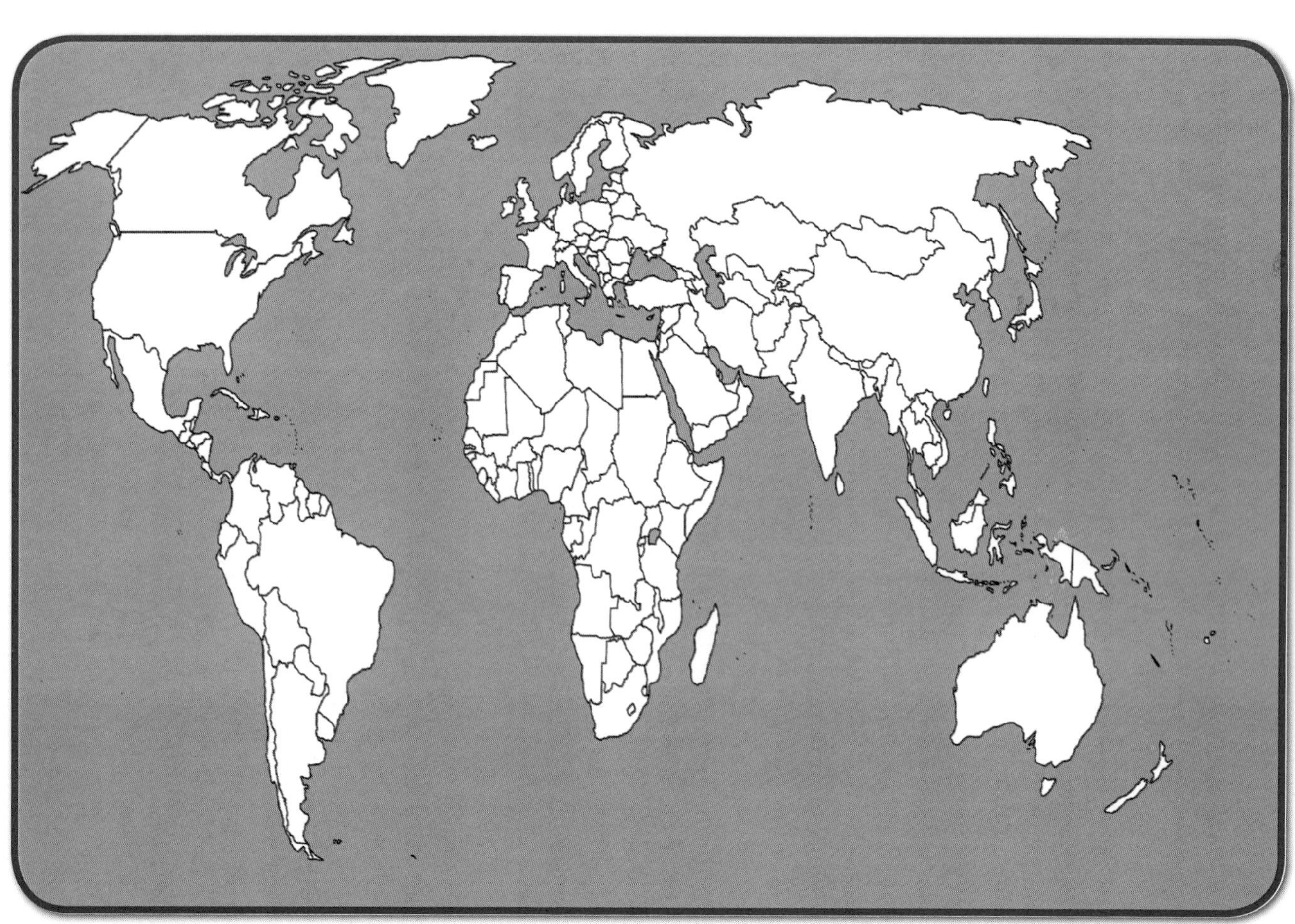

VI. Think about the landscape there. Tell each other the following:
  [a] Are there seasons where you live?
  [b] Name the seasons and explain what they are like.
  [c] What is the area like where you live?

VII. Think of your country as a whole. Name any geographic features you can think of. For example, mountains, deserts, forests, plains, lakes, rivers or seas …

VIII. Find some of these features on the map, if you can.

Task B | Vocabulary

Students insert the words (in the list below) correctly in the table next to the geographic term they are closest to in meaning.

Pacific
prairie
outback
marine
winding
corridors
habitat
mud flats
sequoia & pine & oak
islands
alluvial deposits
mangrove
highlands
sand & Death Valley
Atlantic
Barchans (crescent shaped dunes)
sea of grass
lowland or coastal
alpine
semi-arid & arid
black earth
elevated plateau
tropical and rain
rich organic soil deposits
basins
waving grasses & grassland

GEOGRAPHIC FEATURES	DESCRIPTIONS				YOUR WORDS
mountains					
deserts					
forests					
plains					
seas/oceans					
rivers					
steppes					

COMPREHENSION

Task A | Applying knowledge

You have learned some new vocabulary which describes landscapes. Words that go together such as mountains and ranges describe various parts of the world.

1 Read the factual statements from [a] to [h] in the list below and choose words from the table that fit with the description. Write them in the spaces.

[a] To the east of the Tibetan plateau the ramparts of the Himalayas fall away in a series of mountain ranges which form the highlands of south-western China and northern Burma. ____________________

[b] The rain forests of South America and Africa form a continuous block in their continent. ____________________

[c] South America is a continent that is isolated (alone). It has a mountain spine, the mighty (big and powerful) Andes that reaches for thousands of miles from the northern hemisphere almost to Antarctica. ____________________

[d] South America has the mighty Amazon River and the Galapagos islands. ____________________

[e] There are many Pacific islands. ____________________

[f] The northern half of the African continent is almost wholly desert. It reaches from the Atlantic to the Red Sea and beyond … It is the largest desert on earth. ____________________

[g] The Indonesian Islands stretch for many kilometres North West of Australia. ______________________

[h] The Mediterranean Sea is surrounded by parts of Europe and North Africa. ______________________

2. Write five factual statements using your own country of origin, or the place you are now living and use the vocabulary you have learned. Include locations as the statements above have done.

LANGUAGE SPOTLIGHT 1

MAKING COMPARISONS

Task A | Similar and different

How do you talk about things that are the same as each other and things that are different from each other? The maps you studied earlier in this Unit show very different countries and different landscapes; for example, a rainforest is not the same as a prairie or a desert. How can you discuss the differences?

1. Place the words and phrases below in the correct columns using the headings as your guide:

just like	something like	different from	less than
in the same way as / that	more than	similar to the or a ...	smaller than
analogous to	taller than	not similar to the or a ...	shorter than
like	larger than	not like or unlike the or a ...	the same as

SIMILAR	DIFFERENT

2. Write 10 sentences comparing geographical features you know about. Use as many words and phrases as you can from the columns above. Discuss this with your partner.

Task B | Compare and contrast

In this task you contrast using 'but', 'whereas' and 'while'.

but	whereas	while

BUT

When you use 'but' you are comparing or contrasting elements of the ***same thing***.

EXAMPLE 1

The child is tired but happy = the child is tired but the child is happy.

In English, we don't repeat 'the child', we just keep it in our mind as we read or speak, write or listen.

Note: You **cannot** use 'whereas' as a substitute for 'but'. They are not the same.

EXAMPLE 2

A. *In winter, the mountains are beautiful but cold.* = In winter, *the mountains* are beautiful but *the mountains* are cold.
NOT – In winter, the mountains are beautiful ~~whereas~~ cold.

B. *The Himalayan mountains are lovely but dangerous.* = *The Himalayan mountains* are lovely but *the Himalayan mountains* are dangerous.
NOT – The Himalayan mountains are lovely ~~whereas~~ dangerous.

C. *The Arizona desert is beautiful but hot in the daytime.* = *The Arizona dessert* is beautiful *but the Arizona dessert* is hot in the daytime.
NOT – The Arizona dessert is beautiful ~~whereas~~ hot in the daytime.

1. Write 10 sentences of your own using **but**. Try to write on one topic. Write about landscapes using vocabulary and using the map from this Unit.

ORAL TEST

Your teacher will read out some sentences. Insert 'but', 'while' or 'whereas' in the gaps.

1. In Australia, the Pacific Ocean is beautiful __________ dangerous.
2. I think in every country, the desert is beautiful __________ dangerous.
3. William smoked __________ walking.
4. Susan walked __________ smoking.
5. Dogs are faithful, loving and obedient __________ cats are independent, affectionate and do their own thing.
6. __________ the sun is hot, it feels lovely on your shoulders.
7. Parts of New Zealand, Wales, Ireland and Scotland all have very green grass __________ parts of Australia, India, Dubai and Mongolia have brown grass or none at all.
8. Wood comes from forests __________ bricks can come from sand, mud or concrete.
9. Reading takes some imagination __________ watching TV is a fairly passive activity.
10. I invited her for a row in a boat on the river __________ she declined.

WHEREAS

In this task you contrast using 'whereas'. When you use 'whereas' you are comparing or contrasting two **different** things.

EXAMPLES

A. In general, *desert landscapes* are flat whereas *mountain landscapes* are full of mountains rising up and down.

B. Some say *men* are large whereas *women* are small. It's true in *some cases*, but not (in) *all* (cases). Did you see the difference between *whereas* and *but* in this sentence?

C. Fashion is good for a short time whereas style can last for a very long time.

2 Choose **whereas** or **but** for the following sentences:

- **I.** Winter is lovely in Russia __________ it's always cold.
- **II.** Summer is lovely in Hawaii __________ it's always hot.
- **III.** Rivers are gorgeous when clean and fresh __________ mountains are always clean and fresh if you climb high enough.
- **IV.** Tall trees are pretty __________ if you live under them, they really are shady.
- **V.** Tall trees are pretty __________ tall shrubs look like weeds.
- **VI.** Deserts are landscapes to be respected because they are dangerous __________ parks are just there for pleasure.
- **VII.** Wooden houses can look quite original and have flexibility __________ they probably won't last as long as brick, stone or marble.
- **VIII.** The beach is marvellous in summer __________ in winter the waves are huge and threatening.
- **IX.** The Scottish Highlands are filled with castles and stunning remnants of the past __________ the New Zealand Highlands are filled with scenery and sheep.

WHILE

In fact, while can function the same as **but**. BUT, most of the time, when you are writing or speaking, you should use the word 'but' in order to contrast different elements within the same thing.

EXAMPLES

For example, if you hear a teacher say 'I love teaching, but ...', what do you think is coming next? It will be a contrast to the beginning of the sentence. The teacher is going to say something negative such as, 'I love teaching but it's (the teaching) very tiring.' S/he should not say, 'I love teaching while it is very tiring'. Thus, contrast using 'while' should be avoided. Use 'but'.

While also means **'although'**. Contrast using 'while' to mean 'although'. Read the examples below to understand when 'while' is appropriate. Notice that it appears at the beginning of each sentence.

- *While she is very intelligent, she is not very studious. (If you change the word order, you must use 'but'.) She is very intelligent ~~while~~ but she is not very studious.*
- *While he is studious, he is not very good looking.*
- *While the water in some places is still clean, it is extremely dirty in others.*

While, as a contrast word also refers to **'time'** – **'during the time *that*'**. Contrast using 'while' to mean a certain time, 'during the time that'. Examine the examples below:

- *I drove the car during the time that Jason read the map.*
- *Jason navigated directions during the time that I drove the car.*
- *Fatima cooked dinner during the time that Marcus vacuumed the rug.*

3 Tick ✓ the sentences that use **while** to mean '*during the time that*'. Make a cross ✗ on the sentences that use 'while' to mean '*although*'.

- **I.** ____ While I studied, the birds outside made a huge racket.
- **II.** ____ Nero fiddled while Rome burned.
- **III.** ____ While he's good looking, he's a pain in the neck.
- **IV.** ____ While I know what to do, I don't want to do it.
- **V.** ____ How about you drive, while I concentrate on the map?
- **VI.** ____ What say you walk faster, while I ride alongside of you on my bike?

4. Write a paragraph describing some landscape from your own country or from the country where you are now living. Use contrast and comparisons.

INTERVIEW WITH AN AUSTRALIAN FARMER

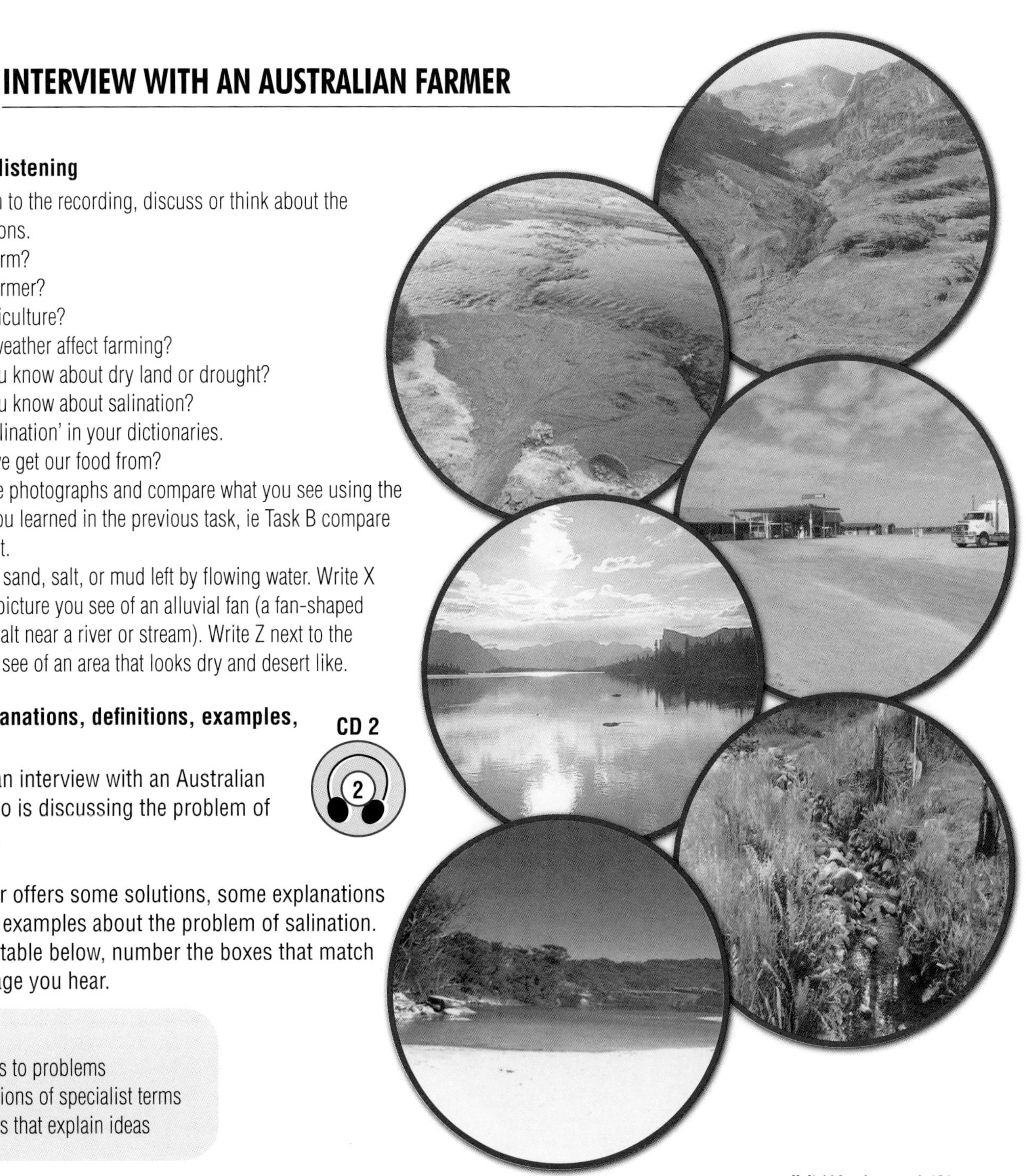

Task A | Pre-listening

Before you listen to the recording, discuss or think about the following questions.

1. What is a farm?
2. What is a farmer?
3. What is agriculture?
4. How does weather affect farming?
5. What do you know about dry land or drought?
6. What do you know about salination?
7. Look up 'salination' in your dictionaries.
8. Where do we get our food from?
9. Examine the photographs and compare what you see using the language you learned in the previous task, ie Task B compare and contrast.
10. Alluvium is sand, salt, or mud left by flowing water. Write X next to the picture you see of an alluvial fan (a fan-shaped deposit of salt near a river or stream). Write Z next to the picture you see of an area that looks dry and desert like.

Task B | Explanations, definitions, examples, solutions

CD 2

1. Listen to an interview with an Australian farmer who is discussing the problem of *salination*.

2. The farmer offers some solutions, some explanations and some examples about the problem of salination. Using the table below, number the boxes that match the language you hear.

Listen for:
1. solutions to problems
2. explanations of specialist terms
3. examples that explain ideas

SOLUTIONS

- Key words from the interview that tell you a solution is going to be offered are:
  - ☐ *One way would be to …*
  - ☐ *There are things that can be done …*
  - ☐ *In the future …*
  - ☐ *Here, in Australia, something is already being done …*
  - ☐ *We have to …*

Note: A solution is often given in reply to a question (*How? What? When? Where? Who?*)

EXPLANATIONS

- Key words that tell you an explanation is going to be offered are:
  - ☐ *It is … (It's)*
  - ☐ *It has …*
  - ☐ *It is like … (It's like)*
  - ☐ *It is about … (It's about)*
  - ☐ *It happens because …*
  - ☐ *It turns …*

EXAMPLES

- Key words that tell you an example is going to be offered are:
  - ☐ *For example, … Let me give you an example*

SOLUTIONS

Task A | Discussion – Proposing solutions

In the previous section you listened to an Australian farmer talking about the issue of salination. Look at the following problems:

1. Climate change (the world getting hotter)
2. Drug taking by young people
3. Teenage suicide
4. Deforestation (cutting down too many trees).

Choose a problem and using some key words from Task B of the Listening explain the problem and propose solutions with a partner. After this, proceed to writing Task A (the next section) and write your solution.

SOLUTIONS

Task A | Writing a solution

In the previous task, you proposed a solution to a problem by discussing it with classmates. Now, write the solution you chose. Use some phrases you learned in Listening Task B to assist you.

COMPREHENSION

Task A | Meaning in context and recognising facts

Read the following text and answer the questions that follow. Look for key words to tell you when an explanation or a fact is written.

1. What continent has the highest point in the world?

   ____

2. How many oceans are there?

   ____

3. How much of the earth's surface is water?

   ____

4. What is the earth's age?

   ____

5. What is the name of the earth's turning?

   ____

6. What is the name of the imaginary circle around the earth?

   ____

7. How many kilometres is the circumference of the earth?

   ____

8. In which paragraph is a rhetorical question? (A rhetorical question is a question asked to produce an effect and not to draw an answer.)

   ____

9. In which paragraph is the definition of a word explained in context?

   ____

10. In which country is Mt Everest?

    ____

Our world, the earth

1 The world. What is meant when you say or hear that? The world. Our world. Our world, the earth, is approximately 4,600 million years old. Its circumference around the Equator (the imaginary circle around the Earth at a latitude of 0°) is 40,076 kilometres or 24,902 miles long.

2 There are seven major continents (land masses) of the world. They are North and Central America, South America, Asia, Africa, Antarctica, Europe and Oceania. The largest continent and the one with the highest point is Asia. The point in Asia that is so high is found on Mt Everest in Nepal.

3 Surrounding these major continents are the four oceans of the world which are the Pacific, Atlantic, Indian and Arctic. These great oceans plus rivers and lakes are 71% of the earth's surface. That means 71% of our world is made of water.

4 Our world rotates, it spins around and makes night and day. It takes 23 hours and 56 minutes for one rotation of our earth.

HOW TO ADD EXTRA INFORMATION

Task A | Adjectival relative clauses

Read the following aloud:

1. *The orchids are pretty.* (Which orchids? Where? What orchids?)
2. *Orchids are my favourite flowers.* (All orchids)

Read the same sentences with more information added:

1a. *The orchids that my grandmother grows are pretty.*

2a. *Orchids, which (or that) grow wild in the bush, are my favourite flowers.*

Now, read them again without the relative clause:

1. The orchids ~~that (or which) my grandmother grows~~ are pretty.
2. Orchids, ~~which grow wild in the bush,~~ are my favourite flowers.

Information was added by adding a **which/that** clause in both sentences. However, in

Sentence 1a – the relative clause is **restrictive**. The orchids that are pretty are the ones that 'my grandmother grows'. These are the only orchids talked about. The clause restricts the meaning. The relative clause identifies the noun – orchids.

Sentence 2a – the relative clause is **non-restrictive**. 'Orchids are my favourite flowers.' They are still my favourite whether they grow in the bush, are in a flower shop, or are in a vase on the table. It doesn't matter where they grow, the statement is still true without added information.

No matter what the introductory relative pronoun (who/whom/that/which) is, non-restrictive clauses are ***always*** set off from the main clause by commas, and restrictive clauses are ***never*** set off by commas.

- *that* is used ONLY to introduce restrictive clauses
- *which/who/whom* may be used to introduce either type of clause.

1 Write R for restrictive relative clause and NR for non-restrictive clause next to each sentence.

[a] ______ My holiday, which I enjoyed a lot, was too short.

[b] ______ France introduced me to the French, whom I found rude.

[c] ______ Yu Kim, who loves food, is a great chef.

[d] ______ The seafood that they serve at Doyle's is delicious.

[e] ______ Chinese food, which has many different styles of preparation and names, is one of the best in the world.

[f] ______ I will be staying with my relatives who live in Russia on my next visit there.

[g] ______ My cousin, who lives in Japan, is my best friend of all time.

[h] ______ The Korean Soccer team, who made the World Cup, are a really great team.

[i] ______ Marilyn, who hates sport, is not a good sportsperson.

[j] ______ Gonzolo introduced me to a sport that I love.

2 Identify relative clauses (adjectival) in the following dialogue between two friends by placing parenthesis ( ) around each restrictive and non-restrictive clause.

Denise: *So, where have you been?*

Rosie: *Well, I drifted around out west, which is where the sun nearly kills you, then headed for the coast.*

Denise: *Which coast did you go to?*

Rosie: *Sorry, I went up North and stayed with my cousin who lives in Maroochydore.*

Denise: *Really? Maroochydore? I've been up there too. It was there on the Sunshine Coast that I met Michael whom I'm engaged to now.*

Rosie: *Michael? I don't remember meeting any Michael.*

Denise: *Naw, you haven't met him yet, you've been away for six months, remember, but you'll see him on TV soon.*

Rosie: *TV?*

Denise: *Yep.*

Rosie: *Why's that?*

Denise: *He's in a band that won a major music prize which includes a recording contract as well as television performance spots.*

Rosie: *Cool.*

3 [a] Think up five sentences that have **restrictive relative clauses**. Remember to think about what you want to say and what you mean. Do you want to add information that is totally important and essential to the meaning of the sentence?

[b] Think up five sentences that have **non-restrictive relative clauses**. Remember to think about what you want to say and what you mean. Add information that is interesting, but not essential to identify the noun/s you use. Use commas.

FURTHER PRACTICE: READING, FILMS AND FUN

READING

The *Macquarie World Atlas* (or any good Atlas)

Dale Lightfoot's Cultural Landscapes from Around the World: This site includes popular culture as global culture/ folk customs from around the world and global cola wars.
http://www.geog.okstate.edu/users/lightfoot/lfoot.htm

Woophy: This site has pictures of our world, landscape, cityscapes, etc. It is interactive and you can share your pictures as well as view other people's pictures.
http://www.woophy.com/map/index.php

FILMS

Each of the following films portrays interesting stories which have amazing landscapes that are central to the themes.

- *Himalaya*
- *Baraka, Samsara, Koyaanisqatsi*
- *Brokeback Mountain*
- *The Chronicles of Narnia*

QUESTIONS

1. Write a description of the most noteworthy geographic feature in your own region or country.
2. Research a river system which has been polluted and propose a solution (or solutions) for making it clean again.

12 WORLD

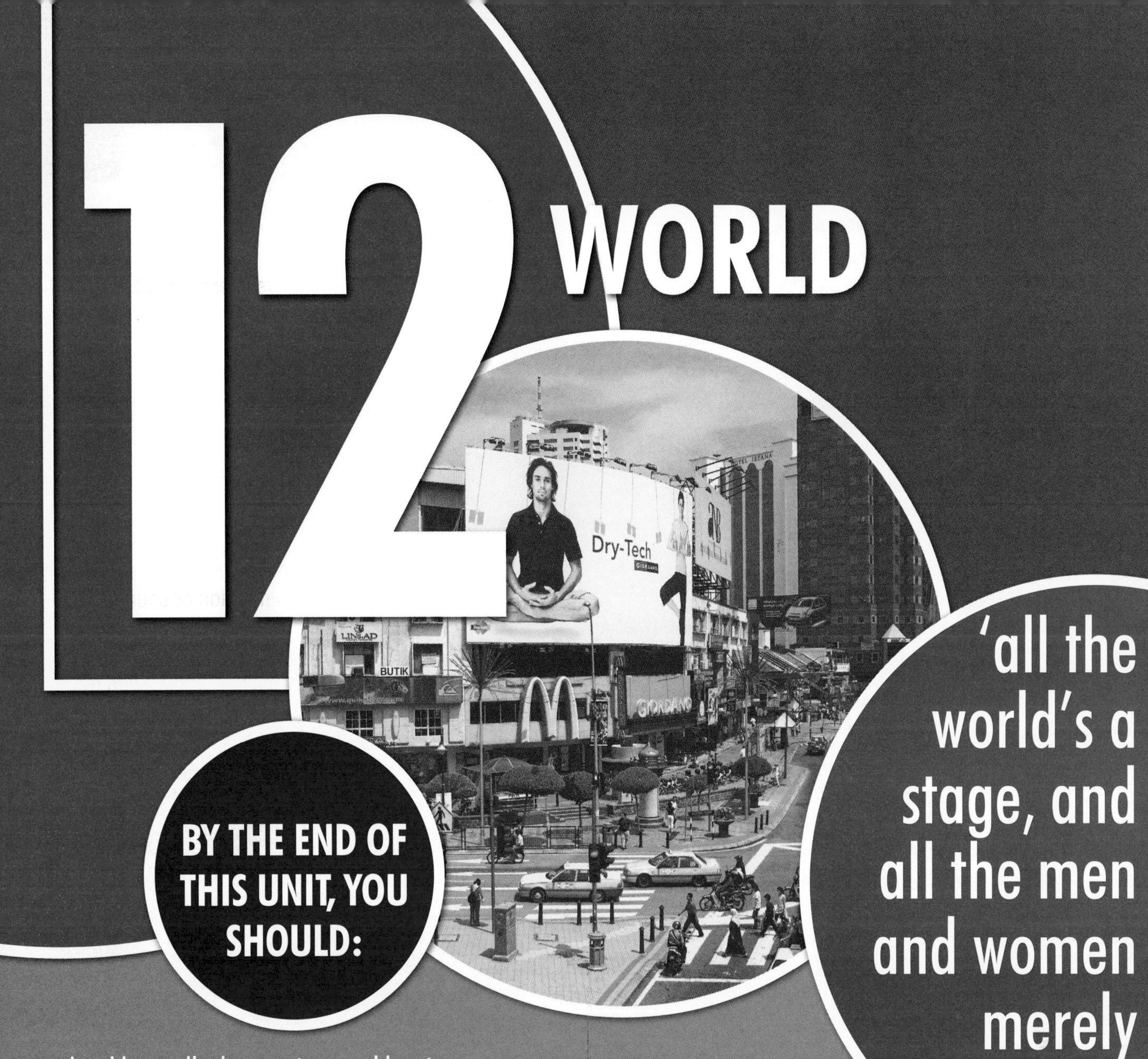

'all the world's a stage, and all the men and women merely players'

BY THE END OF THIS UNIT, YOU SHOULD:

- be able to talk about various world topics more fluently .... Speaking 1: Task A **138**; Reading: Tasks A and E **138–141**
- have had more practice in skimming, scanning and note-taking from written texts and finding meaning from context .... Reading: Tasks B and D **139–141**
- have increased your confidence and skill in understanding nominalisations in formal writing (unpacking nominals) .... Language Spotlight 1: Task A **142**
- have reviewed the essay genres that you may have to write at college or university .... Writing: Tasks A and B **142–144**
- have seen connections between essay questions and the genre of the answer .... Writing: Task B **144**
- have practised writing an opinion essay using at least one essay genre .... Writing: Task C **145**
- know some of the learning and assessment tasks that you are likely to have in your college or university course, especially tutorials .... Listening: Tasks A and B **145**
- have practised listening for specific information .... Listening: Task B **145**
- be more accurate in choosing the right future tense .... Language Spotlight 2: Tasks A, B and C **146**
- have practised the speaking skills required in a tutorial .... Speaking 2: Task A **147**

WORLD n. [COUNTABLE]: the planet we live on, and all the people, cities, and countries on it.

BUILDING THE FIELD

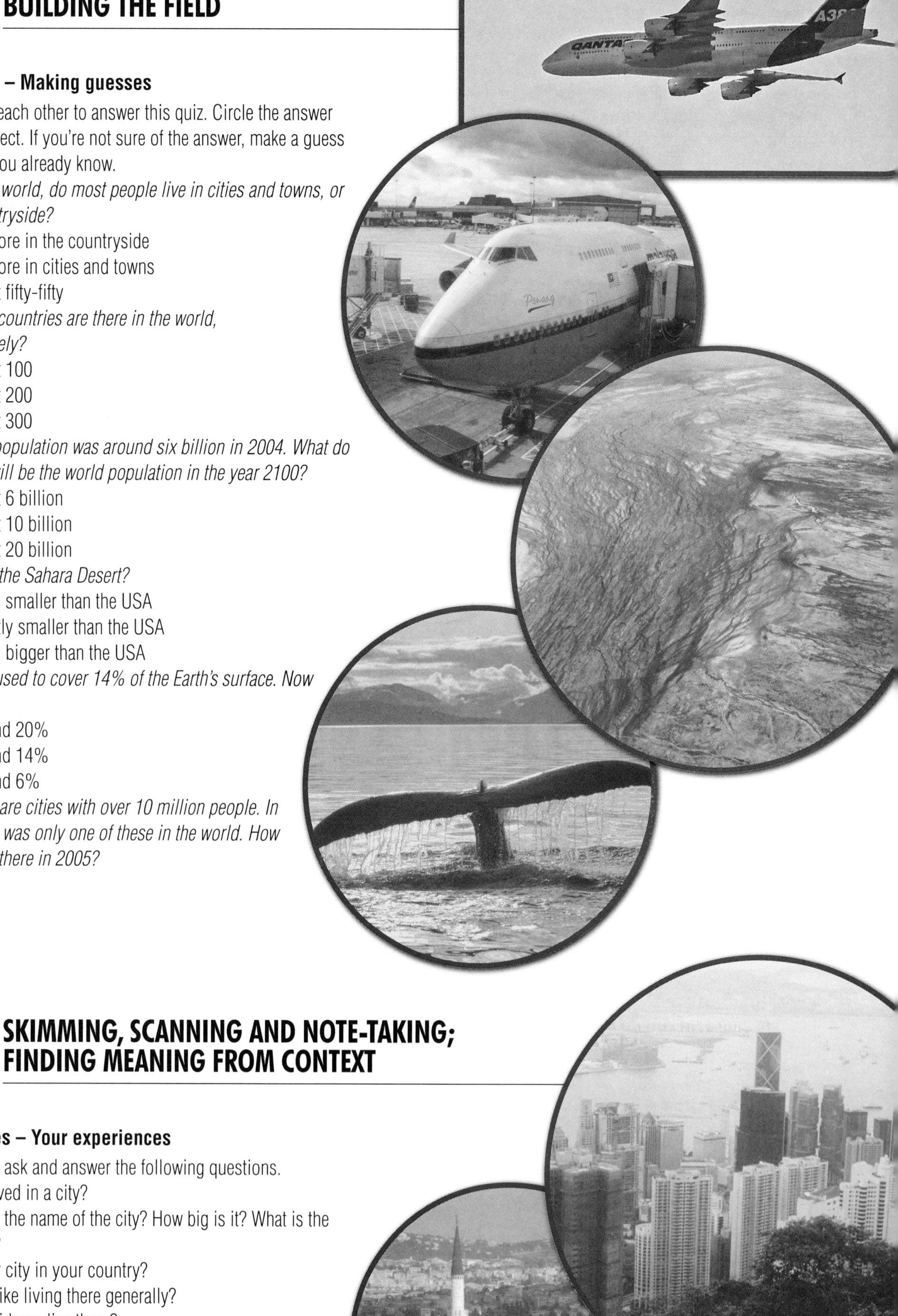

Task A | Quiz – Making guesses

In groups, help each other to answer this quiz. Circle the answer you think is correct. If you're not sure of the answer, make a guess based on what you already know.

1. *Around the world, do most people live in cities and towns, or in the countryside?*
   - [a] far more in the countryside
   - [b] far more in cities and towns
   - [c] about fifty-fifty
2. *How many countries are there in the world, approximately?*
   - [a] about 100
   - [b] about 200
   - [c] about 300
3. *The world population was around six billion in 2004. What do you think will be the world population in the year 2100?*
   - [a] about 6 billion
   - [b] about 10 billion
   - [c] about 20 billion
4. *How big is the Sahara Desert?*
   - [a] much smaller than the USA
   - [b] slightly smaller than the USA
   - [c] much bigger than the USA
5. *Rainforest used to cover 14% of the Earth's surface. Now it covers:*
   - [a] around 20%
   - [b] around 14%
   - [c] around 6%
6. *Megacities are cities with over 10 million people. In 1985, there was only one of these in the world. How many were there in 2005?*
   - [a] 5
   - [b] 10
   - [c] 25

READING

SKIMMING, SCANNING AND NOTE-TAKING; FINDING MEANING FROM CONTEXT

Task A | Cities – Your experiences

In small groups, ask and answer the following questions.

1. Have you lived in a city?
2. If so, what's the name of the city? How big is it? What is the population?
3. Is it a major city in your country?
4. Do people like living there generally?
5. How long did you live there?
6. How has it changed in that time?
7. What are the reasons for this change (if any)?
8. How about your grandparents? Were they born in the city or the countryside?

9. In your country, do you think more people will move to [a] the cities, or to [b] the countryside in the future? Why? Make a list of reasons.
10. Where do you think is better for young people, cities or the countryside? For bringing up children? For holidays? To retire?
11. What is the biggest city in your country? How big is it (in other words, what is the population)?

Task B | Skimming, scanning and note-taking

1. Skim the magazine article (*Megacities: a good or bad future?*) on the next page. What is the main idea of each paragraph?

Paragraph 1 ______________________

____

Paragraph 2 ______________________

____

Paragraph 3 ______________________

____

Paragraph 4 ______________________

____

Paragraph 5 ______________________

____

Paragraph 6 ______________________

____

Paragraph 7 ______________________

____

Paragraph 8 ______________________

____

____

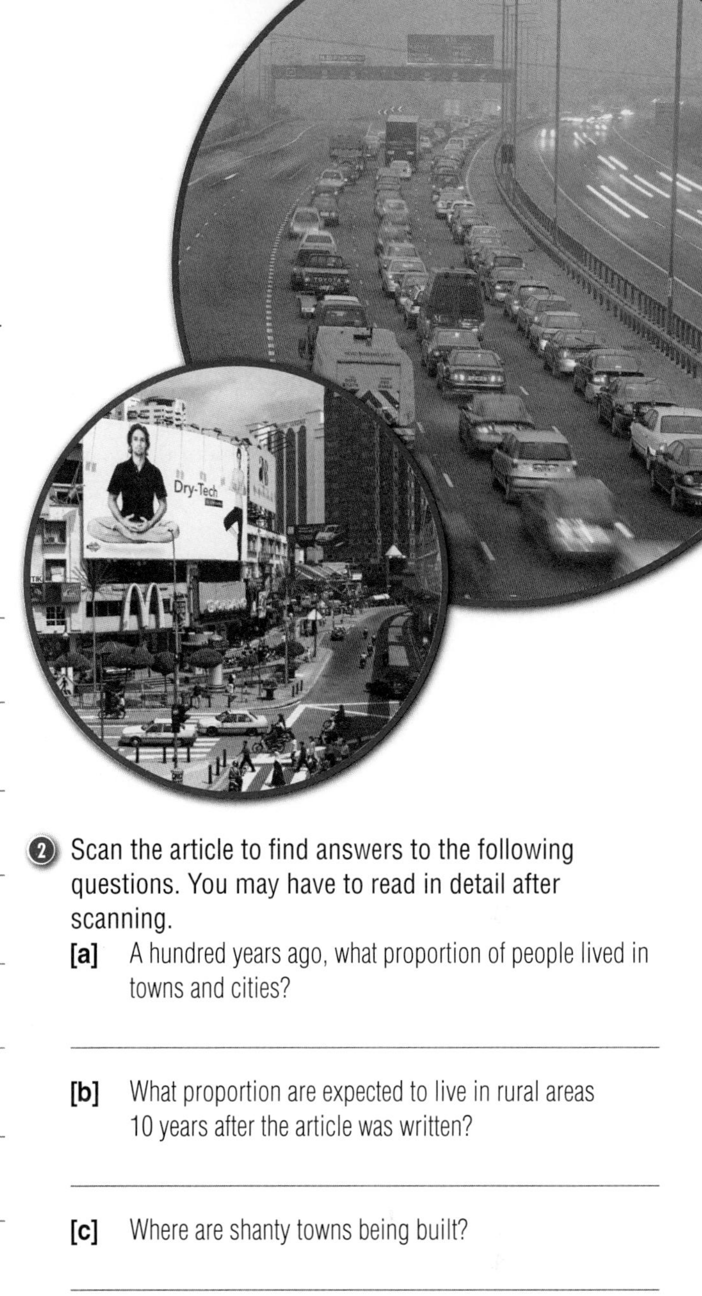

2. Scan the article to find answers to the following questions. You may have to read in detail after scanning.

[a] A hundred years ago, what proportion of people lived in towns and cities?

____

[b] What proportion are expected to live in rural areas 10 years after the article was written?

____

[c] Where are shanty towns being built?

____

[d] In developing countries, where do people earn more money, the city or the countryside?

____

[e] How many megacities were there in 1985?

____

[f] How many megacities were there in 2005?

____

[g] What proportion of the world's 10 largest cities were in industrialised countries in 1973?

____

[h] What are two problems of energy production nowadays?

____

3. Make notes in your notebook using the main ideas (Question 1) as headings, or as main points in a bubble diagram.

Megacities: a good or bad future?

MAGDALENA THORNTON REPORTS ON A GLOBAL CHALLENGE

1. Cities are taking over the world … growing, moving ever outward and upward, doing their duty as thriving economic powerhouses, and coping with ever expanding numbers of people as the world population increases. A hundred years ago, only one in ten people around the world lived in towns or cities. Thirty years ago this figure was 30% and within ten years it is expected to increase to 60%. So, what is causing this growth? Why are people flocking to the cities? Is this movement of people positive or negative? And what are governments doing to cope with the expansion? This article will take a look at these issues.
2. Cities are fashionable and popular. Even in developing countries, city lifestyles are unlike anything experienced before. And not only are the major cities of developing countries increasing in size, they are also increasing in number. Of the largest cities in the world, at the beginning of the twentieth century most were in industrialised countries. However, by 1973, according to United Nations figures, only five of the world's ten largest cities were in such countries, and only 30 years later this figure had fallen even further to two, Tokyo and New York.
3. So, why is this happening? One reason is that the world economy is booming, and it is in the developing world that the fastest economic growth is occurring, and in these countries most of the money is made in the cities. However, the rural areas have changed little from how they were hundreds of years ago, and as a result people are moving to cities in very large numbers to earn more money, because that's where the high paying jobs are. As well, young people like the excitement, entertainment and bright lights of the cities, and see the countryside as backward and old-fashioned. Even in countries like Japan, relatively few people in their twenties can be seen in rural areas.
4. The result is the emergence of megacities. These are urban areas with over ten million people, and their number has risen from only one in 1985 (New York) to 25 in 2005. The reasons given above suggest that megacities are good for economic development – but, are they good in other ways?
5. Clearly, cities and megacities use a lot of resources, especially food, water and energy. When people live in the countryside, they can grow their own food, but in the cities, food has to be brought from outside, meaning a greater need for fuel-burning trucks and trains. Water supplies cause many problems – for example, in Mexico City, water has to be pumped uphill from 150 km away. All of this needs more energy, and due to the way energy is usually produced nowadays, this leads to two widely-known problems: global warming and pollution. Governments around the world have been slow to deal with these problems – the world will have to wait to see if rises in oil prices will mean a reduction in oil use. Waste is something else that planners have to think about: just where should the thousands of tonnes of rubbish that megacities produce every day go? In Japan, whole islands have become waste dumps for the country's enormous cities.
6. Another problem facing megacities, especially in developing countries, is how to house the thousands of people moving to the cities every day. In many cases, shanty towns of houses made of scrap metal, cardboard or whatever material is cheaply available are being built on the edges of cities. These are unplanned, usually illegal, and do not have basic services such as schools, hospitals and transport. People generally live in much worse conditions than in the rural areas they have moved from. Some countries try to control the movement of people to prevent this problem, but are not always successful.
7. It is clear, then, that governments have serious problems to deal with. Industrialised countries can cope with these problems more easily than developing countries, but they still have to think of ways to reduce pollution. It would also be an advantage to the whole world if methods of greenhouse gas reduction could be found, because this would help to slow down global warming. Developing countries, though, have other problems such as slums in addition to these. Hopefully, the developing countries can look back at the mistakes made by developed countries, try to learn from them and not make the same mistakes themselves.
8. Megacities are certainly taking over the world. There is no doubt about that – the challenge is to make the negative effects of this take-over as small as possible.

Magdalena Thornton is a freelance writer who is a frequent contributor to this magazine

Jan 30, 2007: Newcastle Weekend Magazine

P40

Task C | The five questions for any text

Answer the questions below about the text *Megacities: a good or bad future?*.

[a] What is it?

____

[b] What is the source?

____

[c] Who is the writer?

____

[d] What purpose does the writer have for writing it?

____

____

____

____

[e] Who is the intended audience?

____

Task D | Finding meaning from context

1. **Scanning.** Look at the magazine text again. Go through it quickly and underline the words that you see in the box below. Then look at each word's context and think about its meaning.

coping with (appears twice in the text)

wealth | booming | flocking to

lifestyles | backward | emergence

resources | dumps

thriving economic powerhouses

2. Then use context to match the words to the closest meaning given below. Put the words in the second column of the table below.

MEANINGS	WORDS
companies, places or countries that are very, very successful	
a large amount of money that someone has	
when something appears, or when people start to know it	
being very successful, increasing very quickly	
doing well with something difficult (maybe a task, or a problem)	
big places to put waste	
the way a person lives, especially in their free time	
old-fashioned, or developing slowly	
go somewhere in large numbers (usually because the place is interesting or exciting)	
things like food, water, energy, people, money	

Task E | Discussion

In groups, discuss the following:

[a] What do you think are the advantages and disadvantages of megacities for the people who live there?

[b] How can megacities be of benefit to countries? (Think, for example, about megacities you have heard of. What are they famous for? How does this benefit the country? Do smaller cities and rural areas provide the same benefits to the country?)

[c] What problems can megacities cause? (Try to think of ideas beyond what the reading is about.)

[d] Would you like to live in a megacity? Give as many reasons as you can for your answer.

UNPACKING NOMINALS

Task A | Written style

Look at the two following sentences. One is from the magazine text in the Reading section, paragraph 6.

- Some countries try to control where people go.
- Some countries try to control the movement of people.

1. Which sounds more spoken? Which sounds more written?

2. Look at the part of each sentence after the word 'control'. Which carries more meaning through nouns? Which has the more formal vocabulary?

3. For each of the expressions below, write a less formal sentence or sentences with the same meaning (some of the expressions are also from the text in the Reading section).

   [a] The result is the emergence of megacities.

   ____

   ____

   [b] in the cities ... a greater need for fuel-burning trucks and trains.

   ____

   ____

   [c] rises in oil prices will mean a reduction in oil use.

   ____

   ____

   [d] methods of greenhouse gas reduction.

   ____

   ____

   [e] A large majority of people will count megacities as their place of residence in the future.

   ____

   ____

   [f] There is a reasonable possibility that there will be economic problems in rural areas in the future.

   ____

   ____

   [g] A point of significant importance is that there should be participation by all citizens in the reduction of energy use.

   ____

   ____

To help you:
emerge = appear
residence = home
significant = very large, very important

REVIEW OF GENRES; MATCHING GENRES TO TASK

Task A | Review of genres

In pairs, fill in the table showing the features of the genres you might use in any writing task at college or university. The *Unit* column tells you which unit in this book introduced the genre. Try to do as many as you can from memory. You may want to go back to the units to check.

GENRE	UNIT	PURPOSE	STAGES
Information report	2		
Explanation	3		
Argument	4		
Discussion	6		
Review	8		

NOTE: OF COURSE, AT COLLEGE OR UNIVERSITY, ALL GENRES HAVE EXTRA PURPOSES: FOR YOU TO SHOW YOU KNOW ABOUT THE SUBJECT, THAT YOU HAVE THOUGHT ABOUT IT AND THAT YOU CAN APPLY YOUR KNOWLEDGE TO REAL SITUATIONS.

Task B | Matching genres to task

Now, for each of the questions below, write the genre which could be used to best answer it (some questions have almost the same meanings, and some questions can be answered with more than one genre).

[a] What is a megacity?

[b] Why have megacities developed?

[c] Megacities are good for society. To what extent do you agree with this point of view?

[d] What are the factors in the development of megacities?

[e] Are megacities good for society? Give reasons for your answer.

[f] What features are common to most megacities?

[g] Describe a town or city where you have lived. What are the good and bad points of living there? What kinds of people would you recommend live there?

[h] Some people say that megacities are good for society, while others say they are a negative development. Which opinion do you agree with?

[i] What are the advantages and disadvantages of megacities? Overall, are megacities beneficial or non-beneficial?

Task C | Writing

1. Choose one question from Task B above that asks for an opinion.

2. Write your answer. You should aim to write at least 250 words. When you have written your first draft, use the table in Task A to check that you have all the stages. Then revise your writing.

SPECIFIC INFORMATION – TUTORIAL

Task A | What do you do at college or university?

1. Write the following words next to the best description below. Use your own knowledge and the knowledge of other students – only use a dictionary if necessary.

assignment	exam	role play
practical	presentation	lecture
work placement	group project	tutorial

____________ A small group activity focusing on a discussion about the week's lectures or lessons. Students are expected to prepare and take part in the discussion. It can take place in a classroom, the lecturer's office, or even outdoors!

____________ In this, students listen to someone talk. Often, there are many students – sometimes over 100.

____________ This is often used in science, engineering or vocational courses. Students actually do the activities of the job they are studying for. For example, it could be done in a kitchen, or a laboratory.

____________ Students work in a real company, and write reports about this work.

____________ Students sit in silence, writing answers to questions.

____________ Students write an essay or report over a period of a few weeks. They should use books, journals, etc from the library for their information.

____________ Students do work with other students and write a report. Each person writes a section of the report. This is especially common in business subjects, because teamwork is important in business.

____________ Students act out a situation, eg dealing with a customer, and get marks for how well they deal with it. This is common on vocational courses.

____________ Students give a talk to the other students and the lecturer.

2. Has anyone in your group studied at university or college before?

If so, find out from them the following, or ask you teacher.

- Which of the above activities did they do?
- How many people were in each activity?
- How did they feel about each activity?
- Which one helped them to learn the most?

Task B | Listening for specific information

You are going to hear a tutorial discussion, in which geography students are preparing for an assignment.

1. Look at the pictures and predict the topic of the assignment.

CD 2 (3)

2 Read the following questions, then listen for the answers. You don't need to write more than three words for each answer.

[a] How did students first know about the assignment?

____

[b] How many words should the students write?

____

[c] What two things will be covered in the tutorial? Go through what to ____________ in their plans, and ____________ some ideas.

[d] The students' design should last for ________ years.

[e] Students should think about ____________ as well as environmental change.

[f] In the lecturer's opinion, is environmental change the easy part of the assignment?

____

[g] There might be floods because the ____________ is flat and because of ____________ change.

[h] The dike might stop ____________ and access to the ____________.

[i] The example mentioned of something with a temporary purpose is ____________.

[j] Empty nesters are people whose children have ____________.

[k] Empty nesters often move into ____________.

[l] Housing developments often have problems when there are no ____________, ____________ or ____________.

[m] The cost of services can come from ____________ on every new house.

[n] Students can get up to ____________ of their mark just for participating in the tutorials.

[o] The lecturer will pay special attention to students' ____________ of the issues.

REVIEW OF FUTURE TENSES

Task A | Intentions

CD 2 (3)

1 Listen again to the beginning of the tutorial (up to where the lecturer mentions the map the students on the recording have already seen). What does the lecturer want to cover in the tutorial? Which tense does he use for these intentions?

2 Tell your partner what you intend to do:

- today
- this week
- at the weekend
- after you finish this course

(If you're not sure, pretend that you do have some intentions!)

Task B | Decisions, intentions and arrangements

Look at the following extract. Each situation mentions the same future action, but the tense used is different because each situation is different. What is the difference between the situations? Which tense is used to talk about the trip?

Situation 1
John: Oh, by the way, next Friday's lecture is cancelled!
Nick: Great news! I think I'll go away for the weekend!

Situation 2
Melissa: Have you heard, Friday's lecture's cancelled!
Nick: Yeah, John told me a couple of hours ago. I'm going to spend the weekend with my friend in London.

Situation 3
Sally: Hey, Nick, I'm having a party at the weekend. Want to come?
Nick: Oh, sorry, I can't – I'm taking the train to London for the weekend.
Sally: Can't you cancel?
Nick: No, sorry, I can't ... I've already paid for the ticket.

Task C | Practice

Tell your partner about the following. If you pretended in Task A, don't pretend now – choose the tense that really shows what you mean! Don't forget to use *may* or *might* if necessary.

1 Talk about:

- Any fixed arrangements you have.
- Any intentions you have, but which you haven't made arrangements for yet.

2 Think about the following, and tell your partner your plans, intentions or arrangements (or lack of them) to:

- See your parents
- Visit family members who live in another town
- Go to a party
- Meet your friends
- Take a holiday
- Travel somewhere.

PROJECT: ROLE-PLAY

Task A | Role-play

You are going to work on a project similar to the one you heard about in this Unit's Listening.

1. Get together in groups of three or four people. Draw a map. You can draw it any way you like, but it must have on it a river, some mountains and other features. There must also be space to build a suburb.

2. Swap maps with another group. You are going to plan a new suburb using the new map. Without talking to the other group members, think about how you want to develop the area. Think especially about:
   - The risk to areas close to the river from the river level rising (the river is close to the sea).
   - What type of housing to have – eg big houses, high-rise apartments.
   - Where the shopping area, schools, hospitals and other services will be.
   - What form of transport to use – trains, motorways, trams, buses …
   - Where you will get the money – eg levy on new buildings, special tax …

3. Explain your ideas to your group, and listen while the others explain their ideas. Combine the best of your ideas to make a single plan for the group.

4. Present your ideas to the class, including the reasons you think the ideas will work.

5. After you hear each group's ideas, discuss what they have said.

6. Which group's ideas do you think will get the highest marks from the tutor on the listening? (Think back to what the tutor said at the end of the listening about what he will give marks for.)

FURTHER PRACTICE: READING, FILMS AND FUN

As with every Unit, these ideas are provided for further reading and listening, and some suggested questions for discussion and writing practice.

The last essay question refers to issues that you have come across earlier in the book, so you can use it for review.

READING

Go to **http://about.com**, then click on Education ➔ Geography ➔ Lists: Countries Cities etc ➔ largest cities in history. You will find a short article about where the largest cities on earth were located over the last 4000 years.

http://www.cia.gov/cia/publications/factbook/geos/xx.html is an interesting place to find out about any country in the world.

More specifically, as you are learning English, it might be interesting to see what the future holds for the English language. Some interesting predictions are at: **http://www.english.co.uk/FoE/contents/cont.html**, the website of The English Company (UK).

FILMS

Around the world in 80 days, directed by Frank Coraci, starring Jackie Chan. A modern film based on the famous novel written by Jules Verne before the aeroplane was invented.

Waterworld, directed by Kevin Reynolds, starring Kevin Costner. Set on the Earth, but in a time when things are very different from now!

QUESTIONS

1. How do you think your home town or city will change in the future? What are the factors behind your predictions?
2. Some people say that if everyone used less energy, many world environmental problems could be solved. What can ordinary people do to use less energy?
3. Think of a problem that could cause big problems to countries in the future (eg childhood obesity, environmental issues, or demographic problems). What can countries do now to prevent these problems?

REFERENCES

Aitken, R (1992) *Teaching Tenses.* Surrey: Nelson.

Horn, A (ed) (2004) *Newsletter of the Arts Law Centre of Australia. Art + Law,* Issue 3, Sept., pp 1–3.

Belloli, A (1999) *Exploring World Art.* London: Francis Lincoln Limited.

Bird, C (1998) *The Stolen Children, their stories.* Australia: Random House.

Cooinda Gallery (2004) *Aboriginal Art.* http://www.cooinda-gallery.com.au/aboriginal_art.htm, accessed 2 April 2005.

Cox, S (1999) *Report on Aboriginals.* Wollongong, Australia: St Mary's College.

Cox, KK (1994) 'Tertiary Level Writing by Magic – Presto! Nominalisation', *EA Journal* 12/1, Autumn 1994.

Cox, KK & Hill, D (2004) *EAP Now! English for Academic Purposes.* Sydney: Pearson Education Australia.

Coxhead, A (2000) 'A New Academic Word List', *TESOL Quarterly,* 34/2: 213–38.

Encyclopaedia of the Orient (2006) *Sahara.* Accessed from http://lexicorient.com/e.o/sahara.htm, 20 August 2006.

Halliday, MAK & Matthiessen, CMIM (2004) *An Introduction to Functional Grammar* (3rd ed). London: Arnold.

Hartley, Stephen (2002) *The Trainer's Toolbox: Authentic Case Studies and Vignettes for Trainers, Educators, Consultants and Facilitators.* Sydney: Pearson Education Australia.

Heath, J (1997) 'Salination'. *Destinations.* May–June issue.

Hutton, D (ed) (1987) *Green Politics in Australia: Working towards a Peaceful & Achievable Future.* Australia: Angus & Robertson.

Internet Movie Database Inc (2006) *The Internet Movie Database.* http://www.imdb.com, accessed 2006.

Kennedy, G (2003) *Structure and meaning in English.* Harlow: Pearson.

Larsen-Freeman, D & Long, M (1991) *An Introduction to Second Language Acquisition Research.* New York: Longman.

Lewis, M (1993) *The Lexical Approach: The State of ELT and a Way Forward.* Hove: Language Teaching Publications.

Longman Dictionary of Contemporary English. England: Pearson Education.

McMahon, D (2005) 'Voices from the village', *The South Sydney Herald,* Vol 1, No 28, Feb, p 1.

Mehrabian, A (1971) *Silent messages.* Belmont, California: Wadsworth.

Moore Foundation (2005) *Andes-Amazon,* Moore Foundation. Accessed from http://www.moore.org/program_areas/environment/initiatives/amazon-andes/initiative_amazon-andes.asp, 20 August 2006.

Murphy, R (2004) *English Grammar in Use* (3rd ed). Cambridge: Cambridge University Press.

The Oracle Education Foundation (ND) *The Silk Road: Linking Europe and Asia by Trade.* Available: http://library.thinkquest.org/13406/sr/, accessed 30 May 2005.

Oxford University Press (2000) *Oxford Advanced Learner's Dictionary* (6th ed). Oxford: Oxford University Press.

Pwerte Marnte Marnte Aboriginal Corporation (2004) *Aboriginal Australia Art & Culture Centre: Iconography.* http://aboriginalart.com.au/gallery/iconography.html, accessed 2 April 2005.

Reynolds, H (2001) *An Indelible Stain? The Question of Genocide in Australia's History.* Australia: Penguin.

Stavrou, K (2004) Email, Milingimbi, Australia, 21 November.

Stavrou, K (2004) Photographs, Milingimbi children.

Stevens, K (2003) *Aboriginal Art of Australia: The symbols and their meanings.* Available at http://www.mainzdidgeridoos.com.au/art/artsymbols.html, accessed 2 April 2005.

Stevens, FS (ed) (1973) *Racism the Australian Experience, Vol. 2, Black versus White.* Redfern: Australia & New Zealand Book Company.

Timmons, C & Gibney, F (eds) (1980) *Britannica Book of English Usage.* USA: Library of Congress.

United Nations, Department of Economic and Social Affairs, Population Division (2003) *Urban Agglomerations Wallchart.* New York: United Nations.

United Nations, Department of Economic and Social Affairs, Population Division (2004) *World Population Trends Wallchart.* New York: United Nations.

Wikipedia contributors (2006) 'Nuclear and radiation accidents'. *Wikipedia, The Free Encyclopaedia.* Retrieved 08:15, 5 June 2006, from http://en.wikipedia.org/w/index.php?title=Nuclear_and_radiation_accidents&oldid=56035660.

APPENDIX 1

ACADEMIC WORD LIST AND PARTS OF SPEECH

USING THE LIST

The list in this appendix is to help you find the right part of speech, especially when writing. It is a list of the most common words used in academic English. It is adapted from a book called *Structure and meaning in English* (Kennedy, 2003).

There are many ways to use this list. Every student might find a different way; a way that works for you. Some suggestions are:

- At the end of each Unit, read the list and tick the words that you now feel you can recognise.
- You can use the list when writing essays. It can be a quick way to check, for example, which verb or preposition to use with a noun (although you should use a dictionary if the information isn't in the table).
- The list can also help you to improve your writing. After finishing the first draft:
  - Look at the word list and try to find words that can replace more basic words. Use the *important collocations* column, and/or a good dictionary to check, for example, which prepositions, verbs or nouns to use with the new words.
  - Try to change some of the verbs you have used into nouns (nominalisation), adjusting the grammar of the sentence as well. This makes the style of writing more academic.

LEARNING WORDS

This list is a reference for you – we do not expect you to learn the vocabulary just by studying the list. It is much better to learn words when you see or hear them. If you do this, it will be easy to remember the words, because you will be able to connect them with the context, or situation, in which they are used. Below are some tips to help you learn vocabulary – not just the words below, but all vocabulary.

- Also look at the example sentences in your dictionary (try to use a dictionary which gives lots of example sentences).
- Don't forget the words commonly used with the word you are learning. The *Important collocations* column will help you here, and so will a good dictionary.
- Try to notice the words in real life – during the next week, when you are reading or listening, look especially for the words you are learning. The more you pay attention to how the word is used in real life, the easier it will be to learn – and doing this will also help you to sound more natural.
- Notice whether the word is used in written or spoken English, or in formal or informal situations (most of the words below are quite academic and are used mostly in writing).
- Think of other situations in which you might use each word, and try to make a picture in your mind of the situation, think about a story involving the situation, or imagine a conversation where you talk about the situation in English.
- Use the words as much as possible. It is very difficult to remember words if you don't use them.
- Don't expect to remember the word after looking at it only once or twice – people usually have to use a word more than 10 times before they remember it.

In the table that follows, note that the following suffixes change the meaning of the word:

- *–ible* and *–able* both mean 'can' (eg If someone is *contactable*, it means people can contact them, eg their telephone is switched on). Words ending in *–ible* and *–able* are adjectives.
- *–ise* usually means 'make' or 'give' (eg *finalise* means make something final; finish it).

VERB	NOUN	ADJECTIVE	IMPORTANT COLLOCATIONS
access	access	accessible	*... have access to ...*
achieve	achievement	achievable	*... a (big) achievement ...*
acquire	acquisition		
administrate	administration	administrative	
affect	effect		*... have an effect on ...* *... the effect of ...*
aid	aid		
	alternative	alternative	*... an alternative to ...*
analyse	analysis	analytical	*... an analysis of ...*
		annual	
approach	approach		
	appropriateness	appropriate	*... appropriate for ... ing ...*
	area		
assemble	assembly		
	attitude		*... have an attitude ...*
author	author (person)		
authorise	authority	authoritarian	*... have authority to ...*
	availability	available	
	awareness	aware	*... be aware of ...* *... have an awareness of ...*
benefit	benefit	beneficial	*... be beneficial to ...*
categorise	category		
challenge	challenge	challenging	*... challenge someone to ...* *... have a challenge ...* *... give a challenge to ...*
	circumstance	circumstantial	
civilise	civilisation	civil	
	colleague		
comment	comment		*... make a comment about ...*
communicate	communication	communicative	
	community		

VERB	NOUN	ADJECTIVE	IMPORTANT COLLOCATIONS
complicate	complexity	complex complicated	
concentrate	concentration		*... concentration/concentrate on ...*
	concept	conceptual	
conclude	conclusion	conclusive	
confirm	confirmation		
conflict	conflict		*... have a conflict with ...* *... conflict with ...* *... be in conflict with ...*
	consequence	consequent	*... a consequence of ...*
consider	consideration		
consist			*... consist of ...*
construct	construction		
consume	consumption		*... consumption of ...*
contact	contact	contactable	*... be in contact with ...*
contextualise	context	contextual	*... in context ...*
contract	contract	contractual	*... contract someone to ...*
contrast	contrast	contrasting	*... in contrast to ...* *... to contrast something with ...*
contribute	contribution	contributory	*... to contribute to ...*
create	creation	creative	*... a creative person...*
credit	credit	creditable	*... credit someone with something ...* *... credit something to someone ...* *... give credit to someone ...*
	decade		
debate	debate	debatable	*... to debate something with someone ...*
decrease	decrease	decreasing	*... a decrease in ...*
define	(a) definition	definable	*... a definition of ...*
demonstrate	demonstration		
deny	denial		

VERB	NOUN	ADJECTIVE	IMPORTANT COLLOCATIONS
design	design	well designed, badly designed, etc	*... a badly designed (building) ...*
display	display		
distribute	distribution		
document	document	documented	
		domestic	
	economy	economic	
emphasise	emphasis	emphatic	*... put/place/have an emphasis on ...*
enable			*... enable someone to do something ...*
ensure			
	environment	environmental	
	event		
evidence	evidence	evident	*... piece of evidence ...* *... have evidence for/against ...* *... it was evident that ...*
exhibit	exhibition		*... an exhibition of ...*
	expert (person) expertise	expert	*... be expert at ... ing ...* *... be an expert at ... ing ...* *... have expertise in ...*
feature	feature		
finalise	final	final	
finance	finance	financial	
focus	focus	well focused, badly focused etc	*... to focus on something ...* *... it was a (clearly) focused lesson ...*
function	function	functional	*... function (smoothly) ...*
fund	(a) fund funding	well funded, poorly funded etc	*... find funding for ...* *... a well funded (project) ...*
	generation		
	goal		
identify	identification	identifying/identified	
illustrate	illustration	illustrated	
	income		

VERB	NOUN	ADJECTIVE	IMPORTANT COLLOCATIONS
increase	increase	increasing	*... an increase in ...*
indicate	indication	indicative	
injure	injury	injured	*... have a (head) injury ...* *... have an injury to (his head) ...*
instruct	instruction	instructional instructive	*... instruct someone to ...*
		internal	
interest	interest	interesting interested	*... an interest in ...* *... an interesting (film) ...* *He was interested in (the film) ...*
investigate	investigation	investigative	*... an investigation into ...*
involve	involvement		*... involve someone in ...*
issue	issue		
	item		
labour	labour	laborious	
legalise	legality	legal	
link	link	linked	*... a link to ...* *... link something to something ...*
locate	location		
	majority		
manufacture	manufacture (process) factory (building)	manufacturing manufactured	
maximise	maximum	maximum	
	medicine	medical	
		medium	
mention	mention		
	military	military	
minimise	minimum	minimum	
	minority		
normalise	normality	normal	

VERB	NOUN	ADJECTIVE	IMPORTANT COLLOCATIONS
object	objection		*… make an objection to …* *… have an objection to …* *… object to …*
		obvious	
occur	occurrence		
opt	option	optional	*… have an option to …* *… to opt for (the second choice) …*
output	output		
		overall	
	period	periodical	
	policy		
politicise	politics	political	
		positive	
		previous	
	prime	primary	
process	process	processed	
	profession	professional	
protest	protest		*… protest against …*
range	range		*(It) ranges from … to …* *… has a large range …*
react	reaction		*… react to …* *… a reaction to …*
reduce	reduction	reducible	*… a reduction in …*
	region	regional	
regulate	regulation	regulatory	*… make a regulation …*
reject	rejection	rejected	*(He) felt rejected.*
release	release	released	*… release … from …*
	relevance	relevant	*… be relevant to …*
rely	reliance	reliable	*… rely/reliance on …*
remove	removal	removable	
research	research		*… a piece/an item of research …*

VERB	NOUN	ADJECTIVE	IMPORTANT COLLOCATIONS
retain	retention		
reveal	revelation		
	role		
	section		
secure	security	secure	*... make something secure ...* *... have security ...* *... feel secure ...*
search	search	searchable	*... search for ...* *... carry out/conduct/do a search of ...*
select	selection	select	
	sign		
	significance	significant	*... have significance ...*
	similarity	similar	*... similar to ...*
specify		specific	
	structure	structural	
style	style	stylish	
suffice	sufficiency	sufficient	
survey	survey		
survive	survival survivor (person)		
target	target		
	technology technician (person)	technical	
	theme	thematic	
theorise	theory	theoretical	*... a theory about/of ...*
	tradition	traditional	
transfer	transfer	transferable	*... transfer something/someone to ...*
transport	transport transportation	transportable	*... forms of transport/transportation ...*
vary	variation	varying	
	vehicle		
	version		

APPENDIX 2

SELF-CORRECTION MEMORY BANK

Here are some common mistakes made by students. Use the table to add your own mistakes from writing. Add your corrected sentence and the grammar rule.

SENTENCE WITH MISTAKE	CORRECTED SENTENCE	GRAMMAR RULE
It sounds good, *isn't* it.	It sounds good, doesn't it.	verb choice/is/does
In regarding to my study ...	Regarding my study ... In regard to my study ... With regard to my study ... With regards to my study ...	collocation
Her name is Jane, *who is* going to complete her studies in February.	Her name is Jane, and she is going to complete her studies in February. Jane, who is going to ...	pronoun substitution dependent clause
I am writing to inform you that *I have to move the flat.*	I am writing to inform you that I have to move out of my flat. *or* ... from my flat.	verb/object agreement sense requires a preposition (remember: the flat's too heavy to move!)
I am very *appreciate* it.	I appreciate it. I appreciate it very much. I am very appreciative of it.	verb/object agreement word order
I am taking my exam on next Monday.	I am taking my exam on Monday. I am taking my exam next Monday. Next Monday, I am taking my exam.	prepositional phrase (choice of preposition)

SENTENCE WITH MISTAKE	CORRECTED SENTENCE	GRAMMAR RULE

APPENDIX 3

SELF-CHECKING GUIDE – WRITING A PARAGRAPH

STRUCTURE: PARAGRAPH 1	YES	NO
First sentence – the topic sentence – what the paragraph is going to be about.		
Supporting sentences that explain or give a reason after the title sentence.		
A definition within the paragraph that links to the title and topic.		
One or more factual sentences that support the topic.		
A concluding sentence.		

STRUCTURE: PARAGRAPH 2		
First sentence – the topic sentence – what the paragraph is going to be about.		
Supporting sentences that describe the topic sentence.		
A definition within the paragraph that links to the title and topic.		
One or more factual sentences that support the topic.		
A concluding sentence.		

STRUCTURE: PARAGRAPH 3		
First sentence – the topic sentence – what the paragraph is going to be about.		
Supporting sentences that evaluate the topic sentence.		
A definition within the paragraph that links to the title and topic.		
One or more factual sentences that support the topic.		
A concluding sentence.		

STRUCTURE: PARAGRAPH 4		
First sentence – the topic sentence – what the paragraph is going to be about.		
Supporting sentences that list details of the topic sentence.		
A definition within the paragraph that links to the title and topic.		
One or more factual sentences that support the topic.		
A concluding sentence.		

STRUCTURE: PARAGRAPH 5	YES	NO
First sentence – the topic sentence – what the paragraph is going to be about.		
Supporting sentences that contrast or compare after the title sentence.		
A definition within the paragraph that links to the title and topic.		
One or more factual sentences that support the topic.		
A concluding sentence.		

STRUCTURE: PARAGRAPH 6		
First sentence – the topic sentence – what the paragraph is going to be about.		
Supporting sentences that establish a cause after the title sentence.		
A definition within the paragraph that links to the title and topic.		
One or more factual sentences that support the topic.		
A concluding sentence.		

APPENDIX 4

INFORMATION GAPS

UNIT 2, LANGUAGE SPOTLIGHT 1: VOCABULARY, DESCRIBING GRAPHS AND TABLES (page 22)

Student A's graphs

First, describe this graph to your partner, without showing it to him/her. Your partner will draw it, following your instructions.

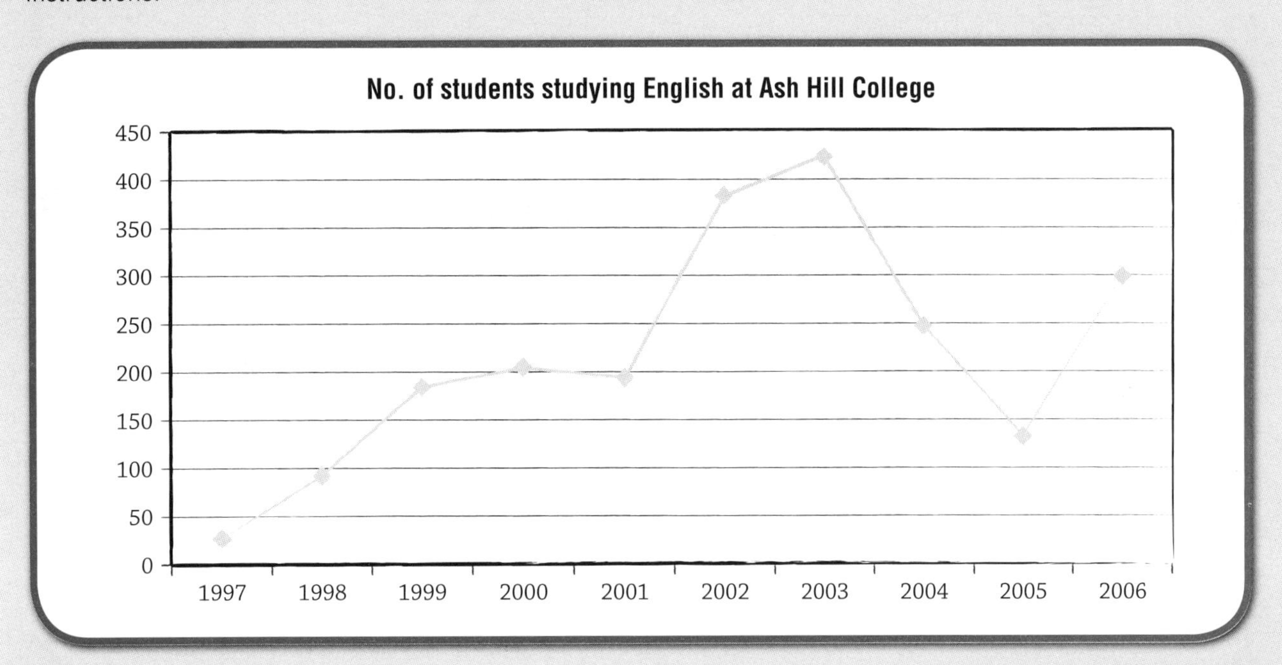

Next, draw below the graph that your partner describes to you.

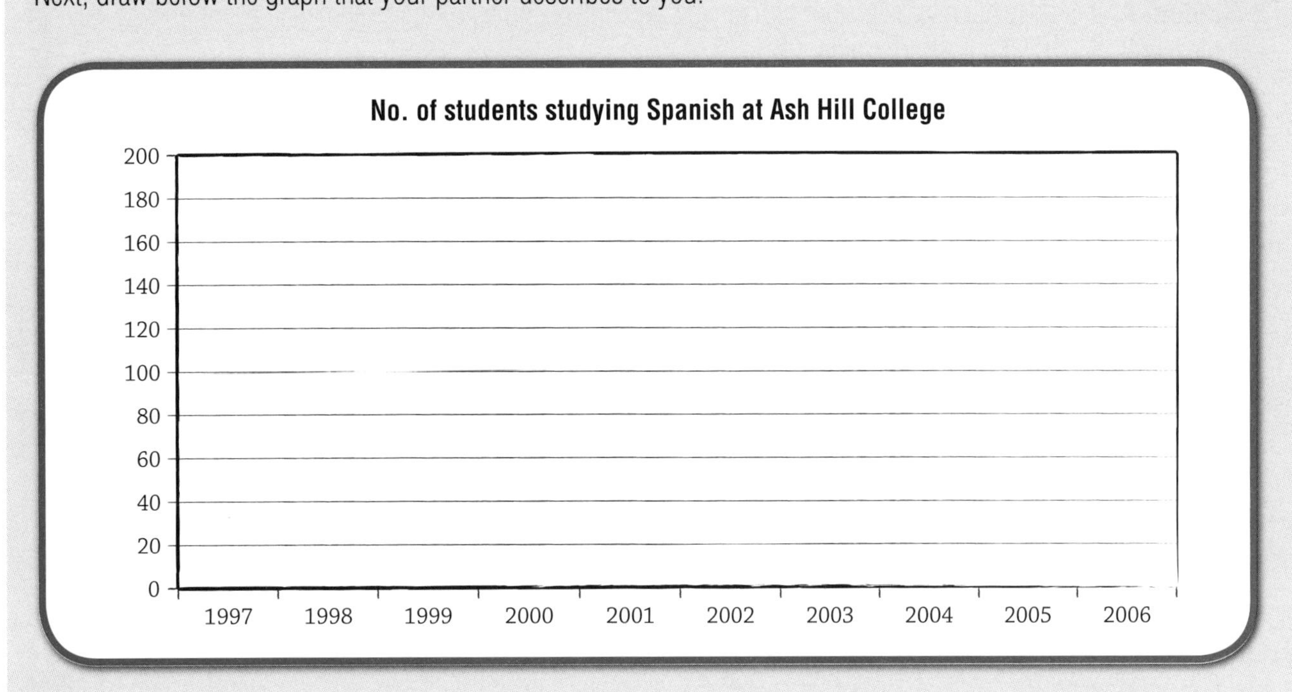

UNIT 5, SPEAKING 2: MAKING REQUESTS (page 60)

Student A's situations

SITUATION 1

Student A: You want to get information about studying ancient history at Auckland University, New Zealand, as an international student. Request:

i) Orientation dates

ii) Whether the university can provide accommodation

iii) Any brochures or leaflets they have about the course or the department to be sent to you.

SITUATION 2

Student A: You work in a car rental company. In order to help the customer who is calling, you need the following information:

i) There are several small cars available next weekend – but it's best to book early

ii) Customers can pay extra for a higher level of insurance. Customer must return the car with a full tank of petrol – if not, they will be charged $2 per litre to fill it up.

iii) Weekend charges for small cars are $89 per day, or $150 total if the car is picked up before 6 pm Friday and returned by 6 pm Sunday.

SITUATION 3

Student A: It is orientation week at your new university, and you are speaking to someone about joining the table tennis club. Find out the following:

i) How much it costs

ii) How often and when the club meets

iii) What competitions the club takes part in, or holds.

UNIT 2, LANGUAGE SPOTLIGHT 1: VOCABULARY, DESCRIBING GRAPHS AND TABLES (page 22)

Student B's graphs

First, your partner will describe a graph to you, without showing it. Draw the graph on the lines (axes) below, following your partner's instructions.

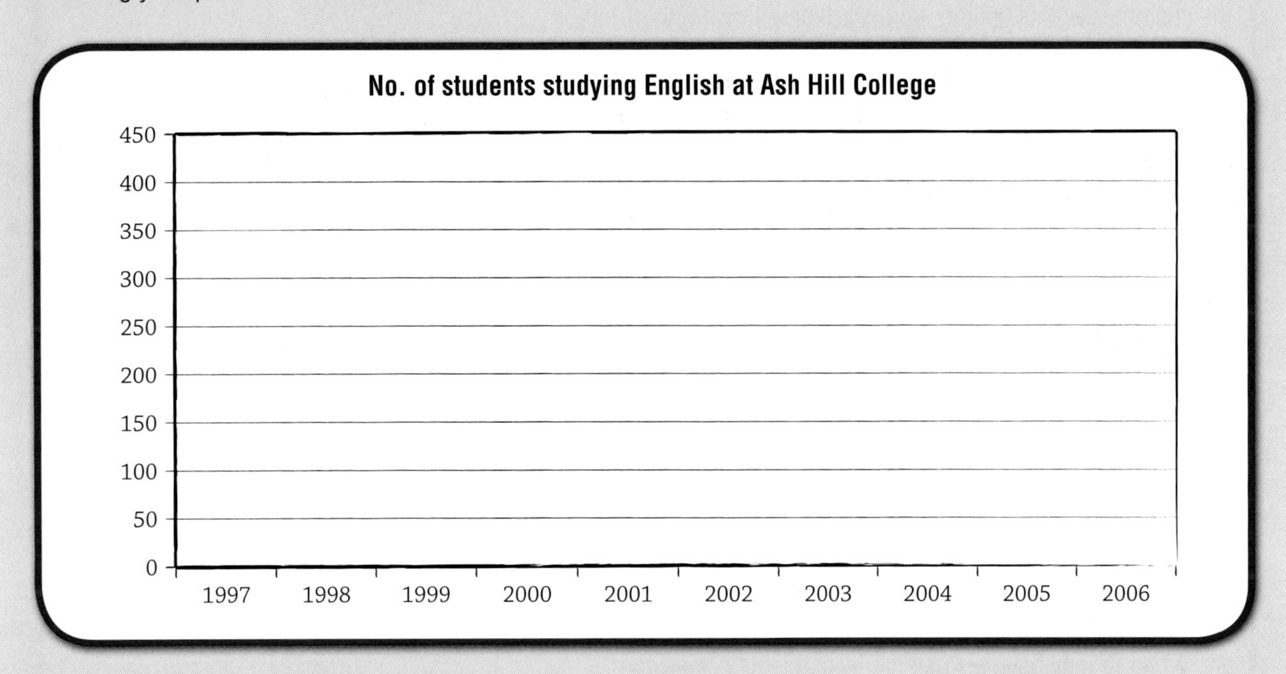

Next, describe the graph below to your partner, without showing it to him/her. Your partner will draw it, following your instructions.

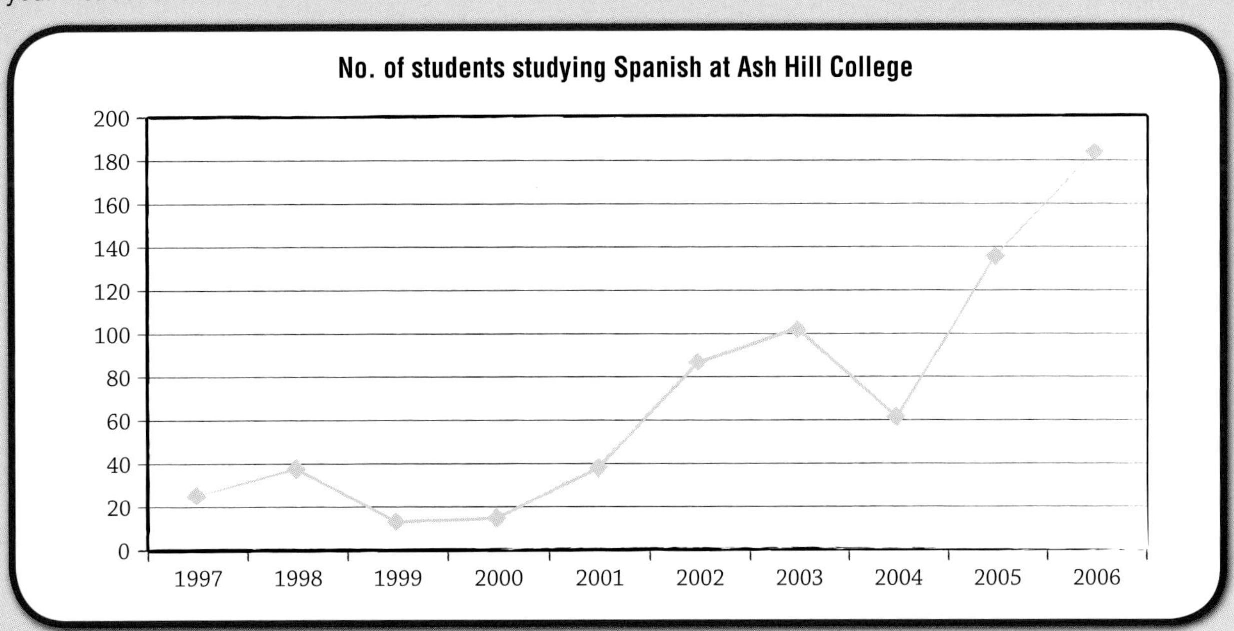

UNIT 5, SPEAKING 2: MAKING REQUESTS (page 60)

Student B's situations

SITUATION 1

Student B: You are an international admissions officer at Auckland University, New Zealand. In order to help the customer who is calling, you need the following information:

i) The university can provide accommodation, but only in the first year. Students must apply early – it's on a first come, first served basis.

ii) Orientation week: 4th to 8th September. Very important to attend.

iii) There is a brochure for international students at the university, and another one about the ancient history department.

SITUATION 2

Student B: You are a university student who wants to explore the local area with a friend at the weekend. You decide to hire a car, but first you need to get some information. Call the car hire company and find out the following:

i) The cost of hiring a small car for the weekend

ii) Whether there are any extra charges for insurance or petrol

iii) Whether they have a small car available next weekend.

SITUATION 3

Student B: You are the membership secretary of a table tennis club at university. An international student, new to the university, is asking you about the club. You will need the following information:

i) The club takes part in the National Inter-University Table Tennis Competition every year, and holds an internal competition every term.

ii) The club meets twice a week, on Monday evening and Wednesday afternoon.

iii) The membership fee is £10 per term, and it costs £2 per meeting to cover room hire.

INDEX